Borderline

and Other Self

Disorders

BORDERLINE AND OTHER SELF DISORDERS

A Developmental and Object-Relations Perspective

Donald B. Rinsley, M.D.

JASON ARONSON INC.
Northvale, New Jersey
London

The Master Work Series

First softcover edition 1997

Copyright © 1982 by Jason Aronson Inc.

Library of Congress Cataloging-in-Publication Data

Rinsley, Donald B.
    Borderline and other self disorders.

    Bibliography: p. 271.
    Includes index.
    1. Personality, Disorders of—Etiology.   2. Separation-
individuation.   I. Title.
    RC554.R56   616.89   81-20538
    ISBN 1–56821–847–8   AACR2

Printed in the United States of America on acid-free paper. For information and catalog write to Jason Aronson Inc., 230 Livingston Street, Northvale, New Jersey 07647-1731. Or visit our website: http://www.aronson.com

CONTENTS

PREFACE

This book is a product of over twenty years of experience in treating seriously disturbed children, adolescents, adults, and their families and contains the bulk of my writings since the 1975 Masterson-Rinsley paper (chapter 2 of this book) on the role of the mother in the psychogenesis of borderline personality disorder. That experience, together with much of the recent psychodynamic-psychoanalytic and psychopharmacologic literature, points to the inference that major personality or characterologic pathology lies midway along a developmental-diagnostic continuum between the psychoses and the psychoneuroses. The concept of such a continuum was originally put forward in classical psychoanalytic stage theory and later elaborated by Mahlerian phase theory. This book attempts to synthesize a coherent view of the developmental etiology of such pathology, drawing in particular on the work of a number of recent and contemporary contributors: Melanie Klein and Ronald Fairbairn, representing the so-called British school of object-relations; Edith Jacobson and Otto Kernberg on internalized object relations; Margaret Mahler and her associates on symbiosis and individuation; John Bowlby on attachment and loss; Heinz Kohut on the psychology of narcissism and disorders of the self; James Masterson on borderline object relations, especially the concept of abandonment depression; and Piaget, whose epochal contributions to the development of cognitive-perceptual structure pervade the evolving body of psychodynamic and "academic" literature devoted to how children become adults.

The essential thrust of this work is based on the assumption that individuals with major personality or characterologic disorders and psychotic illness have never completed the process of separation–individuation. They remain significantly symbiotic and are unable to mourn. They present repetitive approach–avoidance conflicts such that even the prospect of intimacy—or separation—elicits disruptive or near-disruptive degrees of anxiety.

Along with many others, I believe that the pathogenesis of the psychotic and personality disorders originates in the vicissitudes of the mother–infant relationship in the first three to four postnatal years. Of particular importance is the failure of communicative matching, mutual cuing, or "goodness of fit" between mother and child, leading to the latter's depersonification or appersonation. That constitutional factors play a role in pathogenesis cannot be disputed, although I believe that their impact increases in proportion to the degree of psychopathology; thus, they play a negligible role in the higher-level personality and psychoneurotic syndromes. Nonetheless, it must be borne in mind that even the most dedicated, nurturant, and healthy parenting cannot fully overcome the heredo-congenital defects common to autistic and profoundly schizophrenic children.

My view of wider sociocultural determinants is largely in agreement with that of Christopher Lasch (1977, 1978) who has related the decline of the nuclear family and the so-called culture of narcissism to the increased frequency of personality disorders. Dysfunctional childrearing, the failure of the public schools to impart basic literacy skills, and the bloated welfare bureaucracy have spawned a widespread psychology of entitlement with its notions of success without effort and income without productivity. The unfortunate children of perplexed, disarticulated, and dysfunctional families, now graduated from undisciplined schools with "open" and "child-centered" classes, ungraded nonsense curricula, and social promotions, are the next generation's borderline and narcissistic personalities. Thus, the combined failures of the family and the school as vehicles for the child's progressive socialization leave these young people unprepared for the responsibilities and expectations of the wider culture to which they belong.

It comes as no surprise that over the past 20 years these same sociocultural determinants have influenced psychiatry toward a resurgent and simplistic mind-is-brain view of human nature and psychopathology, with an emphasis on enzymes, neurotransmitters, and urinary metabolites, and that these determinants have revived the fruitless search for magic bullets to combat the complex, overdetermined symptomatology derived from sociocultural *anomie.* The rise of a new behaviorism, with its mindless emphasis on *acts* rather than persons, reflects a descent to shotgun pseudo-solutions reflective of a preoccupation with *doing something* to the detriment of thoughtful introspection. "Do it now!" and "Do it if it feels good!" are the catch phrases of those whose regressive narcissism bespeaks little or no patience with the thoughtful, the historical, the painstaking, and the complex.

To paraphrase the late Philip Wylie, we have indeed spawned a generation of narcissists who now flood our public and private therapeutic facilities. To expect that psychodynamically based treatment will assist them easily in resolving their serious adaptive problems is, of course, naive; to expect that psycho-active drugs will in most cases do more than cover up their symptoms is fatuous. It should also be reaffirmed that doctrinaire methodology and technical rigidity are ultimately deleterious to psychotherapeutic work with these patients, who fare best with an expressive approach grounded on the disciplined, yet flexible use of "support parameters." The basic therapeutic task thus amounts to an effort to provide the patient with a "good enough" or "holding" environment within the context of which the application of explanation, clarification, confrontation, and interpretation may lead to the resolution of underlying pathologic determinants.

CHAPTER 1

ECONOMIC ASPECTS OF OBJECT RELATIONS

This chapter represents an attempt to begin to incorporate Federn's economic views on ego psychology into classical metapsychology, specifically into object-relations theory. Federn and the object-relations theorists have much in common. By way of introduction, I shall give a brief overview of the status of both object-relations theory and economics, followed by a condensed review of those of Federn's contributions that bear on object relations and the latter's structural underpinnings.

OVERVIEW

The fundamental importance of object-relations theory, developed by the so-called British School of Psychoanalysis, no longer requires comment. At root, object-relations theory represents a particular view of, and approach to, instinct theory, and it epitomizes the shift within Freud's own writings (Hartmann 1956a) from a predominantly aim-oriented to an object-oriented view of metapsychology. The latter may be said to have coincided, in more than a rough way, with Freud's related shift from an emphasis upon the id to an emphasis upon the ego. The writings of Klein and of Fairbairn and their followers emphasize the primacy of the object of instinct as over against instinctual aim

1

(Guntrip 1964), and they establish the point of view, of great importance for psychoanalysis, that the object is no mere instrumentality, just as Federn (1952) emphasized that the ego is no mere abstraction.

The shift toward object relations within psychoanalysis has evoked research of far-reaching importance by those workers who have been favorably disposed toward the significance of the British workers' efforts to understand intrapsychic events. Related to, if not a direct outgrowth of, this frame of reference has been the work of Jacobson (1964) and others (e.g., Kernberg 1966) on the structural aspects of object relationships, which has yielded an understanding of identity of notable subtlety and profundity.

When we enter the area of economics, however, matters become complex far beyond what is expected of a predominantly structural view. It would not be incorrect to say that the current limits to which research on economics has attained lie essentially where Hartmann (1950, 1955) and his colleagues (e.g., Kris 1955) have left them, and that with one notable exception there have been no fundamental contributions to our understanding of economic matters beyond Freud's (1923) and Hartmann's writings. The exception is Federn (1952, Weiss 1950, 1960). Federn's work illuminates further the economic aspects of object relations because it supplies a comprehensive economic basis for structural considerations. Some of the reasons why Federn's fundamental work has long lain fallow among psychoanalysts are set forth elsewhere in this chapter.

RÉSUMÉ OF FEDERN'S ECONOMIC AND EGO-PSYCHOLOGICAL CONCEPTS

Of the various modern psychoanalytic writers who have made notable contributions to our understanding of the treatment of the major psychoses, particularly of schizophrenia, Federn has been among the foremost. In the exploration of subjective experiential states he had few peers; his writings set forth his comfort with both psychoanalytic and phenomenological concepts; his theoretical contributions to ego psychology or, perhaps better, to the phenomenology of "ego states" are as profound as they are abstruse; his intuitive awareness of the subjective difficulties of the psychotic ego was impressive; his practical recommendations for their treatment, based firmly upon his theoretical work, have attained among dynamic workers a self-evidential acceptance that has long since come to obscure the oft-forgotten fact that it was Federn who first set them down.

The apparent disproportion between general professional acceptance of Federn's therapeutics and ambivalence toward his theoretical formulations constitutes the paradox of the work Federn accomplished and of the kind of person he was. There are, at casual inspection, several reasons for this paradoxical state of affairs with respect to the general body of Federn's contributions to psychoanalysis and psychiatry.

First of all, Federn was an intensely introspective, self-perceptive individual. Second, he possessed a thorough grasp of phenomenology, a subject with which many psychoanalytic workers are not familiar. Third, the subjective, introspective nature of the material with which he dealt does not readily lend itself to facile verbal description—there is, certainly, no easy way to explicate variations in "ego feeling," or shifting ego states, or the vicissitudes of depersonalization and estrangement, to mention but a few of the exceedingly self-intimate phenomena with which Federn wrestled. Again, Federn was not endowed with a gift for brilliant writing; indeed, some of his formulations are prolix, his metaphors too condensed, his phraseology at times burdensome to the point of inducing boredom. Finally, some of Federn's most important formulations regarding, for example, narcissism, differed sharply from those set forth by Freud. Thus, although Federn deemed himself a faithful student of Freud and emended certain of Freud's ideas only after he reluctantly had to admit that clinical evidence strongly supported his point of view, his "deviations" were, as could be expected, received with suspicion by many of his colleagues.

It cannot be denied, in addition, that Federn, like Aichhorn, was at home in the treatment of the kind of cases which Freud could personally hardly tolerate, much less treat: the major psychotics, infantile and impulse-ridden characters, borderline types, and the "psychologically dishonest," whom Freud often found distasteful. Federn's extraordinary gifts as a therapist could be said to have been among the most important factors which led him to apply psychoanalytic treatment to the more difficult cases with whom he came into contact; in consequence of this, his pioneering demonstration of the power of psychotic transference ran counter to Freud's generally pessimistic view that "narcissistic" cases could not be expected to respond to psychoanalytic treatment (E. Federn 1962). The attitude persists to this day, among some members of the profession, that, for example, one cannot analyze adolescents, psychotics, character neurotics, and other infantile-narcissistic patients because their egos are too "weak," their narcissistic fixations too profound to bear the burden of analytic work.

To understand Federn's concept of the psychotic, immature, or "weak" ego, one must bear in mind his assertion that such an ego suffers from a "deficiency disease," which will be discussed in detail later in this chapter.

THEORETICAL CONSIDERATIONS

As already noted, Federn's approach to metapsychology draws heavily upon phenomenology. We may therefore begin our consideration of his theoretical contributions with his positive assertion that the ego is to be viewed, not merely as a theoretical construct, or a "postulated reference-point of thought," or, like Sherrington's reflex, a convenient fiction, but rather, as a fact of human experience. One therefore feels, perceives, apprehends, *is aware of* one's ego. Federn's assertion signifies much more than is contained within the classical view of the *perceptive* (including the self-perceptive) *function* of the ego, ordinarily deemed but one of its many properties; instead, it ascribes to the ego a more *fundamental perceptibility.* To account for this fundamental property of the ego, namely, its *inherent experientiality,* Federn postulated the operation of a specific ego cathexis. This ego cathexis, in turn, consisted of both libidinal and aggressive drive energies, but its ultimate origin was left undecided. The ego cathexis, according to Federn, conveys to both conscious and preconscious experience the entire range of the individual's awareness of his continuity in time, of his position and extension in space, and of his apprehension of causal or deterministic sequences of events.

A further refinement of Federn's formulation of the ego cathexis is his assertion that its attainment of preconscious and conscious awareness finds expression in a fourfold congeries of feelings, which he termed *ego feelings.* Thus, *active ego feelings* find expression in an active perceptual valence attached, in turn, to aggressive, exploitive, acquisitive, controlling, and mastering acts or behavior; *passive ego feelings* become attached to the aim of absorbing or submitting; *reflective ego feelings* come to be associated with the retroflexion of perceptual awareness upon the *ego as object of self-awareness* (reflective or reflexive narcissism; reflective *cogito* of Sartre; the ego's self-perceptive function according to classical concepts); while *medial ego feelings* signify the most basic awareness of one's existence, or the fact that one simply *is* (prereflective, primary, "objectless" narcissism; prereflective *cogito* of Sartre). Although all four kinds of ego feelings contribute to the totality of self-awareness, medial ego feeling lies very close to the core of the ego; disturbances of it lead to depersonalization, the paradox of which lies in the sufferer's relatively well-preserved reflective ego feeling concomitant with an intimate, almost indescribable feeling of inner strangeness and "deadness."

A second major contribution to ego psychology was Federn's concept of *ego boundaries.* Stated briefly, the ego boundary constitutes a vaguely perceived line of demarcation between what is, as it were, within the ego and what is outside it. The ego boundary may thus be said to delimit those perceptions and experiences which the individual identifies as personal, intimate, subjective, and hence, within the ego boundary ("egotized"; invested with "Me-ness" [Claparède 1911]), from those which he identifies as "real" or "external" to him, and hence, outside the ego boundary. Federn distinguished, as parts of the ego boundary, an *inner ego boundary*, arrayed against (internal) unconscious mental contents and invested with countercathexes directed toward precluding such contents from access to conscious awareness, and an *external ego boundary*, by which what is "outside" ("in reality") is separated from what the individual perceives as within the ego's sphere of intimate subjectivity. According to Federn, the ego boundary plays a critically important role in the maintenance of what he called the sense of reality, or what Janet termed *le sentiment du réel*. Federn concluded that the ego cathexis guaranteed the integrity of the ego boundary, both internal and external; hence one may speak of the ego boundary cathexis.

On the basis of these formulations, we may specify two interrelated functions or, more properly, effects of the ego cathexis, viz., maintenance of the individual's self-awareness in space, time, and causality (hence, the essential continuity of experience), and the integrity of the ego boundary, which in turn determines one's sense of reality.

Essential to these concepts is Federn's assertion that the normally fluctuating "extent" of the ego boundary waxes and wanes with variations in the ego cathexis; hence the ego boundary ordinarily undergoes a process of dynamic, expansile and contractile flux; this state of relative flux in turn allows explanations for a variety of clinical phenomena. For example, in sleep the ego boundary contracts, and thoughts, ideas, emotions, images, and wishes previously "within" it proceed to fall "outside" it; thus, since what is outside the ego boundary is sensed as real, mental phenomena assume the quasi-realistic characteristics of the transformed figures and images of the dream and are, in the dream, perceived as real. Similarly, for reasons to be discussed later, the ego boundary contracts in psychoses, whereupon thoughts, ideas, and feelings previously perceived as one's own fall outside the ego boundary, and hence, are perceived as real. It is thus possible to explain the etiology of hallucinations and illusions as internal elaborations which fall outside the ego boundary.*

Yet a third important contribution to the phenomenology of the ego boundary may be found in the manner in which Federn viewed the relationship of the ego boundary and the bodily ego, a subject developed more thoroughly in another context by Schilder (1935). Embedded within the external ego boundary, according to Federn, are the body's sense receptor organs. He concluded that failure of the ego cathexis to invest, and hence vivify, the external ego boundary, for whatever reasons, brings about functional impairment of the sense organs, the "windows" through which external object-representations enter the territory of the ego. When this occurs, the individual perceives the external world as estranged (derealized).

From these formulations one may distill the following generalizations concerning the phenomenology of ego function:

1. Impaired medial ego feeling results in perceptual alienation of the core of the ego, leading to depersonalization;
2. Impairment of the cathexis of the external ego boundary leads to estrangement;
3. Impairment of the sense of reality follows upon contraction of the ego boundary.

Finally, these various disabilities, which comprise a wide range of psychiatric symptomatology, result, in turn, from impairment or impoverishment of the ego cathexis.

---

*It will be seen that the process by which egotized mental contents proceed to fall outside the external ego boundary could be equated with the defense mechanism of projection. As I shall later show, the two are not equivalent; hence such terms as *externalization, extrusion,* and *extrajection* are preferable for the former process.

THE "WEAK" EGO

The aforementioned disabilities—depersonalization, estrangement (derealization), and impaired sense of reality—comprise predominantly sensori-perceptual symptoms; it may be said, in line with Federn's views, that they bespeak underlying ego weakness since they are predicated upon a deficiency or impairment of the ego cathexis. Various degrees of these symptoms are ubiquitous among individuals ordinarily labelled psychotic, borderline, or "as-if," or who are diagnosed as schizophrenic, character-neurotic ("psychopathic"), immature, infantile-narcissistic, polymorphous-perverse, or impulse-neurotic.

Clinical study of such people reveals a variety of characteristics ordinarily associated with the so-called "weak" ego. Thus, one discerns various of the following: failure of normal repression; persistence of primitive mechanisms of defense, with reliance upon projection, introjection, regression, and denial; impairment of the ego's synthetic function (Nunberg 1955), leading to disruption of self-environment relationships and breakdown of perceptual, cognitive-ideational, affective, and motoric functions; predominance of anxiety of the instinctual type; lack of "basic trust"; impairment of object relations; failure of sublimation of "raw" instinctual impulses; persistence of primary process thinking with reliance upon transitivism, infantile-megalomanic modes of thought, magical gestures and words, and scotomatization and negative hallucination; and, finally, serious difficulties with pre-Oedipal and sexual identity.

The view that these manifestations of ego weakness result from a relative deficiency or impoverishment of the ego cathexis appears to contradict the classical view, derived from Freud (1911a, 1914b, 1917a, 1924a,b), which conceptualizes ego weakness in terms of withdrawal of "object-cathexis" with corresponding concentration of (narcissistic) libido upon the ego itself. In Federn's view, however, a "withdrawal of object-cathexis" may be seen to ensue from a contraction of the external ego boundary, such that the mental representations of external objects fall in increasing numbers outside the external ego boundary, and hence, are extruded from the territory of the ego; as such, they lose "Me-ness," or cannot any longer be experienced as part of one's self; hence they undergo de-egotization and proceed to seem "real."

At the risk of oversimplification we may therefore assert, in accordance with this view, that what appears as a loss of interest in external objects in fact represents the ego's loss of a sense of familiarity with its internal object-representations. It was Federn's merit to show that the psychotic individual does not, in fact, lose interest in "external" objects. On the contrary, the extruded internal object-representations assume, in such cases, an extraordinary perceptual intensity, and the individual must resort to ever more protean defenses to ward it off.*

We may now generalize as follows:

1. Where there is significant ego weakness, the ego loses a sense of familiarity with its internal objects;

2. This loss of familiarity results from the extrusion of these objects to the "outside," which ensues from a relative contraction of the external ego boundary. As a further result, the extruded internal objects assume a quality of intense vividness (they are sensed as unduly "real") which, among schizophrenics, is oppressive and requires near-Herculean efforts to ward off;**

---

*According to the view expressed here, impoverishment of the ego cathexis brings about two interrelated syndromes. One comprises de-egotization of mental contents with concomitant extrusion of these contents to the "outside." The other is clinical estrangement or derealization, which Federn attributes to libidinal decathexis of the sensory organs embedded in the external ego boundary. It should be noted that estrangement of "external objects" is often experienced as a disquieting heightening of their perceptual intensity, most often centering upon the eyes; thus, as these objects are perceived to be estranged, their illumination is felt to be excessive, and estranged patients are wont to complain that "the lights are too bright." It is not unexpected that individuals with significant degrees of estrangement are found to be paranoid types for whom the environment, populated with oppressive, persecutory objects, is excessively vivid to the point of pain.

**The usual view of these phenomena would conceptualize them in terms of breakdown of the "stimulus barrier" against sensory input (Bergman and Escalona 1949, Freud 1920). Wordsworth stated it poetically: "The world is too much with us."

3. Loss of familiarity with internal objects and their extrusion to the outside, in consequence of contraction of the external ego boundary, constitutes a *splitting* of the ego;

4. The oppressive intensity with which the ego perceives its extruded internal objects in part accounts for the view that they are predatory or persecutory external objects. Also, as contraction of the ego boundary causes the extrusion of more and more internal objects, the ego feels, as it were, emptied out of them. During the period in which these transformations normally occur, as I hope later to show, the "purified pleasure ego" perceives all that is "not-me" as "bad," and all that is "me" as "good." Thus, the extruded objects become "bad objects" while the ensuing paucity of familiar internal objects leads to a condition which could be described as one of "bad" or "negative" identity.

SOME COMMENTS ON EGO STATES

Although the term "ego state" finds frequent expression in the literature, it is necessary to specify its exact meaning for the purposes of the present discussion. Federn's conception of an ego state is set forth by Weiss (1960) as follows:

> In Federn's opinion only the ego feeling is permanently conscious, not the preconscious material over which it extends. He calls an ego state the mental material which—at one time or another—was or is unified by a coherent ego cathexis and has its own boundaries. Furthermore . . . ego states, like id contents, can undergo repression. In such cases ego states lose their current ego cathexis, but remain preserved by a cohesive force intact in the unconscious.

This concise statement implies that ego states have the character of mental structures, that they are therefore internally coherent, that they are in part composed of ego feelings (including, of course, the fourfold ego feelings set forth above), that they may be conscious or repressed, and that they are held together through the operation of an energy cathexis.

A not dissimilar formulation of the nature of ego states, drawn from a very different background of research, is found in the work of Kernberg (1966), who in turn draws upon the work of Jacobson (1964). According to Kernberg, all ego states are composed of three elements, viz., self-representations, object-representations, and affects (or, the perceptual equivalents of instinctual drives striving toward discharge). The self- and object-representations constitute the perceptual contents of ego states, while the affective component represents instinctual drives; hence, ego states, according to this view, are *mental substructures composed of both perceptual and economic components.* It is important to note, for the purposes of the present discussion, that the economic aspect of mental structures may be introduced at the level of ego states, and furthermore, that both Federn, who approaches metapsychology from a phenomenological vantage point, and Kernberg, a careful student of the structural "derivatives" of object relations, introduce it similarly.

We must bear in mind, of course, that the mental representations of "self" and "object" about which Jacobson has written constitute perceptual mental contents, if by "perceptual" we mean akin to images of some sort. The assimilation of affects to these mental representations introduces into ego states their particular quality of propensity toward discharge, or of "valence," which implies that they possess a directed or vectorial quality. This quality of "intentionality," developed originally by Brentano (1874) and inherent in the concept of cathexis itself, is further set forth by Federn in his concept of the fourfold ego feelings, a fundamental property of which is innate directionality (active, passive, reflective) or its absence (medial). A purely classical view of "tendency toward directional discharge" would conceptualize it in terms of a reduction of instinctual drive tension according to the pleasure principle. The very directedness of ego states, however, is in turn a component linked to representational content; hence self- and object-representations are inseparable from drive discharge itself. It would not seem importunate, therefore, to consider that Federn's implications for, and Jacobson's and Kernberg's more explicit formulations of, ego states have much in common—most significantly, the concept that objects and instinctual drive systems are indivisible aspects of each other.* This view therefore asserts that, in a certain sense, one could with justification number Federn among the object-relations theorists, since the concept of inseparability of object and instinct is a fundamental tenet of object-relations theory.

INFANTILE DEFENSES AND THEIR PRECURSORS

By the time the child has reached the end of the first year of life, self and nonself have undergone limited differentiation from each other. The beginnings of this differentiation are to be found in the operation of those unconditioned physiological mechanisms by which the infant literally incorporates—swallows—that which tastes good to him, and rejects—spits out—that which tastes offensive to him. The metapsychological concomitants of these processes constitute the purified pleasure ego of Freud, according to which "All that is good is me; all that is bad is not-me" (Freud 1915a). At this stage of ego development, the "good : me" perceptions and the "bad : not-me" perceptions may be said to constitute the earliest manifestations of what will later become, respectively, self-representations and object-representations; hence they may be viewed as precursors of the latter.

We must ask, however, by what means these representational precursors come to serve as vehicles, so to speak, for the affect-charges which, in turn, represent the emotional expression of the infant's primitive instinctual drives. If we assume, with Klein

*The interrelatedness of "instinct" and "object" was, of course, first put forward by Freud (1905, 1915a) and was further developed by Schilder (1953).

(1932, 1935), that the infant harbors a vast reservoir of un-neutralized aggression which must be gotten rid of lest his very existence be threatened, then we shall look to extrusive or expulsive mechanisms which the infant already has at hand for the accomplishment of that task. It would appear that the mechanisms inherent in the operation of the purified pleasure ego are equal to it: that which the infant experiences as offensive is perceived as "not-me" and is rejected, and to these offensive external oral items (potential food substances), which the infant will of necessity spit out, become attached the aggressive affect-charges which must be gotten rid of. Thus, aggressive affect-charges are extruded as they come to be affixed, so to speak, to the "real" items which the infant literally spits back into the surround. At this point of ego development, the fusion of aggressive affect-charge with offensive "external item" could be said to constitute the precursor of projection; and projection per se will have come into functional significance when, at a later time, the aggressive instinct becomes separated from the "real external item"—split off, as it were—and externalized qua itself, without further necessity for a "real item" to serve as its vehicle.

From the foregoing, we may infer that the mechanism of splitting already figures prominently in at least two interrelated processes that have assumed importance by the time the third trimester of infancy has been traversed, viz., the operation of the purified pleasure ego, by which representational precursors of "me" and "not-me" have been differentiated, and the separation of aggressive instinct from the "real items" by which it was initially extruded into the surround, thus initiating the operation of true projection. It is axiomatic for this stage of ego develop-ment, in addition, that the extruded or projected "not-me" regularly undergoes scotomatization, and hence, is denied exist-ence in the perceptual field. Thus, a third mechanism comes into operation which leads to the perceptual extinguishment of offensive "real items" and, later, of intolerable aggressive instinct—denial. These three interrelated mechanisms—splitting, projection, and denial—are the earliest defenses of which the primitive ego is capable, and in turn represent the deepest point of genetic regression attainable by the psychotic child or adult.

The unremitting—indeed, perseverated—operation of infantile projection tends to lead the infantile ego into a state of relative imbalance, such that a welter of "bad" objects is perceived to reside outside the self, while a minimum of "good" objects is perceived to reside within it (Fairbairn 1941). Insofar as "good" internal objects carry a "positive valence" (Kernberg 1966) or, in other words, carry a libidinal cathexis which imparts a hedonic quality to the infant's primitive self-awareness, then a relative paucity of good internal objects bespeaks a relative deficiency of libido. Furthermore, the welter of projected bad objects, including the extruded aggressive affect charges as well as the need-frustrating feeding object (= breast), return unremittingly to plague the early ego's perceptual apparatus. As noted before, we have good if indirect reasons for believing that the infant experiences these bad objects as terrifyingly vivid, and that their perceptual intensity threatens to overwhelm the infantile stimulus barrier and thus precipitate the ego into a traumatic state; hence they assume the quality of persecutory objects.*

It is now possible to bring together several inherently interrelated lines of thought that have to do with basic structural, economic, perceptual, and boundary aspects of early ego function. We may, first of all, view projection as a product of the more basic process of splitting. Second, it is clear that splitting is fundamental to the modus operandi of the purified pleasure ego. Third, Klein's "paranoid position" (later, following Fairbairn's ideas, more correctly termed by her "paranoid-schizoid position"), and Fairbairn's so-called paranoid transitional mechanism (1941) may be viewed as later derivatives of the purified pleasure ego.

---

*It is necessary to point out that, in the interest of succinctness, the term "object" is here used to mean "part-object-representation."

Returning now to Federn's view of the economic basis of ego states, we shall recall his postulate that a relative deficiency of ego libido is the cause of contraction of the external ego boundary, and that under these circumstances, as in the case of the "weak" or "psychotic" ego, formerly egotized mental contents come to fall outside the territory of the ego delimited by that boundary; such contents therefore come to be perceived as "real." Since, as we know, the ego's libidinal affect-charges (= "ego libido") are carried by its reservoir of good internal objects, it becomes possible to assert that deficiency of ego libido, and hence, impoverishment of the ego cathexis, is a consequence of a deficiency of good internal objects.

THE TODDLER

The end of the first year and the inception of the second are of momentous significance for the elaboration of all that has gone before. The foreordained maturational spurt that marks this stage of development in part engenders the cessation of the child's abject dependency on the mothering object as two basic forms of mastery now begin to make their appearance: walking and talking. As sphincter dominance shifts from mouth to anus, under pressure from both the maturing physiological apparatus and the expectancies of the social milieu, prior splitting and projective defenses continue to operate for a time, displaced as they are toward the anorectal zone. Thus, Abraham (1912, 1921, 1924) spoke of an early anal-expulsive or anal-aggressive stage of psychosexual development, in which the need to extrude anal waste material is prepotent. Thus, the "meaning" of the first anal "gift" of feces is multifold: to get rid of something bad, to attract the good parental object, and magically to ward off the parental object as well.

Toward the end of the second year, however, a significant alteration of the child's partial aims makes its appearance; this alteration is represented in a shift from predominantly anal-expulsive to anal-retentive mechanisms. In Fairbairn's terms

(1941), the "transitional mechanism" shifts from a paranoid mode to an obsessional mode, the hallmark of which is *retention of both the good and the bad objects.* From this point on, the operation of the purified pleasure ego falls rapidly away, and a concomitant recession in splitting, with persistent efforts to cling internally to the whole-object (both "good" and "bad"), now becomes evident. There is good reason to believe that the fateful shift from part-object aims to whole-object aims, with percipient efforts to retain the whole-object, occurs in consequence of those myriad needs and experiences which propel the child toward separation from the maternal object. Thus, retention of the whole-object represents a need to cling to that from which one is proceeding to separate.

To explain these matters more fully, we have recourse to Freud's (1917b, 1923) conclusion that object loss is attended by reintrojection of the loss object, and that the reintrojected object becomes ensconced within the "differentiating grade within the ego"—the superego. Freud further pointed out that reintrojection brings about a defusion of instincts, an *Entmischung,* which separates primary aggression and libido from each other. Following Hartmann (1950, 1955), the defused instincts become available for ego functions according to the process of neutralization.* Thus, aggression becomes available, in deinstinctualized form, to energize the defenses of the unconscious part of the ego as well as for a variety of actions oriented toward the attainment of mastery (secondary autonomy), while libido, in deinstinctualized form, serves to energize the ego's synthetic function and its representational content. The operation of the obsessional mechanism, through which both good and bad objects are retained within the ego, is now seen to occur as a result of the gradual separation of the child from the mother. But what we have been describing here is, after all, nothing more than

---

*It is recognized that the "defused" instincts must ultimately re-associate as whole-object relations are attained (see chapter 3).

mourning attending the loss of a loved object, as set forth by Freud, and by Abraham (1912, 1921, 1924). And this, it now seems reasonable to assert, is what accounts for Klein's "depressive position" of later infancy.*

We have now brought into connection several processes of great importance for the developing ego during the second year of life. Separation from the primary maternal object sets in motion the mechanism of reintrojection with whole-object retention; as a result, instinctual defusion occurs, making neutralized energy available to the ego's defensive, representational, and synthetic functions.

As already noted, reintrojection associated with mourning the separated object and the operation of the obsessional mechanism together have the effect of bringing back a multiplicity of bad part-objects previously extruded from the territory of the ego through the mechanism of projection. During this stage of ego development, self- and object-representations have become progressively clearly differentiated as the child's perceptual apparatus has matured. These representations, according to Kernberg, have become progressively assimilated to instinctual affect-charges of either "positive" (libidinal) or "negative" (aggressive) valence, and hence, have become either positive or negative ego states. The assimilation of self- and object-representations to affect comes about, of course, as a result of the operation of the ego's synthetic function; the latter is energized by deinstinctualized libidinal cathexes resulting, in turn, from instinctual defusion consequent upon whole-object reintrojection. Thus, the territory of the ego is expanded, its "contents" increased.

Of great importance is the whole matter of what, in general, could be termed internalization. The entire congeries of both split-off and retained good and bad part-objects is, in consequence of the reintrojective and obsessional mechanisms, trans-

---

*The signal importance of the relationship between object-loss and splitting as a defense mechanism, so basic to the work of Bowlby (1953, 1960a, 1961) on childhood bereavement, is set forth by Freud (1917b, 1927, 1940b).

ferred, as it were, into the ego itself. When this internalization has reached a sufficient degree, and when mental contents have in significant measure undergone structuralization into ego states through the operation of the ego's synthetic function, projection, scotomatization, and splitting give way, now, to repression.

An understanding of Federn's ego cathexis may be developed in terms of the matters so sketchily discussed here. We shall recall that the ego cathexis maintains the functional integrity of the external ego boundary and of the sensory receptors embedded in it, thus delimiting egotized (subjective) from unegotized (objective, "real") mental contents, and guaranteeing that the latter are perceived with appropriate vividness. The ego cathexis also maintains the functional integrity of the internal ego boundary, directed against unegotized, unconscious mental content; hence it drives and modulates the ego's defense mechanisms against unconscious material. *We may therefore take the concept of ego cathexis to mean a neutralized (deinstinctualized) energy cathexis derived from whole-object introjection.*

FURTHER CONSIDERATION OF REPRESSION

We have set forth the view, in accordance with that of Kernberg (1966), that internalization and structuralization, in the sense developed above, are absolute prerequisites for the defensive shift from splitting to repression. As he has shown, repression consists of dissociation of negative introjections or, more properly, negative ego states from the core of the ego. We shall recall that these negative ego states comprise self- and object-representations assimilated to aggressive affect-charges which repression causes to be excluded from the ego's awareness. Failure of repression is attended by a return of these negative ego states, with their "bad" self- and object-representations, to the core of the ego. Their return, bringing a welter of aggressive affect-charges into the ego core, dilutes and displaces, as it were, the preponderance of positive ego states, organized around libidinal affect-charges, which are necessary for the ego's core perceptions. It is this state of affairs which results in the "perceptual alienation" of the ego core to which Federn originally ascribed depersonalization.

The return of "dissociated" (repressed) aggressive affect-charges and their associated representations signals failure of repression. It is no wonder, then, that in the incipient stages of psychotic disorganization, depersonalization is so regularly experienced. By the same token, failure of the ego cathexis brings about contraction of the external ego boundary and decathexis of the sensory receptors that are a part of it, with ensuing estrangement and deepening impairment of the sense of reality. Also, further withdrawal of libidinal cathexis of mental contents engenders their de-egotization; thus they may be perceived as foreign bodies loosely and unaccountably aggregated within the territory of the ego, such as ego-alien ideas and feelings, or else as extruded "hyperreal" entities of oppressive perceptual intensity.*

Let us now recall Federn's assertion that investment of the ego core with ego cathexis yields medial ego feeling, the impairment of which leads to depersonalization. Medial ego feeling corresponds to a prereflective sense of self or, in other words, to the sense of self inherent in the state of primary or "objectless" narcissism; it represents the individual's more or less vague perception of his extension in time and space prior to that point beyond which he is able to "cathect" himself as an object of his own awareness (Rinsley 1962).

In accepting the view that repression signifies dissociation or exclusion of negative ego states from the ego core, we must ask,

---

*All these regressive processes, consequent upon re-entry of negative ego states into the ego, are evidence of failure of the ego's synthetic function, resulting in a return to part-object-relations and leading to the well-known "fragmentation" of all ego functions; hence, such innately shrewd descriptive terms for *schizophrenia* [sic] used by the earlier, preanalytic psychiatrists: *dementia sejunctiva, intra-psychic ataxia* (Stransky), *folies discordantes* (Chaslin), etc.

conversely: of what is the ego core otherwise composed? Clearly, at the outset, one could say that, *under ideal conditions,* the ego core should be composed exclusively of positive ego states. But what is the fate of the negative ego states, and particularly of the aggressive affect-charges which drive them, following their repression? The more classical answer would hold that these negative ego states, driven by aggressive cathexes, press unremittingly against the internal ego boundary for readmission into the territory of the ego, to "return," as it were, from the Ucs.

Granting Hartmann's view that deinstinctualized aggression serves to maintain the defensive countercathexes of the ego, then clearly the aggressive cathexes associated with repressed ego states cannot be deemed deinstinctualized, and hence, cannot be viewed as available to the ego for the purposes of defense. On the other hand, lest we jettison the dual instinct theory, we must conclude that neutralized energy must ultimately be derived from the vast pool of "raw" aggression in the Ucs, and that its source must be other than that derived from reintrojection of "lost" objects. The latter point follows from at least two antecedent considerations: first, the usual circumstances of life do not witness such a high frequency of object loss as would account for the continuous availability of neutralized energy required for the ego's autonomous functions; were this not so, the individual would be in a constant state of mourning, a condition found only among depressed persons. Second, overwhelming use of introjective mechanisms is a major sign of ego weakness, and at best yields a characterologic structure appropriately termed "borderline" or "as-if" (Deutsch 1942).

The problem may be nearer to solution if we consider that repression of negative ego states from the ego core into the Ucs, however mature a defense it is, nonetheless bears certain of the characteristics of its earlier precursors—splitting, projection, and scotomatization or denial. For in repression too, the ego acts as if the repressed object-representations are, in fact, "lost." One may thus infer that the ego treats the contents of the Ucs in some ways like those of the external world, the most notable indication for which is the fact that the unconscious contents conform to the primary process and are uninfluenced by the ego's synthetic function.

We may with some little justification say, therefore, that repressed objects are lost objects. As with all lost objects, the ego will make strong efforts to get them back, as it were. The striving of the repressed to "return" is, therefore, a more complex process than can be explained in the usual dynamic terms for, in addition, we must add the basic consideration that the ego actively strives to regain its repressed objects, to bring them once again under the hegemony of its synthetic function. The ego's unremitting efforts to do this lead to endlessly repetitive re-entry of Ucs content into the ego's territory; thus, "reintrojection from the side of the Ucs" leads to no less palpable economic results than the analogous process from the side of the external world. In accordance with this view, therefore, with re-entry of Ucs contents into the ego, the previously "fluid" or unbound cathexes and their perceptual representations once again agglomerate according to the synthetic function; the cathexes thus re-bound to mental representations proceed in part to undergo defusion; hence they are available to the ego for the purposes of sublimation.

FURTHER COMMENTS ON THE SOURCES OF NEUTRALIZED ENERGY

We may now recapitulate and expand upon our previous concepts of the origin of neutralized energy. To begin with, our view is that such energy becomes available at that point of psychosexual development when reintrojection of the whole-object begins to take place, and that the latter occurs in consequence of the child's necessary efforts to separate from its mother, to "defuse" or to "desymbiotize," as it were. This early move toward separation serves as a paradigm for the many later efforts to separate from the primary parental figures, such as at the time the child begins school and during adolescence, when further crucially important efforts to separate come about. The earliest definitive move toward separation, beginning in the last trimester of the first year and extending into the anal stage of psychosexual development, is characterized by whole-object cathexis, and by the reintrojection described above; the latter process accounts for the mourning inherent in the separation, and contributes to it the qualities of the "depressive position" described by Klein (1935, 1946). All these interrelated processes, including efforts physically to separate, whole-object invest-ment, reintrojection with accompanying mourning, and defusion of instincts with its issue of neutralized energy, contribute to the child's self-objectification and coincide with his entry into the period of childhood negativism. Indeed, Spitz views the early "No" response as the first indication of the child's use of judgment (1957, 1959).

Another way to view these processes, in accordance with Federn's contributions, would be in terms of the formation and maintenance of the ego boundaries. Thus, the growth of self-objectification (secondary narcissism), based as it is upon rein-trojection, may be viewed as directly related to the growing functional importance of the external ego boundary, which delimits the ego from the "environment" and its "objects," and of the internal ego boundary, which delimits it from its "re-pressed objects." We shall recall, of course, that the integrity of the ego boundaries is guaranteed by the ego cathexis which, as we have seen, is in turn derived from whole-object introjection.

With the child's progressive entry into the stage of self-objectification and mastery, internalization and repression assume ever-increasing importance. With this, splitting mech-anisms fall away, and the processes by which the ego dynami-cally "takes in" and "puts out" its representational contents shift from the side of the external world to the side of the Ucs. Deinstinctualized energy now becomes increasingly available to the ego from the energy cathexes of repressed ego states as these alternatively re-enter and are repressed and re-repressed from the ego's territory under the pressure of the ego's need to regain its repressed objects (or, better, the repressed representational parts of its ego states).

Thus, the ego's need for "good objects" may be equated with its need for neutralized energy, and we may justifiably begin the task of intertranslating the language of economics and the language of object relations.

SUMMARY

The view expressed here asserts the following: (1) it emphasizes the primacy of objects (or, better, object-representations) in respect to the instinctual needs mediated by the ego; (2) it offers somewhat more parsimonious explanations for defensive functions, in particular as it holds to certain basic similarities between the ways in which the ego deals with the Ucs and the so-called external world; (3) it holds, in effect, that the reservoir of the ego's neutralized energy is derived from a process, "from the side of the Ucs," which resembles the repetition-compulsions by which the ego ordinarily works through object loss; (4) it holds that all "mental structures" are in part object-representations; (5) it attempts to show the close relationship between Federn's contributions to the dynamic phenomenology of economics, ego feelings, and ego boundaries, and the general approach of object-relations theory; and (6) it attempts to formulate a conception of ego strength (hence, of ego weakness) which asserts that the "amount" of energy available to the ego's autonomous functions and the relative preponderance within the ego of "good" object-representations are mutually interrelated.

CHAPTER 2

THE ROLE
OF THE MOTHER

This chapter describes the role of the mother's faulty libidinal availability in the development of the borderline syndrome. It describes, in terms of object-relations theory, the effects of alternating maternal libidinal availability and withdrawal, at the time of separation-individuation (rapprochement subphase), upon the development of the psychic structure of the borderline patient—the *split ego* and the *split object-relations unit* (Fairbairn 1954, Guntrip 1961, 1968, Klein 1935, 1946, Parens and Saul 1971, Rinsley 1968, 1971a,b). It then demonstrates how these find expression and proceed to function in the therapeutic alliance, and in transference and resistance.

KERNBERG'S CONTRIBUTION TO THE OBJECT-RELATIONS THEORY OF NORMAL DEVELOPMENT

Object-relations theory may be defined as the psychoanalytic approach to the internalization of interpersonal relations (Kernberg 1971a). Kernberg (1972a, see also chapter 3) postulates four stages in the development of normal internalized object

---

Dr. James F. Masterson was the senior coauthor of this chapter in its original version.

relations. Stage 1 of development, roughly coincident with the first postnatal month of life, precedes the establishment of the primary, undifferentiated self-object constellation built up in the infant under the influence of his pleasurable, gratifying experiences in his interactions with the mother (Jacobson 1964). Stage 2, roughly occupying the first to the third postnatal months, comprises the establishment and consolidation of an undifferentiated self-object image or representation (Jacobson 1964) of a libidinally gratifying or rewarding (= "good") type under the organizing influence of gratifying experiences within the context of the mother-child unit; concomitantly, a separate, primitive intrapsychic structure, comprising an undifferentiated "bad" self-object representation, is built up under the influence of frustrating and painful (i.e., traumatogenic) psychophysiological states. Thus, two sets of opposite primitive self-object-affect complexes are built up and fixed by memory traces as polar opposite intrapsychic structures. Stage 3 is reached when the self-image and the object-image have become differentiated within the core "good" self-object representation; the differentiation of self-image from object-image within the core "bad" self-object representation occurs later and is complicated by early forms of projection, that is, intrapsychic mechanisms which attempt to externalize the "bad" self-object constellation (chapter 1, as well as Kernberg 1966, Spitz and Wolf 1946). This stage is said to occupy the period between the fourth postnatal month and the end of the first year. Stage 4 has its inception at some point between the end of the first year of life and the second half of the second year and continues to evolve throughout the remainder of childhood. During this stage, "good" and "bad" self-images coalesce into an integrated self-concept; in other words, self-images establish coherence and continuity under the impact of polar opposite emotional-interpersonal experiences; affects become integrated and toned down and undergo further differentiation, and the child's self-concept and his actual presentation of behavior in the social field become closer. At the same time, "good" and "bad" object-images also coalesce such that the "good" and the "bad" images of the mother become integrated into a whole-object maternal concept which closely approaches the actuality or reality of the mother in the child's perceptual-interpersonal field.

Kernberg (1972a) emphasizes the progressively integrative aspects of these stages for both ego and superego development, for the establishment of ego identity, and for the development of the capacity for deep and consistent relationships with other persons.

KERNBERG AND THE EGO FIXATION OF THE BORDERLINE

Kernberg theorizes that the fixation peculiar to the borderline syndrome takes place during the third stage of this developmental scheme, when there yet remains a dissociation of libidinally determined (= "good") from (= "bad") self- and object-representations, that is, "good" self- and object-representations and "bad" self- and object-representations are perceived as separate and unrelated.* He then outlines the structural consequences of this fixation, which determine the clinical manifestations of the borderline (Kernberg 1967, 1968): pathological persistence of the primitive defense of splitting; failure to develop an integrated self-concept; chronic overdependence upon external objects; and development of contradictory character traits in relation to contradictory ego states, resulting in chaotic interpersonal relationships. Superego integration suffers as a result of failure of the guiding function of an integrated ego identity, with persistent contradictions between exaggerated "ideal" object-images and extremely sadistic "all-bad" superego forerunners. The failure to develop an integrated object-represen-

---

*It will be evident that Kernberg and Mahler differ significantly with regard to the timing of the occurrence of the fixation underlying borderline personality development, the former citing the period of 4–12 months, and the latter, the period of the "rapprochement subphase," coinciding with 16–25 months postnatally.

tation inhibits and ultimately limits development of the capacity for understanding of, and empathy for, other persons.* Ego strength depends in particular upon the neutralization of "raw" energies, which occurs in intimate connection with the process of integration of libidinally derived (= "good") and aggressively derived (= "bad") self- and object-images, and it is precisely this integration which fails to occur in future borderline personalities. Failure of neutralization, in turn, compromises specific aspects of ego strength, including anxiety tolerance, control of impulses, and the potential for true sublimations (chapter 1).

Kernberg's view of the etiology of this failure places predominant emphasis upon constitutional factors—an excess of oral aggression, a deficiency in the capacity to neutralize aggression, or a lack of anxiety tolerance (Kernberg 1966):

> More characteristic for the borderline personality organization may be a failure related to a constitutionally determined lack of anxiety tolerance interfering with the phase of synthesis of introjections of opposite valences. The most important cause of failure in the borderline pathology is probably a quantitative predominance of negative introjections. Excessive negative introjections may stem both from a constitutionally determined intensity of aggressive drive derivatives and from severe early frustration.

A predominantly heredo-congenital view of the etiology of the developmental failure peculiar to the borderline personality would emphasize the infant's a priori propensity to form pre-

---

*Associated failure to develop an integrated self-representation and an integrated object-representation, normally accomplished during stage 4, may be viewed in terms of failure to develop whole-object relations from antecedent part-object relations. It may be noted that developmental fixation at stage 3 corresponds with fixation at Fairbairn's late oral stage of infantile dependence (Fairbairn 1941), during which the (maternal) whole-object is characteristically perceived and treated as part-object (breast). The borderline's cathexis of whole-objects *as if they were part-objects* leads in turn to a welter of later interpersonal depersonifications and appersonations described elsewhere (Rinsley 1971a,b).

ponderantly negative introjections, which Mahler (1968) considers to be typical in infantile psychosis. Although, as Weil (1970) has recently stated, there is considerable evidence for a wide range of "basic core" variation, predominantly heredo-constitutional views can readily lead to underestimation of the importance of the mother's libidinal availability to the infant during the developmentally critical period of separation-individuation (6–30 months of age).

GENESIS OF THE FIXATION OF THE BORDERLINE: NATURE–NURTURE VERSUS CONSTITUTION–EXPERIENCE

In discussing this often polemical issue with respect to infantile psychosis, Mahler (1968) suggests the complementary relationship between nature and nurture. She states:

> If, during the most vulnerable autistic and symbiotic phase, very severe, accumulated, and staggering traumatization occurs in a constitutionally fairly sturdy infant, psychosis may ensue. . . . On the other hand, in constitutionally greatly predisposed, oversensitive, or vulnerable infants, normal mothering does not suffice to counteract the innate defect in the catalytic, buffering, and polarizing utilization of the human love object or mothering agency in the outside world for intrapsychic evolution and differentiation [p. 48].

Mahler clearly avers that, in her view, constitutional defect serves as the basis for infantile psychosis, the victims of which she describes as lacking or failing to acquire the capacity to internalize the representation of the mothering object as a guide for the differentiation of internal and external stimulation.

The presence of excessive oral aggression in the borderline leads Kernberg to favor a constitutional etiology for the borderline syndrome. Although undue degrees of oral aggression do indeed characterize the borderline individual, their presence per se does not justify a purely or predominantly constitutional view of borderline psychopathology, and Kernberg adduces no other evidence in support of his view. There is, to be sure, a parallel deficiency of libidinal cathexis of both self- and object-representations which could as likely lead to a theory of deficiency of libidinal energy, constitutional or otherwise, a view originally put forward by Federn (1952) (see chapter 1). The issue becomes largely academic, however, in view of incontrovertible clinical evidence, drawn from reconstructive analytic psycho-therapy and from intensive residential treatment, that both adolescent and adult borderlines demonstrate a full capacity for internalization once their abandonment depression has been worked through (Masterson 1971a,b, 1972a,b, 1976, Rinsley 1965, 1971b, 1974a).

Our contention is that the determining cause of the fixation of the borderline individual is to be found in the mother's withdrawal of her libidinal availability (i.e., of her libidinal sup-plies) as the child makes efforts toward separation-individuation during the rapprochement subphase;* and further, that the fix-ation comes into existence at exactly that time because the child's individuation constitutes a major threat to the mother's defensive need to cling to her infant and, as a consequence, drives her toward removal of her libidinal availability.**

---

*The normal developmental vicissitudes of the rapprochement subphase—i.e., the surge of individuation accompanying the acquisition of locomotion and speech, as well as the increased awareness of the separateness from the mother which triggers the child's increased sensitivity and need for the mother—become unique vulnerabilities for the borderline child. The very surge of individuation which brings with it a greater need for the mother's support, actually induces withdrawal of that support—i.e., the vital process in which he is engaged produces the withdrawal that arrests that process and results in the stereotypical clinical pattern—individuation, depression, defense.

**The early mother-child interaction is so complex yet so fateful for a child's development that it is both difficult and hazardous to try to tease out principal themes which can be generalized. Nevertheless, the stereotyped repetition of maladaptive themes in our patients' lives and in the transference impels us to undertake this task, in spite of its hazards and limitations, in the hope of unraveling

The twin themes (*reward and withdrawal*) of this interaction are subsequently introjected by the child, become the leitmotif of his psychic structure, and reappear in his pathologic split self- and object-representations as these are recapitulated within the therapeutic transference.

In view of these considerations, it may be argued that the child's excessive oral aggression becomes entrenched in consequence of the mother's withdrawal of supplies in the wake of the child's efforts toward separation-individuation, further aggravated by the latter's inability to integrate positive and negative self- and object-representations, since such integration would require further separation-individuation, which, in turn, would provoke further withdrawal of maternal libidinal supplies. There thus comes about a situation in which aggression is repetitively provoked without any constructive means conducive to its neutralization.

---

some of its mysteries. It is essential if we are to understand our patients' problems and their therapeutic needs.

Since publication of this article in 1975, the point of view expressed above has been broadened as follows. The basic issue is the mother's libidinal unavailability to the child's need for supplies for separation-individuation. In most of our patients, that unavailability was due to the specific nature of the tie between the mother and that particular child—i.e., the mother's need to extend specific regressive projections on the child to defend herself against an abandonment depression. The child's individuation interfered with these projections, exposed the mother to an abandonment depression, and impelled her to withdraw as a defense.

We emphasized the unique, intimate, and specific nature of that tie by stating that the mother had a borderline syndrome herself and required the child's compliance with her projections to defend against an abandonment depression. Although most of our mothers were, indeed, borderline, it now appears that mothers with even more serious disorders, including psychosis, can have a similar effect since they may also be libidinally unavailable for separation-individuation needs. Theoretically, this would also apply to mothers who are depressed as well as to those who are physically absent during this crucial period. The key issue again is the mother's libidinal unavailability for these needs, which itself may be due to a variety of causes. The child would respond to the unavailability as an absence or withdrawal of a vital need and introject it as a withdrawing maternal part-object. Nevertheless, the relationship stands out with the most clarity where the specific tie can be identified.

MAHLER AND THE ROLE OF THE LIBIDINAL AVAILABILITY OF THE MOTHER IN THE DEVELOPMENT OF NORMAL OBJECT RELATIONS

Mahler's work is replete with references to the fundamental importance of the mother's libidinal availability for the development of normal object relations. In discussing Hartmann's view that infantile psychosis results from a defect in the ego's capacity for drive neutralization, with ensuing interference with the development of other ego functions and object relations, she states: "My theory places special emphasis, however, on the interaction of both these factors with the circular processes between infant and mother, in which the mother serves as a beacon of orientation and living buffer for the infant, in reference to both external reality and his internal milieu" (1968, p. 229). She also writes:

During the course of the normal separation-individuation process, the predominance of pleasure in separate functioning, in an atmosphere in which the mother is emotionally available, enables the child to overcome that measure of separation anxiety that makes its appearance at that point of the separation-individuation phase at which a differentiated object representation, separate from the self, gradually enters conscious awareness . . . [1968, pp. 220–221].

In a quasi-closed system or unit, the mother executes vitally important ministrations, without which the human young could not survive. The intrauterine, parasite-host relationship within the mother organism . . . must be replaced in the postnatal period by the infant's being enveloped, as it were, in the extrauterine matrix of the mother's nursing care, a kind of *social symbiosis*. . . .
The mutual cuing between infant and mother is the most important requisite for normal symbiosis . . . [1968, p. 34].

It is the mother's love of the toddler and her acceptance of his ambivalence that enables the toddler to cathect his self-representation with neutralized energy [1968, p. 222].

The question concerning the manner in which the mother's libidinal availability determines the development of the child's intrapsychic structure is answerable in terms of the child's internalization of his interactions with her to form self- and object-representations, the nature of which will have profound consequences for ego integration (Jacobson 1964, Kernberg 1972a, Mahler 1968). Functioning according to the pleasure principle, which both constitutes and determines his initial orientation in the extrauterine field, the infant will draw away, or will attempt to expel or eliminate in the face of painful or unpleasurable interactions with the mother. Of critical importance, especially in early infancy, is the equation, *"good" = pleasurable = minimally stimulating*, as well as the equation, *"bad" = unpleasurable (painful) = overstimulating (traumatogenic)*, as they apply to the quality of the mother-infant interactions. These interactions are introjected to form scattered "good" and "bad" memory islands which are integrated into the progressively differentiated self- and object-images which Kernberg (1966) has described.*

Mahler articulates the mother's role as follows:

> It is the specific unconscious need of the mother that activates, out of the infant's infinite potentialities, those in particular that create for each mother "the child" who reflects her own *unique* and individual needs. This process takes place, of course, within the range of the child's innate endowments.
>
> Mutual cuing during the symbiotic phase creates that indelibly imprinted configuration—that complex pattern—that becomes *the leitmotif for "the infant's becoming the child of his particular mother"*. . . .
>
> In other words, the mother conveys—in innumerable ways— a kind of "mirroring frame of reference," to which the primitive self of the infant automatically adjusts [1968, p. 19].

---

*It should be noted here that, with reference to mother-infant interactions during the first postnatal year, and in particular during its first half, the term *mother* in fact has reference to the maternal part-object (breast); thus the term *mother* is used here in this connection for convenience and simplicity.

Mahler suggests the possible developmental consequences of the mother's libidinal unavailability to the infant. She asserts that in instances in which the mother, in fantasy or in actuality, fails to accept the infant, the latter experiences a deficit in self-esteem and a consequent narcissistic vulnerability. She goes on to say:

> If the mother's "primary preoccupation" with her infant—*her* mirroring function during earlier infancy—is unpredictable, unstable, anxiety-ridden, or hostile; if her confidence in herself as a mother is shaky, then the individuating child has to do without a reliable frame of reference for checking back, perceptually and emotionally, to the symbiotic partner. . . . The result will then be a disturbance in the primitive "self feeling". . . . [1968, p. 19].

On the other hand, while emphasizing the importance of the mother's libidinal availability for optimal infantile ego development, Mahler also points out the normal infant's striking capacity to extract supplies from any available human contact. In support of this view, she cites Spitz's (1945, 1946, 1965) investigation of infants who experienced the loss of a symbiotic love object during the second half of the first year; although the infants perished if a substitute object was not found, they recovered when one was found.

Mahler also cites studies of children who spent their first year of life in a concentration camp (A. Freud and Dann 1951); she states: "While these experiences left their traces on these children's object relationships, the children developed strong ties to each other and none of them suffered from a childhood psychosis" (1968, p. 50). She further cites Goldfarb's (1945) studies of children placed in foster homes who, "amidst the most trying circumstances . . . were able to extract, as it were, substitutions for the actual loss of mothering. Although they may have paid the price for this object loss with neurotic disorders, character distortions, or psychopathic difficulties later in life, they *never* severed their ties with reality" (1968, pp. 50–51).

Mahler's cited evidence may be adduced in support of her argument for a constitutional etiology for infantile psychosis, since the children studied did not develop such severe psychopathology despite having been subjected to severe stress, particularly as a result of having been deprived of their mothers. On the other hand, her evidence may indeed be taken as favorable to the concept of an environmental etiology of the borderline, particularly in view of her suggestion that these same children might well have later developed neurotic-characterological disorders typical of borderline personalities.

It is, in fact, impossible to compare the children reported on in these cited studies (A. Freud and Dann 1951, Goldfarb 1945, Spitz 1946, 1965) with borderline children. The former had lost their mothers at an early age and were subsequently able to "find" substitutes for them. *On the other hand, the borderline child has a mother with whom there is a unique and uninterrupted interaction with a specific relational focus, that is, reward for regression, withdrawal for separation-individuation.* As we shall attempt to show in what follows, the unique "push-pull" quality of this sort of mother-infant interaction becomes powerfully introjected and forms the basis for the progressive development of the borderline syndrome.

THE ROLE OF THE MOTHER'S LIBIDINAL AVAILABILITY IN THE DEVELOPMENT OF THE PSYCHIC STRUCTURE OF THE BORDERLINE

The mother's withdrawal of her libidinal availability in the face of her child's efforts toward separation-individuation creates the leitmotif of the borderline child, with the result that the child becomes the unique child of the borderline mother. The borderline mother, herself suffering from a borderline syndrome, experiences significant gratification during her child's symbiotic phase. The crisis supervenes at the time of separation-individuation, specifically during the rapprochement subphase, when she finds herself unable to tolerate her toddler's ambiva-

lence, curiosity, and assertiveness; the mutual cuing and communicative matching to these essential characteristics of individuation fail to develop. The mother is available if the child
clings and behaves regressively, but withdraws if he attempts to
separate and individuate. The child needs the mother's supplies in
order to grow; if he grows, however, they are withdrawn from
him (Masterson 1971a,b, 1972a,b, 1976). The images of these two
mothers are powerfully introjected by the child as part-object-
representations, together with their associated affects and self-
representations. Thus is generated the *split object-relations unit*
(SORU), which forms so important a part of the intrapsychic
structure of the borderline case.

The evidence in support of this formulation and of what
follows in greater detail is derived from several sources (Masterson 1971a,b, 1972a,b, Rinsley 1965, 1971a,b):

OBSERVATION. (a) Casework family therapy on a once- or
twice-weekly basis, for as long as four years, of the parents of
inpatient and outpatient borderline adolescents; (b) treatment of
borderline mothers in private office practice; (c) detailed observation and study of borderline mothers in conjoint interviews
with their borderline adolescent children; (d) long-term, intensive residential psychiatric treatment of borderline adolescents.

RECONSTRUCTION. The memories and associated affective responses of borderline adolescents in intensive psychotherapy as
they worked through their underlying abandonment depression.

INTRAPSYCHIC STRUCTURE OF THE BORDERLINE

As noted before, the terms "split ego" and "split object-
relations unit" are employed to define and describe the intrapsychic structure typical of the borderline personality; these
terms require further definition.

SPLITTING (Kernberg 1967). Splitting is a mechanism of defense, the function of which is to keep contradictory primitive

affective states separated from each other; the contradictory states remain in consciousness but do not mutually influence each other. Splitting also keeps apart the internalized self- and object-representations mutually linked with these affective states. Used normally by the immature ego, splitting ordinarily becomes replaced or supplanted by repression. The ego of the borderline, however, retains splitting as its principal mechanism of defense, while the capacity for normal repression remains underdeveloped.

SPLIT EGO (Kernberg 1967). Along with its reliance upon the splitting defense, the ego of the borderline is itself split into two parts, one of which functions according to the pleasure principle, and the other according to the reality principle.

SPLIT OBJECT-RELATIONS UNIT (Kernberg 1972a). The object-relations unit is derived from internalization of the infant's interactions with the mothering object. The unit comprises a self-representation, an object-representation, and an affective component which links them together.* The object-relations unit of the borderline turns out to be split into two part-units, each of which in turn comprises a part-self-representation and a part-object-representation, together with their respective associated affects.

MATERNAL LIBIDINAL AVAILABILITY AND THE SORU

In the case of the borderline, the object-relations unit remains split into two separate part-units, each of which comprises a part-self-representation, a part-object-representation, and an affective component which links the former two together. These two part-units are derived from internalization of the two

---

*The object-relations unit, with its triadic representational-affective structure (Kernberg 1966) has been defined elsewhere as an ego state (chapter 1).

principal themes of interaction with the borderline mother: the mother responds to the child's regressive behavior by maintaining her libidinal availability, and to the child's efforts toward separation-individuation by withdrawing. Thus are produced, in effect, the two aforementioned part-units, which may be termed the *withdrawing part-unit* and the *rewarding part-unit*, each of which has its own component part-self-representation, part-object-representation, and predominant linking affect; the withdrawing part-unit is cathected predominantly with aggressive energy, the rewarding part-unit with libidinal energy, and both remain separated from each other, as it were, through the mechanism of the splitting defense. It will be recalled that this situation comes about through fixation at Kernberg's stage 3, with ensuing failure of integration of "good" (positive, libidinal) and "bad" (negative, aggressive) self- and-object representations into whole (positive + negative) self-representations and object-representations, which would otherwise be expected to have occurred during stage 4. Table 2-1 summarizes the two part-units that constitute the borderline's split object-relations unit.*

MATERNAL LIBIDINAL AVAILABILITY AND THE SPLIT EGO

Freud (1911a) originally emphasized that in the beginning the child's behavior, under the domination of the primary process, is motivated by the pleasure principle, that is, the need to seek pleasure and to avoid pain. Governed "by the peremptory

---

*The reader will immediately discern the similarity of the split object-relations unit to Fairbairn's split internalized "bad" object, and Fairbairn deserves full prior credit for having perceived its basic structure in his analysands. Thus the withdrawing part-unit may be seen to correspond with Fairbairn's *rejecting object* (R.O.) while the rewarding part-unit may be seen to correspond with his *exciting object* (E.O.) (see chapters 4 and 14).

TABLE 2-1. SUMMARY OF THE BORDERLINE'S SPLIT OBJECT-RELATIONS UNIT

WITHDRAWING OR AGGRESSIVE PART-UNIT		
Part-object-representation	*Affect*	*Part-self-representation*
A maternal part-object which is attacking, critical, hostile, angry, withdrawing supplies and approval in the face of assertiveness or other efforts toward separation-individuation	Chronic anger, frustration, feeling thwarted, which cover profound underlying abandonment depression	A part-self-representation of being inadequate, bad, helpless, guilty, ugly, empty, etc.

REWARDING OR LIBIDINAL PART-UNIT		
Part-object-representation	*Affect*	*Part-self-representation*
A maternal part-object which offers approval, support, and supplies for regressive and clinging behavior	Feeling good, being fed, gratification of the wish for reunion	A part-self-representation of being the good, passive, compliant child

demands of internal needs" the child originally made use of hallucination to provide for their satisfaction. Freud added, however, that

> It was only the non-occurrence of the expected satisfaction, the disappointment experienced, that led to the abandonment of this attempt at satisfaction by means of hallucination. Instead of it, the psychical apparatus had to decide to form a conception of the real alteration in them. A new principle of mental functioning was thus introduced; what was presented in the mind was no longer what was agreeable but what was real, even if it happened to be disagreeable. This setting-up of the *reality principle* proved to be a momentous step.

Freud proceeds to trace the development of the use of the sense organs, perception, memory, consciousness, and thought as

agencies of the developing ego's capacity for reality testing. He
goes on to say: "Just as the pleasure-ego can do nothing but *wish*,
work for a yield of pleasure, and avoid unpleasure, so the reality-
ego need do nothing but strive for what is *useful* and guard itself
against damage." Of central importance is Freud's emphasis
upon the gradual transformation of the pleasure ego into the
reality ego in the wake of the child's increasing experience with
the failure of hallucinatory wishfulfillment.

In the case of the borderline individual, the term *split ego* has
reference to a persistent stunting of ego development such that a
substantial part of the pleasure ego fails to undergo the expected
transformation into the reality ego, with resultant pathological
persistence of the former; thus a large part of the ego of the
borderline continues, in effect, under the domination of the
pleasure principle. It should be emphasized that, in the case of
the borderline, the concept of ego splitting implies, not that a
previously former structure had undergone regressive splitting,
but rather, that a coherently functioning ego, operating in
accordance with the reality principle, had failed to develop.
Thus that part of the ego which Freud termed the pleasure ego
could, in the case of the borderline individual, be termed the
pathological ego, while the "remainder" could be termed the
reality or *healthy ego*.

It is necessary now to inquire into the basis for the persistence
of the pathological (pleasure) ego in these cases. To begin with,
the future borderline child finds himself caught between his
genetically determined drive toward separation-individuation
and the perceived threat of withdrawal of maternal supplies in
the face of it. As the child's self-representation begins to differentiate from the object-representation of the mother, that is,
as the child begins to separate, he experiences the abandonment
depression* in the wake of the threat of loss or withdrawal of

---

*As here employed, the term "abandonment depression" refers to the core
affect structurally linked to the part-self- and part-object-representations which
together constitute the withdrawing (aggressive) part-unit. The subjective state

supplies; at the same time, the mother continues to encourage and to reward those aspects of her child's behavior—passivity and regressiveness—which enable her to continue to cling to him.

Thus the mother encourages and rewards in the child the pathological ego's key defense mechanism of denial of the reality of separation, which in turn allows the *persistence of the wish for reunion, which later emerges as a defense against the abandonment depression.* Thus part of the ego fails to undergo the necessary transformation from reliance upon the pleasure principle to reliance upon the reality principle, for to do so would mean acceptance of the reality of separation, which would bring on the abandonment depression.

The mother's clinging and withdrawing, and the patient's acting out of his wish for reunion, promote the failure of one part of the ego to develop, resulting in an ego structure which is split into a pathological (pleasure) ego and a reality ego, the former pursuing relief from the feeling of abandonment, and the latter pursuing the reality principle. The pathological ego denies the reality of the separation, which permits the persistence of fantasies of reunion with the mother; these are then acted out through clinging and regressive behavior, thus defending against the abandonment depression and causing the patient to "feel good." Extensive fantasies of reunion are elaborated, projected onto the environment, and acted out, and are accompanied by increasing denial of reality. The two, operating in concert, create an ever-widening chasm between the patient's feelings and the

---

conveyed by the term includes a core anxiety component and a more differentiated component. The former is of an instinctual quality and corresponds with the primal experience of impending loss of the maternal stimulus barrier against endopsychic and external stimulation, with ensuing gross ego trauma. The latter, more structuralized, conveys the feeling of guilt which signifies the ego's anxiety over impending "abandonment" or sadistic assault by the superego, also perceived as a threatened loss or withdrawal of supplies. The basic feelings common to the state of abandonment depression thus comprise *a profound sense of emptiness* and, as an aspect of estrangement, *a sense of the meaninglessness of the "external" world.*

reality of his functioning as he gradually emerges from the developmental years into adulthood.

Again, it should be emphasized that such an arrest of ego development in all likelihood reflects, not a sudden or acute occurrence at the time of separation-individuation, but rather, a persistent, ongoing developmental failure, dating possibly from the mother's ambivalence toward the infant's earliest moves toward differentiation at about four to five months of age.

THE RELATIONSHIP BETWEEN THE SORU AND THE SPLIT EGO

As already noted, the splitting defense keeps separate the rewarding and the withdrawing object-relations part-units, including their associated affects. Although both the rewarding and the withdrawing maternal part-objects are pathological, the borderline experiences the rewarding part-unit as increasingly ego-syntonic, as it relieves the feelings of abandonment associated with the withdrawing part-unit, with the result that the individual "feels good." The affective state associated with the rewarding part-unit is that of gratification at being fed, hence, "loved." The ensuing denial of reality is, in the last analysis, but a small price to pay for this affective state.

An alliance is now seen to develop between the child's rewarding maternal part-image (rewarding part-unit) and his pathological (pleasure) ego, the primary purpose of which is to promote the "good" feeling and to defend against the feeling of abandonment associated with the withdrawing part-unit. This ultimately powerful alliance further promotes the denial of separateness and potentiates the child's acting out of his reunion fantasies. The alliance has an important secondary function, the discharge of aggression, which is both associated with and directed toward the withdrawing part-unit by means of symptoms, inhibitions, and various kinds of destructive acts. The aggression, which gains access to motility through the agency of the pathological (pleasure) ego, remains unneutralized, and hence, un-available for the further development of endopsychic structure (chapter 1).*

The withdrawing part-unit (part-self-representation, part-object-representation, and feelings of abandonment) becomes activated by actual experiences of separation (or of loss), as a result of the individual's efforts toward psychosocial growth, and by moves toward separation-individuation within the thera-peutic process, all of which inter alia symbolize earlier life experiences which provoked the mother's withdrawal of supplies.

The alliance between the rewarding part-unit and the patho-logical (pleasure) ego is in turn activated by the resurgence of the withdrawing part-unit. The purpose of this operation, as it were, is defensive, that is, to restore the wish for reunion, and thereby to relieve the feeling of abandonment. The rewarding part-unit thus becomes the borderline's principal defense against the painful affective state associated with the withdrawing part-unit. *In terms of reality, however, both part-units are pathological; it is as if the patient has but two alternatives, that is, either to feel bad and abandoned (withdrawing part-unit) or to feel good (rewarding part-unit), at the cost of denial of reality and self-destructive acting out.*

---

*Again, the reader will discern the similarity of these formulations to those of Fairbairn. Fairbairn originally postulated a splitting within the infantile ego in correspondence with the split internalized "bad" object, and in effect postulated an alliance between their parts. He postulated, on the one hand, an alliance between the *exciting object* (E.O.) and what he termed the *libidinal ego* (L.E.), and another between the *rejecting object* (R.O.) and what he termed the *anti-libidinal ego* (Anti-L.E.). The E.O.-L.E. alliance corresponds fairly directly with the one herein presented between the rewarding part-unit and the pathological (pleasure) ego. For Fairbairn, the Anti-L.E. came to represent the punitive, sadistic aspect of the superego, allied with the R.O. as a split mental structure. The view of mental structure herein developed presents no structural components analogous with Fairbairn's Anti-L.E.-R.O. alliance, in part reflective of the fact that Fairbairn had not developed a concept of the tripartite object-relations unit. His profound insights, however, deserve further study aimed at exploring the possible relationships among his basic structural formulations and those presented here (see chapter 4).

THERAPEUTIC CONSIDERATIONS

It is necessary now to consider the impact which this intra-psychic structure exerts upon therapeutic transference and resistance. In brief, the transference which the borderline develops results from the operation of the SORU—the rewarding part-unit and the withdrawing part-unit—each of which the patient proceeds alternatively to project onto the therapist. During those periods in which the patient projects the withdrawing part-unit (with its part-object-representation of the withdrawing mother) on to the therapist, he perceives therapy as necessarily leading to feelings of abandonment, denies the reality of therapeutic benefit, and activates the rewarding part-unit as a resistance. When projecting the rewarding part-unit (with its reunion fantasy) on to the therapist, the patient "feels good" but, under the sway of the pathological (pleasure) ego, is usually found to be acting in a self-destructive manner.

THE THERAPEUTIC ALLIANCE

The patient begins therapy feeling that the behavior motivated by the alliance between his rewarding part-unit and his pathological (pleasure) ego is ego-syntonic, that is, makes him feel good. He is furthermore unaware of the cost to him, as it were, which is incurred through his denial of the reality of his self-destructive (and, of course, destructive) behavior.

The initial objective of the therapist is to render the functioning of this alliance ego-alien by means of confrontative clarification of its destructiveness. Insofar as this therapeutic maneuver promotes control of the behavior, the withdrawing part-unit becomes activated, which in turn reactivates the rewarding part-unit with the appearance of further resistance. There results a circular process, sequentially including resistance, reality clarification, working through of the feelings of abandonment (withdrawing part-unit), further resistance (rewarding part-unit), and further reality clarification, which leads in turn to further working through.

In those cases in which the circular working-through process proves successful, an alliance is next seen to develop between the therapist's healthy ego and the patient's embattled reality ego; this therapeutic alliance, formed through the patient's having internalized the therapist as a positive external object, proceeds to function counter to the alliance between the patient's rewarding part-unit and his pathological (pleasure) ego, battling with the latter, as it were, for ultimate control of the patient's motivations and actions.

The structural realignments which ensue in the wake of the working-through process may now be described. The repetitive projection of the patient's rewarding and withdrawing part-units (with their component maternal part-object-representations) on to the therapist, together with the latter's interpretative confrontation thereof, gradually draws to the patient's conscious awareness the presence of these part-units within himself. Concomitantly, the developing alliance between the therapist's healthy ego and the patient's reality ego brings into existence, through introjection, a new object-relations unit: the therapist as a positive (libidinal) object-representation who approves of separation-individuation + a self-representation as a capable, developing person + a "good" feeling (affect) which ensues from the exercise of constructive coping and mastery rather than regressive behavior.

The working through of the encapsulated rage and depression associated with the withdrawing part-unit in turn frees its component part-self- and part-object-representations from their intensely negative, aggressively valent affects. As a result, the new object-relations unit (constructive self + "good" therapist + "good" affect) linked with the reality ego becomes integrated into an overall "good" self-representation, while the SORU linked with the pathological (pleasure) ego becomes integrated into an overall "bad" self-representation; both are now accessible to the patient's conscious awareness, as are their counterparts within the therapist. At this point, the patient has begun in earnest the work of differentiating good and bad self-representations from good and bad object-representations as prefatory to the next step, in which good and bad self-representations coalesce, as do good and bad object-representations. The stage is now set for the inception of whole-object relations, which marks the patient's entrance into stage 4 (Kernberg 1972a).

The de-linking, as it were, of "raw" instinctual energies from the rewarding and withdrawing part-units renders these energies increasingly available to the synthetic function associated with the patient's expanding reality ego, and hence, available for progressive neutralization. With this, and concomitant with the progressive coalescence of good–bad self- and object-representations, splitting is replaced by normal repression, with progressive effacement, as it were, of the personified or "unmetabolized" images associated with the disappearing SORU (Kernberg 1966). The patient is now able to complete the work of mourning for these "lost" images, which characterizes his final work of separation from the mother.

CLINICAL EXAMPLES

The following clinical examples illustrate the foregoing considerations, particularly the operation of the rewarding and withdrawing object-relations part-units, the pathological (pleasure) ego, and the therapeutic alliance.

Case 1

A 27-year-old married woman, a college graduate with a successful career as a television actress, came to treatment with a depression against which she had been defending herself through drinking, abuse of drugs, and by having an affair. She complained that her husband did not care for her because he spent too much time at his work.

The patient's history included an alcoholic mother who spent most of her time sitting at home drinking, and who rewarded the patient, at least verbally, for passivity, inactivity, and regressive behavior but who withdrew whenever her daughter demonstrated any form of constructive behavior; for example, when the patient, as an adolescent, cooked a meal, the mother would withdraw and assume a critical attitude; the same reaction ensued whenever the patient attractively decorated her room or had success at school.

In what follows, the patient clearly describes the withdrawing maternal part-image, that is, the mother's withdrawal from the girl's assertiveness, activity, or need to grow up, with the associated feelings of abandonment and the accompanying part-self-representation of being bad, ugly, inadequate, unworthy. She also clearly reports the rewarding part-unit: a rewarding maternal part-image, "feeling good," and the self-image of a child who is taken care of. The mother's commands and the patient's behavior are thus linked together as the basis for the alliance between the rewarding part-unit and the pathological (pleasure) ego.

Therapeutic progress had activated the withdrawing part-unit, which in turn activated the rewarding part-unit as a defense, with the patient's behavior coming under the control of the pathological (pleasure) ego, that is, passivity, drinking, the affair. As the patient improved, as if despite herself, every step symbolized separation-individuation and proceeded to activate the withdrawing part-unit with its feelings of abandonment. She experienced her improvement as a loss, a frustration of the wish for reunion, and each time she improved she became resistant and hostile, projecting her anger at the mother's withdrawal on to the therapist and the therapeutic situation.

After a year of individual therapy three times a week, during which time she had gained control over the behavior motivated

by the alliance between the rewarding part-unit and the pathological (pleasure) ego, she reported,

> This week I pulled myself more into reality. . . . I felt you
> had left me but told myself it wasn't true and the feelings went
> away. . . . (*Note in what follows, however, the activation of the
> withdrawing part-unit and attendant resistance.*) Yet today I don't
> want to tell you . . . I'd like to report that I was fucked up all
> weekend . . . I guess I felt healthy over the weekend. Last
> night I made a big drink but threw it out rather than drank it.
> (*Note that the improvement brings on further resistance.*) I woke up
> angry at you this morning. . . . I recognize I'm doing better
> and I'm afraid you'll leave me. When my work went well, one
> side of me was pleased. (*Note rewarding part-unit.*) The other side
> said why did I do that and I wanted to drink. I don't think I can
> maintain a mature way of living . . . when I have to do
> something responsible one side of me says no and wants to go
> out and get drunk. (*Note wish for reunion.*) The better I do the
> more I want to hang on to the fantasies of lovers and drink.
> (*Note withdrawing part-unit.*) If I'm grown up, independent, on
> my own, I'll be all alone and abandoned.

A little later the patient reports that, in effect, the alliance
between the rewarding part-unit and the pathological (pleasure)
ego has become ego-alien:

> I had a fight with my bad side—the baby. . . . (*Note
> the rewarding part-unit and the pathologic [pleasure] ego.*) I was
> enjoying myself reading and it was as if I heard a little voice
> saying have a drink. I could feel myself turn off feeling, then I
> took a drink. The bad side is my mother's commands. . . .
> I'm ten years old and I can't decide myself . . . I have to
> follow the command but as I become aware of the command I
> can now disregard it and decide for myself.

In the next interview the patient reports,

> I had two successes—each time it was as if I heard my
> mother's voice get started but each time I overcame it and went
> ahead. (*Again, however, control of the rewarding part-unit activates
> the withdrawing part-unit, which is then projected onto the therapist as*

a resistance maneuver.) I wasn't going to tell you today as you'd think I was better and act like my parents. If I get better you'll leave me. I worry about this, especially when you go on vacation. I feel you're leaving me because I'm doing better. My image of myself is of a person who drinks and has affairs, or of a young little girl who has to be taken care of.

As another example of how improvement had activated the withdrawing part-unit and produced resistance, the patient stated,

I didn't want to come today. I saw my old boyfriend. The baby side of me made me feel angry that I didn't want those old satisfactions. I don't want you to think I'm doing too well or I'll want to leave you . . . as if I want to get back at you . . . angry at you, you're doing this, making me better to get rid of me . . . I'm losing you. The baby side of me is angry that you think I can handle myself. Whenever I have five good days, the baby side of me gets angry at you but I can't verbalize it or you'll leave me for sure! I like to sit here and say nothing just to piss you off! I see getting better as your withdrawing affection. Last night as I saw I had fixed up my apartment nicely I got furious at you. Mother used to resent any creativity in me. . . . I never imagined verbalizing this anger at mother . . . fantasies and the feeling were all action—hitting, stabbing, killing her!

As illustrated by this case, the alliance between the rewarding part-unit (rewarding maternal part-object-representation) and the pathological (pleasure) ego had as its objective the restoration of the wish for reunion and the relief of feelings of abandonment (separation anxiety and resultant rage), the latter being acted out, and hence, discharged in behavior. Thus aggression otherwise available to build intrapsychic structure gains access to motility via self-destructive behavior.

Case 2

The second case example concerns a 20-year-old man who had dropped out of college because of severe depression and a work inhibition; he reported that he felt unable to perform, study, or even think. The patient's frankly paranoid mother had openly attacked him throughout childhood, both verbally and physically, for any assertion or expression of individuality; the father, rather than come to his son's aid, demanded that the boy submit to the mother's assaults as the price for the father's approval.

Analysis of the patient's withdrawing part-unit revealed the following structure: a part-object-representation consisting of a condensed image which included elements of the attacking mother and the withdrawing father; the predominant affect was, as expected, that of abandonment; the part-self-representation was that of a person who had caused the abandonment, who had leprosy, who was no good, inadequate, "crazy," and "bad." The rewarding part-unit included the affect of "feeling good" and the part-self-representation of an obedient child, both dependent upon the pathological (pleasure) ego's use of avoidance, inhibition, and passivity with denial of reality in pursuit of the wish for reunion. The patient's efforts to assert himself, to study, and to learn activated the withdrawing part-unit, which in turn activated the rewarding part-unit, leading to the defensive use of avoidance, inhibition, and passivity.

As the patient improved in treatment and attempted to resume studying, he would block; however, he was now able to report the maternal part-image, the part self-image, and the abandonment feelings (the withdrawing part-unit), as well as the results of activation of the rewarding part-unit, that is, inhibition, avoidance, passivity, and blocking. He stated,

> When I sit there trying to study I feel hurt, stepped on, crushed, and I want to give up. I never felt any support or connection with my mother. It's a feeling of complete loss, helplessness, inability to cope with reality. . . . I feel adrift, alone . . . Mother has no love for me. My image of Mother's face is one of an expression of disgust like despising, criticizing, mocking me. I want her to love me but she hates me and she acts as if I did something against her and she wants to get back

and she attacks me. I haven't done anything for her to hate me . . . she used to discourage my interest in girls or in my taking any activity in the home or outside. When I appealed to my father for help, he was never home and he would tell me to cut it out because I was upsetting his relationship with my mother.

When they left me alone they took part of me with them. They take something with them that leaves me empty. They double cross me. . . . no feeling of worth or meaning . . . the feeling of being deserted kills me. I can't handle the aftermath of asserting myself or speaking out, studying or learning. I feel it's wrong to be myself and I can almost hear my father's voice telling me to cut it out, that if I don't he will leave me. Mother told me that Father didn't care about me . . . she was the only one who cared . . . if I didn't stay with her she'd leave me.

Trying to learn is tempting fate, risky, treacherous. It brings them down on me . . . I can almost hear their voices . . . I can't break their hold . . . I feel I'm dying. I can't think and not feel hurt so I give up. I feel they don't care and they're laughing at me. I can't fight them every second. I have to block out. When I sit down to study, it's as if I hear my father saying, "Don't you see the anguish you're causing me?"

I feel completely abandoned and I yell: "Help me out! Where is everybody?" And they say, "He's crazy!" Father tells me it's my fault . . . the way I see things is all wrong. They feel sorry for me. I say: "Please forgive me for having leprosy." I can't scream or beg any more because they think I'm crazy. I'm so afraid if they don't protect me I'll die!

As the above communicative sequence reveals, the activation of the withdrawing part-unit in the wake of the patient's efforts toward self-assertiveness leads the patient into a condition of abandonment which brings him close to experiencing delusions, somatic delusions, and auditory hallucinations. The untrammeled operation of his SORU brought him close, at times, to regression into stage 2, with consequent blurring of the distinction between self-representations and object-representations.

Case 3

The third case example concerns an unmarried, 19-year-old girl, a freshman in college who had been an outstanding high school student and who had subsequently dropped out of college because of depression and "panic."

The patient's father, a manic-depressive professional man, had had an explosive temper. Throughout the patient's childhood, the father had behaved as a dependent child in his relationship with the mother, had openly attacked the patient for her "childhood inadequacies," but had envied her achievements. The major role obfuscations within the family found the mother playing the role of the father's mother and demanding that the patient not only submit to the father's attacks but also serve in the role of her own (the mother's) mother (Rinsley 1971a,b, chapter 11).

The patient's withdrawing maternal part-image was that of a mother who exploited her and who was deliberately cruel and enjoyed the patient's helplessness and dependency; the associated affect included abandonment depression and the fear of engulfment; the part self-image was that of being inadequate, worthless, guilty, an insect, a bug. The patient harbored cannibalistic fantasies and fears throughout childhood, relieved during that time by masturbation; in the fantasies she was at times the victim and at other times the cannibal. The rewarding maternal part-image was that of a strong, idealized ("all-good") mother who would save her from death; the associated affect was that of "feeling good" and the part self-image was that of a helpless, clinging child.

After some five months of treatment, the patient had begun to separate, with emergence of the withdrawing part-self-image (withdrawing part-unit), which precipitated her into near-panic. She reported,

> I feel everybody's angry at me. I'm about to be attacked. I feel like an insect, a bug. It's all because I don't want to be like my mother, I don't want to hold on to her. The role she puts me

in fit her needs but also gave me security. She would love me no matter how bad I was. I want her and I want to be taken care of and I can't breathe without her. I don't have a separate existence and I feel guilty if I try. I can't stop wanting my mother like a baby. I can't seem to make a life of my own.

Whenever the withdrawing part-unit was activated as a result of a move toward separation-individuation, the patient projected her resultant anger at the withdrawing maternal part-image and became resistant to treatment, which she then viewed as conducive to abandonment. Thus she expressed her wish to kill the therapist, her mother, and herself:

> Over the weekend I felt completely independent but cut off. I talked about my job very self-confidently, then I got frightened and went into a rage. I wanted to tear myself apart, rip my mother apart or you apart and I felt terribly depressed. I realize I'm getting better and I don't want to admit it. I don't need my mother. I lost my motivation, my desire to go on. I feel humiliated, defeated, dead, and cold, I hate you! I don't think you can help me and I want revenge on my mother and you!

This patient's pathological (pleasure) ego, shaped by her mother's "rewarding" responses, comprised regressive-defensive behavior, such as acting helplessly, clinging, a variety of somatic symptoms, and carrying out the mother's assigned role of an inadequate, hysterical child.

Case 4

The fourth case example concerns a 22-year-old unmarried college graduate who lived alone. She complained of anxiety, depression, and hysteriform fears that her legs "might not work" and that she might be unable to eat or swallow; she had, in addition, experienced several episodes of impaired consciousness. There were also feelings of helplessness and inability to cope, and she almost constantly contacted her mother for reassurance.

The mother had idealized the family unit and had rewarded infantile-compliant behavior, which she viewed as a religious virtue; conversely, she vigorously attacked her child's efforts toward self-assertiveness or originality, an example of which had been her refusal to attend the patient's high school graduation exercises when she had learned that the girl had participated in a demonstration against the war in Vietnam. The mother had particularly attacked heterosexual relations as "the work of the devil." The father, an emotionally distant man, served in the role of the mother's figurehead.

The patient's withdrawing maternal part-image was that of an angry, punitive, and vengeful mother who would kill her; the associated affect was a compound of fear and abandonment depression; the part self-image was that of being guilty, worthless, despicably bad. The rewarding maternal part-image was that of an omnipotent, godlike mother; the associated affect was relief from anxiety and "feeling good"; the part self-image was that of a helpless, compliant child. The pathological (pleasure) ego, which functioned to maintain the wish for reunion, abetted the fulfillment of the mother's wishes by being helpless, dependent, unassertive, clinging, and asexual. Again, therapeutic progress activated the withdrawing part-unit, which then triggered the rewarding part-unit with ensuing helpless clinging, passivity, and phobic and hysteriform symptomatology.

Following resolution of the patient's initial resistances, she reported,

> I think I'm destined to die because I'm growing up. I can envisage no life outside of my mother or family. I'm made up of two parts—one me, one her. The part that she has worked on, taken care of, and given to me. . . . If I move away from her the part of her that's in me would turn against me. . . . Mother will make it turn against me and it will punish me. I don't feel strong enough to battle in spite of myself. Mother insists that I remain helpless and not grow up.

The patient continues:

I'm afraid if I grow up I'll lose her. I will take away her reason for living. I carry out what mother says—I'm an empty shell. Mother puts in the values, otherwise I will be nothing. I'm empty except for her. Mother sees me as a tool for herself. She instructed me in the one thing I can't do—grow up and leave her—or I'll be punished for it.

The patient experienced intense guilt over her hostility toward the mother:

I feel dirty and disgusting! Mother equates growing up with stealing and murder. Defying her is like defying God—you feel guilty and frightened. I've been frightened into believing that growing up is wrong. If I do anything that mother doesn't approve of, like have sex or smoke grass, I'm throwing myself to the winds and anything can happen to me. Mother suggested that sexual intercourse before marriage would make me mentally ill. If I smoke or have intercourse I'm violating the bargain I made with her not to leave her. I'm afraid she will leave me. When I assert myself rather than complying I feel nasty and impudent and that everybody will be angry with me. I'm just beginning to realize the extent to which I carry out Mother's wishes. If I don't do what she says, it's wrong. . . . If I reject one thing, it's like rejecting all. In other words, having sex is like lying, stealing, or rejecting my mother. She would rather I die than go out and do something she didn't want. Mother wanted me in order, just like she wanted the nice, clean bathroom in order. When I go and do something that is not in order she goes into a rage and would like to kill me.

In this case the alliance between the rewarding part-unit and the pathological (pleasure) ego engendered the patient's feeling of panic over anticipated punishment if she attempted to grow; the punishment she expected would take the form of her "going crazy," and of paralysis of walking, talking, and swallowing. In her case, the pathological (pleasure) ego discharged aggression by means of autoplastic symptom formation.

SUMMARY

This chapter describes the contribution of maternal libidinal availability and withdrawal to the etiology of the borderline syndrome. It underscores Mahler's emphasis upon the mother's vital contribution to normal ego development and relates the effects of deficiency in that contribution to the development of the intrapsychic structure of the borderline: *the split ego* and *the split object-relations unit* (SORU). The latter, which develops from internalization of the two major themes of interaction with the mother, produces the leitmotif of the borderline's intrapsychic structure: *the rewarding* and *withdrawing object-relations part-units*. The rewarding part-unit becomes allied, as it were, with the pathological (pleasure) ego to defend against the withdrawing part-unit, but at the cost of failure to cope with reality.

The relationship of these borderline intrapsychic structures to each other and to the therapist's intrapsychic structures, as developed in the therapeutic transference and resistance, is described and illustrated by means of clinical case examples.

CHAPTER 3

A VIEW OF
OBJECT RELATIONS

This chapter attempts to delineate and classify borderline disorder from a developmental viewpoint, as well as to suggest a viable approach to psychoanalytic therapy with borderline patients. Historically, there has been—and continues to be—great controversy among clinicians regarding the concept of the borderline personality. For some, the borderline personality is a clinical syndrome intermediate between two other differentiable categories of psychopathology, namely, psychosis and psychoneurosis (chapter 2, as well as Kernberg 1972a, Masterson 1973, 1974). Others view borderline patients basically as neurotics who periodically or episodically display the signs and symptoms of psychotic illness (Fenichel 1945). Or, in accordance with the work of Hoch and Polatin on "pseudoneurotic schizophrenia" (1949), the borderline patient may be considered the victim of a basically schizophrenic disorder, the symptoms of which, to a greater or lesser degree, masquerade as neurotic. This view reflects the opinion of many clinicians, such as Kolb (1973), who classifies patients suffering from "borderline syndrome" under the rubric of schizophrenia; Ekstein (1966), who considers psychotic and borderline children in terms of a similar proneness to regression; and Pine (1974b), who concludes that there is no significant difference between borderline and psychotic childhood disorders.

The concept of the borderline personality may also be used to encompass a wide variety of persons suffering from one or another form of "character" pathology (Boyer and Giovacchini 1967). One may thus subsume under the rubric borderline the spectrum of schizoid, infantile, narcissistic, hysterical, paranoid, inadequate, impulse-ridden, polymorphous-perverse, and alloplastic personalities whose symptomatology falls short of more florid psychoses. Of notable historical significance in this regard is Helene Deutsch's formulation (1942) of the "as if" personality. As-if personalities, who are basically schizoid, correspond to Grinker, Werble, and Drye's third subgroup of borderline patients (1968): those devoid of the capacity for warmth and affection, and deficient in self-identity.

The distinction between the neuroses and the borderline conditions emphasized by some (Kohut 1971) is disputed by others (Ritvo 1974). Whereas the former conceptualizes neurotic conditions in terms of the classical transference neurosis and borderline conditions in terms of pathologically persistent narcissism, the latter consider such a distinction overdrawn (Loewald 1974). The distinction between borderline disorders and psychosis, especially in childhood, appears equally unclear. The borderline child is characterized as unable successfully to separate self- and object-representations, with an associated failure of introjection (Kut Rosenfeld and Sprince 1963). Impairment or failure of self-object differentiation is likewise cited as the basis for child psychosis (Mahler 1968). Similarly, Kernberg (1968) cites a "quantitative predominance of negative introjections" as the prime contributing factor in the etiology of borderline psychopathology, while Mahler (1968) cites a predominance of negative introjections as etiologic for infantile psychosis.

Even so cursory a review as that presented here readily confirms the unsettled nature of the nosology and psychodynamic significance of the concept of borderline disorders. The wide range and pleomorphic nature of borderline symptomatology certainly add to the confusion. In contrast, the view of borderline disorders I shall develop here is based on the following considerations:

1. The diagnosis "borderline syndrome" constitutes a theoretically, clinically, etiologically, and heuristically valid and specific nosologic category.

2. The clinical symptomatology, level of developmental fixation, and therapeutic response of borderline patients allow their placement along a spectrum of psychopathology between the psychoneurotic and the psychotic.

3. The etiology of the borderline syndrome, and the developmental arrest basic to it, are known.

4. The particular deficiency in object relations common to borderlines, which differentiates them from psychoneurotics and psychotics, is likewise known.

5. Based upon these considerations, a rationale for the treatment of borderline patients may be developed.

HISTORICAL ANTECEDENTS TO AN OBJECT-RELATIONS THEORY OF BORDERLINE PERSONALITY

The historical basis for the development of an object-relations theory of borderline personality organization may be said to have been laid down in the early, classic psychoanalytic studies of depression (melancholia). Abraham (1912) describes depressed persons' feelings of inner impoverishment, emptiness, and "badness," and their inability to love, coupled with the need to project aggression (hate) onto others to create, as it were, a congeries of what Melanie Klein (1932) later termed "external persecutors." Abraham (1916) postulates the melancholic's regression to the stage of oral cannibalism, such that the "lost" object is devoured. Later (1924), he postulates the anal expulsion and subsequent annihilation of the lost object and advances the important distinction between the melancholic who expels it and the obsessional who retains it. Abraham theorizes that the melancholic at first expels, then later reintrojects, the lost object and narcissistically identifies with it, a sequence based in turn on Freud's (1917b) earlier formulation concerning the

melancholic's regression from object love to narcissistic identification as a consequence of the persistence of narcissistic object
choice. Freud clearly perceived in the melancholic the persistence
of that form of object relations that proceeds from failure to
achieve the differentiation of self from object, so that the latter
variously and significantly reflects ("mirrors") the former (Kohut
1971; Mahler 1968, 1974).

Rado (1928) develops a concept of depression, sometimes
termed his "double-introjection" theory which, despite certain
theoretical shortcomings, nonetheless contains important inferences concerning the metapsychology of depression. According
to Rado, the melancholic introjects the lost object as a split,
dyadic "good object" and "bad object"—the former, symbolic
of the beloved but potentially punitive parent surrogates, is
incorporated into the superego, and the latter into the ego.
Rado's concept of the split good-bad introject had important
echoes in the later contributions of such theorists as Melanie
Klein and Fairbairn.

Melanie Klein's (1932, 1935, 1940, 1946) contributions to the
metapsychology of depression and to object-relations theory are
too well known and extensive to permit a comprehensive restatement here. Of particular importance for this discussion,
however, is her concept of the depressive position of infancy,
during which the infant experiences a transition from reliance
upon part-object relations to reliance upon whole-object relations. In accordance with her view, while in the depressive
position, and due to his inability to perceive a preponderance of
good internal objects, the infant denies the terror associated
with the potential loss of his good object by denying the object's
complexity. The object thus becomes either "all good" or "all
bad"—in effect, a split-object. Klein concludes that the infant is
able to mourn only if the good lost object is a whole-object. The
persistence of splitting thus precludes adequate mourning, and
hence, adequate working through of object loss. Her view of the
infant as, in effect, "unsure" of his good objects recalls
Abraham's earlier description of the melancholic's feeling of

inner impoverishment, which is accompanied by a perceived inability to love.*

Fairbairn's (1941) further elaboration of these and related considerations must now be looked at. He differentiates three sequential stages in the development of object relations:

1. Infantile dependence includes: (a) an early oral stage, during which the infant seeks only a part-object, i.e., the maternal breast; and (b) a late oral stage, termed "mother-with-the-breast," during which the whole-object (mother) is dealt with as a part-object (breast).

2. Quasi-independence, which Fairbairn considers a stage of transition between infantile and later adult dependence, is characterized by progressive relinquishment of relations based on primary identification in favor of relations with differentiated objects, and by "desperate endeavors . . . to separate from the object and . . . to achieve reunion with the object." During this stage, developmental progress occurs in terms of "dichotomy and exteriorization" (externalization) of the object, thereby differentiating self from object, and endowing the externalized object with the characteristics of reality.

3. Mature dependence, during which both accepted and rejected objects become externalized, involves the achievement of the ability to perceive and interact with the "external" object as a whole-object, that is, as an object that combines within itself both "good" (or libidinal) and "bad" (or aggressive) characteristics.

Fairbairn places particular emphasis on the vicissitudes of the splitting of "good" and "bad" objects during the transitional or quasi-independent stage, and he cites his now famous transitional techniques, by means of which the person attempts to regulate

---

*I have elsewhere (chapter 1) commented on the important relation between deficiency or impoverishment of ego libido and a dearth of internalized good objects, as noted in schizoid states.

the process of differentiation of self from object. Schematized in somewhat revised form, these techniques are:

1. Paranoid technique: "good" (accepted, libidinal) object is internalized; "bad" (rejected, aggressive) object is externalized.

2. Hysterical technique: "good" object is externalized; "bad" object is internalized.

3. Obsessional technique: both "good" and "bad" objects are internalized.

4. Phobic technique: both "good" and "bad" objects are externalized.

Fairbairn (1951b) goes on to postulate the infant's need to split the internalized bad object into two parts, which he terms, respectively, an *exciting object* (E.O.) and a *rejecting object* (R.O.). The endopsychic consequences of this are of pervasive importance in the genesis of borderline and schizoid conditions, to which reference will be made later.

Jacobson's (1954a, 1964) contributions to an understanding of the metapsychology of borderline and psychotic states may be said to center upon two basic conceptions. The first of these involves the developmental vicissitudes of self- and object-representations, while the second concerns the degree to which these representations retain the characteristics of, and in psychotic states regress to, early infantile self- and object-images. With respect to the former, progressive development entails and signifies the progressive differentiation of self-representations from object-representations such that "self" and "other" become demarcated from each other. In regard to the latter, progressive development signifies the ongoing depersonification ("metabolization") of primitive self- and object-representations (Kernberg 1966) and their transformation or assimilation into otherwise smoothly functioning defensive and representational structures (chapter 1). By the same token, reanimation of primitive, infantile self- and object-images signals the onset of pre-Oedipal regression with entrance into prepsychotic or frankly psychotic states of function and experience; it represents a de-structuralization symbolic of an effacement of internal structural boundaries and of the boundary between "self" and "outside."

Influenced strongly by Jacobson's work, Kernberg, who defines object-relations theory as the psychoanalytic approach to the internalization of interpersonal relations (1971a), postulates four sequential stages in their normal development (1972a):

STAGE 1. Roughly coterminous with the first postnatal month, this earliest stage of development antedates the establishment of the primary, undifferentiated self-object constellation built up in the infant as a consequence of pleasurable, gratifying mother-infant interactions (Jacobson 1964). Mahler (1968) applies the phrase "normal autism" to this period; the term "presymbiotic" (Rinsley 1972, 1974a,b) is similarly applicable to it.

STAGE 2. Roughly spanning the second and third postnatal months, this second stage of development witnesses the establishment and consolidation of an undifferentiated self-object image or representation of a libidinally gratifying or rewarding ("good") type under the organizing influence of pleasurable or gratifying mother-infant interactions. Concomitantly, a separate "bad" self-object image or representation evolves under the influence of painful or frustrating (i.e., traumatogenic) psycho-physiological states. Two self-object affect complexes are thus built up and fixed by memory traces as polar-opposite endo-psychic structures. In accordance with Mahler's (1968) formulations, the chronology of this developmental stage includes the inception of the mother-infant symbiosis, which she dates from the second postnatal month and which reaches its peak some two to three months later.

STAGE 3. The third developmental stage is reached when the self-image and object-image have become differentiated within the core "good" self-object representation. Similarly, a start is made toward differentiation of self-image and object-image within the core "bad" self-object representation. According to

Kernberg, this stage spans the latter three quarters of the first postnatal year, a period of time which is noted to overlap Mahler's symbiotic phase and her subsequent differentiation and practicing subphases (6–16 months).*

STAGE 4. Kernberg's fourth developmental stage witnesses the coalescence of "good" and "bad" self-images into the beginnings of an integrated self-concept. Self-images establish coherence and continuity, affects become integrated and undergo further differentiation, and the child's self-concept and social behavior become progressively congruent. At the same time, "good" and "bad" object-images also coalesce and the "good" (libidinal) and "bad" (aggressive) images of the mother become integrated into a whole-object maternal concept which progressively faithfully reflects the mother's actuality. Kernberg dates the inception of this stage at some point between the end of the first postnatal year and the second half of the second year, and considers that it continues to evolve throughout the remainder of childhood. In accordance with this chronology, stage 4 is seen to overlap Mahler's practicing and rapprochement subphases and her on-the-way-to-object-constancy phase.*

Kernberg's formulation of the developmental events specific to stage 4 resembles Fairbairn's conception of how the individual achieves mature dependence, in particular through the mechanism of externalization ("exteriorization") of *both* "accepted" (good, libidinal) and "rejected" (bad, aggressive) objects with ensuing replacement of splitting, as exemplified in his transitional mechanisms, with repression and the assumption of whole-object relations.

---

*Kernberg's timing of the stage 3 and stage 4 developmental-representational events appears, on both theoretical and clinical grounds, to be premature. Stage 3 events, including the inception of differentiation of self- and object-images, and hence, awareness of one's separateness from the maternal object, typify Mahler's rapprochement subphase of separation-individuation (16–25 months), while stage 4 events typify her on-the-way-to-object-constancy phase.

In accordance with the phenomenology of Kernberg's developmental schema, psychotic syndromes may be said to result from developmental fixation or arrest at stages 1 or 2. In those cases that suffer arrest at stage 1, basically autistic (autistic-presymbiotic) syndromes may be expected to ensue, while arrest at stage 2 may be expected to result in predominantly symbiotic syndromes. Common to both is failure of differentiation of self from object, and to both the diagnostic term schizophrenia may be said to apply (Rinsley 1972).

By contrast, developmental arrest at stage 3, during which self and object begin to differentiate from each other, but only within the core "good" or "bad" self-object representations, yields borderline personality organization. In such cases, self and object remain partially differentiated, whole-objects are in effect dealt with as part-objects, introjective-projective defenses remain prominent, alternating efforts toward separation from and reunion with the (primal) object are characteristic, and paranoid-hysterical mechanisms typify object relations.

Attainment of stage 4 signifies arrival at, at worst, a psycho-neurotic modus vivendi, and, at best, an essentially healthy one. Borderline personalities, fixated at stage 3, at their best approach, and often appear to achieve, this degree of integration, while at their worst they regress toward the undifferentiated representational state characteristic of fixation at stage 2. Persistent reliance upon splitting as a defense mechanism is typical for both psychotic (stages 1 and 2) and borderline (stage 3) personalities and accounts for the various manifestations of their respective "weak" egos (Rinsley 1968).

Mahler's numerous and fundamental contributions to an understanding of the development of personality (1968, 1971, 1972a, 1974, Mahler et al. 1975) emphasize and explicate the complex process of mother-infant symbiosis and the ensuing processes of desymbiotization and separation-individuation. Her now famous subphases of separation-individuation (*differentiation*: 6–10 months; *practicing*: 10–16 months; *rapprochement*: 16–25 months) comprise a chronology of mother-child interactions which center upon the growing child's drive toward progressive self-differentiation as an object separate from the mother and the latter's complementary facilitating responses in relation to it.

It is during the rapprochement subphase that the child begins to perceive the possibility of his own separateness and uniqueness apart from the person of the mother. The child will tolerate the ensuing separation anxiety and utilize it in the service of his ongoing psychological development provided that the antecedent "maternal beacon" has served him well. This means that his prior interactions with the mother have caused him introjectively to distill a preponderance of "good" (libidinal) object-representations, which in turn have strengthened the *anlagen* of his corresponding self-representations. At about this time, the child also begins to develop the capacity for object permanency (Piaget 1937), precursory for the later development of true object constancy, as exemplified in the capacity for evocative recall (Fraiberg 1969). It may be said that evocative recall represents the achievement of a stable endopsychic state of representational configurations, having superseded the infant's reliance upon magical hallucination and, later, simple recognition memory. The achievement of evocative recall may likewise be taken to signify the inception of replacement of the earlier splitting defense by repression. The healthily developing child's repository of "good" (libidinal) self- and object-representations serves, in turn, as an impetus for his increasing use of evocative recall, as what is recalled is positive. In those cases that reflect a preponderance of "bad" (aggressively valent) introjects, the child persists in his reliance upon riddance mechanisms of a projective nature (chapter 1), with the ever-present possibility of return of the "projects" (i.e., as persecutors).

In accordance with these considerations, a predominance of "bad" introjects fosters the persistence of splitting defenses, precludes the adequate development of evocative recall, inhibits the inception of whole-object relations and hence, following Klein, effectively thwarts the working through of the depressive position, thereby preventing completion of the developmental tasks associated with the separation-individuation phase. In such cases, whether juvenile or adult, the persistence of paranoid and hysterical transitional mechanisms, as set forth by Fairbairn, is readily discerned clinically. Either one's self or others are "all good" or "all bad," the one remaining, in effect, split from the other. Under such circumstances, where some degree of differentiation of self-representations from object-representations has occured, one legitimately speaks of a borderline disorder; where such differentiation has essentially failed to occur, one legitimately speaks of psychosis. Common to all such cases is the persistence of pre-eruptive or actually disruptive degrees of separation anxiety. In psychosis, such anxiety is of the instinctual variety, with its gross threat to what yet remains of intact ego functions; in borderline disorders, such anxiety assumes a partially structuralized form (chapter 2) with both instinctual and superego (guilt) components, which Masterson (1972b, 1973) has termed "abandonment depression."

THE SORU AND BORDERLINE DISORDERS

In accordance with the view espoused by Masterson and myself (chapter 2) regarding the split object-relations unit (SORU) characteristic of the borderline personality, the term borderline may be applied to those cases that demonstrate the interrelated problems of pathologically persistent narcissism and incomplete self-object differentiation, regardless of specific or predominant autoplastic or alloplastic symptomatology. In such cases, clinical experience reveals the seemingly endless alternation of feelings of infantile megalomania, and of impotence and worthlessness, which reflect the persistence of the "all-good"/"all-bad" split. The term borderline may be seen to apply to a wide spectrum of personality disorders, including the schizoid-inadequate, the hysterical, and the more purely narcissistic, central to which is the continued operation of the SORU.

THERAPEUTIC CONSIDERATIONS

From the outset of therapy, the therapist confronts and clarifies the borderline patient's symptomatic behavior; initially, such confrontation evokes the patient's efforts to control his self-destructive behavior, as a result of early, if transient, efforts toward identification with the therapist. Such efforts are relatively short-lived, however, as they quickly activate the withdrawing part-unit, replete with its hostile, rejective, persecutory, maternal part-image; feelings of "badness" and worthlessness; and its repository of unneutralized aggression. Thus, the patient's earliest attempts to exert control over his self-defeating and self-injurious behavior activate his long-harbored persecutory representations, which are then willy-nilly projected onto the therapist who in turn becomes, for the patient, an evil predator. The borderline mother of a hospitalized adolescent girl stated this clearly to her family therapist: "You made me very mad last time . . . after I listened to you Tuesday I felt rotten . . . I tried to stop stuffing myself before I went to bed and the more I thought about what you said about overeating the madder I got . . . I think you just want me to get mad and that's how you'll get your kicks!"

Among other things, this communication conveys the patient's projection of her "bad" and aggressive representation onto the therapist, as well as her counterphobically defended anxiety that the therapist wants her to be "bad" in order to find a basis for rejecting her. Quickly, however, she communicates her subjective experience of activation of the rewarding part-unit: ". . . so then you know what I did . . . I went to the 'fridge' and ate myself blue in the face . . . I got so stuffed I couldn't breathe and I fell asleep."

Now the patient, to "spite" (i.e., demonstrate and exert control over) the therapist, regresses to an infantile, oral-narcissistic state symbolic of the fed, satiated infant who subsequently falls asleep. She feels "good" and full and has flaunted her self-injurious symptom (overeating) in the face of the now fantasied impotent therapist. The split between the projected, with-drawing part-unit (therapist), who now embodies the patient's partially differentiated "bad" part self-image and rejecting mater-nal part-image, and the retained rewarding part-unit, with its hedonic part self-image and its soothing, consoling maternal part-image (i.e., food), is evident.

The therapist is now in a position to confront and clarify these split representations and to begin to link them, with the help of the patient's memories, dreams, and waking fantasies, to earlier actual or fantasied historical events which reinforced and overdetermined the splits as derivatives of the push-pull quality of the mother-child relationship. Many therapeutic hours later the patient notes, "Yes, I remember mother used to tell me I was crap . . . no good . . . that I'd never amount to any-thing. . . . No matter what I did it wasn't good enough for her." She continues, "You know, that's what I thought about *you* [therapist] . . . that you'd find fault with everything I did or said . . . you'd put me down."

The patient now refers to the therapist in terms of transference expectations, utilizing the subjunctive ("would") rather than the immediate present or future tenses. The therapist is be-coming differentiated from the parental representations, in part as a result of vigorous, ongoing interpretation of the patient's transference projections, especially the negative ones (Kernberg 1975). Of particular importance is the sensitive manner in which the therapist must handle the confrontation and interpretation of the rewarding part-unit, with its powerful secondary gain associated with the "good" feeling connected to essentially passive, regressive-compliant, and ultimately self-defeating be-havior. Within the transference, and by displacement outside it, the patient's repeated efforts to provoke the therapist's approval in the wake of such behavior repeatedly fail; the withdrawing part-unit is, in consequence, reactivated and its representations, together with its encapsulated aggression (anger, rage), are in turn reprojected onto the therapist: "You really want me to be nothing . . . I do what you want and all I get is your 'interpre-

tations'. . . . Abuse, that's what it is. . . . You abuse me.
. . . Sometimes you make me feel like I'm your slave!''

As the therapeutic work proceeds, the patient becomes aware
of her redoubtable tendency to project the SORU onto the
therapist, and, in consequence, she perceives increasingly clearly
the presence and operation of the SORU within herself. She
further comes to realize that both part-units are deleterious to
her (cf. the split internalized "bad" object) and that another
part of herself coexists with this "bad" object. As a sixteen-
year-old adolescent girl stated: "You know, there's a part of me
that wants to grow . . . to grow up and accomplish things
. . . I want to prove I can make it . . . I guess you [therapist]
want me to make it too. . . . Boy, it took me a long time to
believe that!''

The "part that wants to grow" is the emergent, long-inhibited,
healthy object-relations unit comprising *a self-image* of a maturing,
increasingly successfully coping individual, *a maternal image* of
a person (therapist) who accepts, encourages, and rewards (i.e.,
provides libidinal supplies for) success, and *a linked affect* composed of mixed aggressive and libidinal valences (libidinalized
aggression in the service of successful coping and mastery). The
last is seen to represent essentially neutralized energy available
for sublimations, the inverse of the *Entmischung*, with the
emergence of "raw" instinct, which typifies regression.

As previously noted, the progressive emergence into the
patient's conscious awareness of *both* the split ("bad") object-
relations unit and the healthy object-relations unit, the latter as a
consequence of the therapist's judicious interpretation of the
therapeutic transference, signals the patient's entrance into
Kernberg's stage 4. It conveys the patient's beginning assumption of mature dependency (Fairbairn 1941), his awareness of his
separateness, and of the coalescence within himself of *both*
"good" (libidinal) and "bad" (aggressive) valences and representations. It thus represents the inception of whole-object
relations. Table 3-1 shows the healthy object-relations unit as
schematized in terms of the therapeutic transference.

TABLE 3-1. NEW, HEALTHY OBJECT-RELATIONS UNIT

Object-representation	Affect	Self-representation
A (parental) image of the therapist, who approves, encourages, and rewards effective and realistic planning and coping behavior (i.e., efforts toward mastery)	A feeling of gratification ("good feeling") in the wake of achievement (libidinal + aggressive)	A self-image of a successfully coping, achieving person

The integration of both "good" and "bad" representational structures within one's self, and the recognition that such integration exists also within the therapist, lead to strikingly gratifying responses from the patient. The aforementioned adolescent girl states, "Wow . . . I guess I'm really one person after all . . . I've got good and bad in me and what I do with them is pretty much up to me . . . just like you [therapist] . . . you can do it too."

A poignant sequence shortly before termination of therapy of a seventeen-year-old girl of superior intelligence is illustrative:

P: I was reading *You Can't Go Home Again* . . . you know, the book by Thomas Wolfe. He said it . . . and I thought to myself that I couldn't go home either . . . and I cried a lot when I thought that. . . . I guess Thomas Wolfe cried a lot too . . . maybe he cried through his work, his writing.
T: You're crying now and grieving, aren't you?
P: Yeah. . . . I remember what you said about mourning and grieving . . . that I couldn't do that when my mother took off. . . . Boy, have I been doing it now.

The final signal that resolution of the SORU has begun in earnest is conveyed in the inception and completion of working through of the departure of the "lost" object, the final mourning of which can only occur in relation to a whole-object, which leads ultimately to acceptance of the fact of one's separateness. With this depart the last vestiges of the long-harbored, pre-eruptive abandonment depression, with its guilt-laden separation anxiety and the persistent and profound vulnerability to real and fantasied "losses" which characterize all essentially unindividuated personalities.

SUMMARY

The following inferences and conclusions concerning borderline personality organization and its clinical expression may be developed from the foregoing discussion:

1. Viewed from a developmental standpoint, borderline disorders comprise a protean symptomatic group which is indeed intermediate or transitional between psychotic disorders and psychoneurotic disorders.

2. Subsumable under the borderline rubric is a wide spectrum of personality disorders otherwise classified as schizoid, inadequate, infantile, narcissistic, hysterical, cyclothymic, sociopathic, and so on.

3. The developmental arrest or fixation etiologic for the borderline syndrome occurs during the separation-individuation phase of infantile development, more specifically, during its rapprochement subphase (16–25 months).

4. The basis for the developmental arrest common to borderline personalities is to be found in the relatively stereotypical "push-pull" nature of the mother-infant interaction during that period, specific to which is the borderline mother's libidinal availability (reward, approval, reinforcement) in response to her infant's dependent, regressive, and clinging behavior, and her withdrawal of her libidinal availability (rejection, disapproval, abandonment, negative reinforcement) in response to her infant's efforts toward separation-individuation.

5. The infant's powerful introjection of the essentially doubly binding, "push-pull" relation with the borderline mother in turn establishes and fixates the *split object-relations unit* (SORU) with

its incompletely differentiated self- and object-representations, ongoing reliance upon splitting defenses, reservoir of unneutralized aggression, persistent reunion-refusion fantasies, and, in alliance with the infantile pleasure ego, denial of separateness with associated impairment of reality testing.

6. As a consequence, the borderline personality continues to deal with whole-objects *as if* they were part-objects and struggles persistently, and not rarely desperately, with them after the fashion of "transitional" objects (Fairbairn 1941). The persistence of part-object relations, based in turn upon untrammeled reliance upon splitting defenses, precludes the infant's negotiation of the depressive position, with ensuing failure to mourn and persistence of that particular form of partially structuralized separation anxiety which Masterson has termed "abandonment depression," with resultant ongoing vulnerability to real and fantasied separations and "losses."

7. The "all-good"/"all-bad" nature of borderline endopsychic and derivative "external" interpersonal relations, and the various "mirroring" phenomena (Kohut 1971) and infantile grandiose and persecutory projections common to borderline personalities are considered to result from failure of differentiation of self- and object-representations characteristic of fixation at Kernberg's stage 3 in the development of object relations.

8. Psychoanalytic therapy of borderline personalities requires confrontative and interpretive exposure of the SORU within the therapeutic transference which, if successful, catalyzes the development of the therapeutic alliance with ensuing restructuring of the patient's endopsychic representations ("healthy object-relations unit"). The resultant depressive working through enables the patient to achieve Kernberg's developmental stage 4, typified by a sense of personal separateness and wholeness.

CHAPTER 4

FAIRBAIRN'S
OBJECT-RELATIONS THEORY

> The ego does not simply accept orders and
> carry them out. Rather, it generates an activity
> of its own toward the outer world as well as
> toward the other forces in the individual him-
> self. (Waelder 1976, p. 70)

This chapter constitutes a reconsideration of object-relations
theory, with particular reference to the internal object relations
of borderline personalities, in light of Fairbairn's powerfully
intuitive inferences regarding schizoid phenomena and experience.* I shall begin with a discussion of Fairbairn's contributions,
offering a critical review of his 17 claims for a theory of object
relations, which he set down in his 1963 "Synopsis." My critique
will differ from Abenheimer's (1955), especially in view of his
Jungian bias, and because of the unavailability at the time his
critique was written of the later contributions to the metapsychology of representations by Carter and Rinsley (chapter 3),
Jacobson (1954a, 1964), Kernberg (1966, 1972a), Mahler (1968,
1971, 1972a, Mahler et al. 1975), Masterson, (1975, 1976),

---

*I offer no excuse for my strongly favorable bias toward Fairbairn's work in
what follows, or, within that context, for my criticism of what I consider to be
some of his theoretical shortcomings.

Masterson and Rinsley (chapter 2), and Rinsley (chapters 3 and 5).

In a series of publications beginning in 1940, Fairbairn set forth the development of his views and conclusions regarding the structure of personality, laying great emphasis upon the splitting defense as fundamental to all object relations. His analytical work had convinced him of the determinative importance of schizoid phenomena for psychological development, his clinical insights into which were profound. Nevertheless, as Modell (1968) has pointed out, Fairbairn's contributions have fallen short of general acceptance within the mainstream of psychoanalysis, and several features of his work may be cited as reasons.

To begin with, Fairbairn considered his theoretical contributions as a significant break with traditional or classical psychoanalytic metapsychology, indeed, as supplanting and superannuating it. He thereby proceeded to jettison much of Freud's structural approach, managing to dismiss the id, to modify the concept of the superego, and to radically revise and complicate the concept of the ego.

Fairbairn sought to replace what he regarded as Freud's drive psychology with what he regarded as a relationship psychology, and, in particular, a psychology based upon *internal* (object) relations; his criticism of classical metapsychology's Helmholtzian underpinnings, like that of numerous others, appears increasingly beside the point in light of newer knowledge (Pribram and Gill 1976). His manner of conceptualizing internalized object relations, derived from the pioneering contributions of Melanie Klein, rendered his ideas suspect for many psychoanalysts (Glover 1949, 1968).

It has rightly been said that many of the problems of the acceptance of classical psychoanalysis may be traced to semantic causes, viz., to Freud's particular use of words or to their unfelicitous translation; indeed, one need only be reminded of Brill's translation of *Trieb* as *instinct* instead of as *drive* to account for the many irrelevant and meaningless controversies that then ensued, particularly from nonanalytic quarters, surrounding such terms as *instinctive, instinctual*, and the like, which served to obfuscate many of the substantive matters to which Freud's work had addressed itself. And Fairbairn's work has often suffered a similar fate.

In the first place, Fairbairn coined new terms, such as "accepted" and "rejected" objects, "internal saboteur," "libidinal ego," and "antilibidinal ego," all of which added to extant terminology. His apparent multiplicity of "egos" could fairly boggle the mind, especially as they appeared to introduce an unwarranted complexity into traditional concepts of mental structure.

Again, Fairbairn's theorizing often appeared to flout in egregious fashion the doctrine of Occam's razor; as he proceeded, he seemed ever ready to revise and expand his earlier concepts, to add a burgeoning congeries of ad hocs to his formulations, therewith to explain less and less with more and more. A good example will be found in his classic 1944 paper devoted to endopsychic structure, in which his efforts to bring his (then) current formulations into line with his earlier ones (as in his "schizoid factors" [1940] and "revised psychopathology" [1941] papers) appeared prolix. Indeed, a careful study of Fairbairn's understanding and interpretation of his patient's dream material in the 1944 paper is necessary before the reader may rightly conclude that it constitutes far more than a persuasive effort to fit it into the procrustean bed of his evolving theoretical elaborations.

Another problem for Fairbairn and for his evolving ideas on human personality is his style of written exposition. His writing is highly precise and full of balanced antitheses, and he gives careful attention to dependent and independent clauses. As Abenheimer (1955) has pointed out, Fairbairn's writing is also highly abstract. The reader is thus tempted to focus upon and be lulled by his convincing form, and often becomes impressed with Fairbairn's phrasing instead of paying attention to what he is writing about.

Of particular importance in any attempt to understand the limited acceptance of Fairbairn's insights by classical psychoanalysts have been his and his protégé Guntrip's (1961, 1968, 1971) efforts to divorce object-relations theory from any connection with classical metapsychology's mechanistic, neurological foundations. Here, Fairbairn's doctrinaire stance has done harm to the acceptability of his clinical insights and theoretical formulations, the more so because his muted polemics against grounding object-relations theory upon physicalistic assumptions, in contravention of Freud's own views, are both mistaken and irrelevant. Quite obviously, without brain there is no mind, and the fact that extant knowledge has not precisely revealed or proved their relationship in no way disproves that it exists. Fairbairn's staunch opposition to physicalism turns out, of course, to be unnecessary for the acceptance of his metapsychological formulations; it has, however, had the effect of sundering object-relations theory from the mainstream of psychoanalysis and of placing its adherents among the prime defectors from classical ideas, such as Adler, Jung, and Rank (Glover 1968).

It may indeed be said that the vast body of Freud's work may ultimately be traced back to his "Project" (1895), from which emanated the complexly interwoven conceptual threads which produced the fabric of classical psychoanalytic metapsychology. There is no reason to believe, moreover, that the major constructs of object-relations theory may not likewise find their source in the "Project"; it must also be admitted that the enormous insights which Freud set forth in that seminal work, including its arresting anticipation of much of contemporary neurophysiology (Pribram and Gill 1976), long remained as obscure to classical psychoanalysts as to the major psychoanalytic "deviants." As Fairbairn had indeed raised polemical objection to Freud's devotion to neurology, so have others such as Peterfreund (1971) and Schafer (1976) in their efforts to construct one or another variety of "uncontaminated" psychoanalytic psychology. Indeed, even so revisory a theorist as Federn never doubted the validity of Freud's genetic-dynamic, structural, and economic concepts, but rather, utilized them in his own psychoanalytic phenomenology to explicate more satisfactorily both major psychopathology and the variations of human perception (Weiss 1960).

FAIRBAIRN'S 17 CLAIMS

In a final summary statement in 1963, written shortly before his death, Fairbairn enumerated the theoretical views he had expounded over the years. I shall discuss his claims 1 through 8 and claims 14 and 17 separately and in some detail. Claims 9 through 13 will be considered together for the purpose of coherent exploratory exposition, as will claims 15 and 16.

1. AN EGO IS PRESENT FROM BIRTH. Note that Fairbairn uses the indefinite article "an" and not the definite article "the" in this statement. In this connection, a great deal depends upon how one chooses to define the term *ego*. Freud originally viewed the ego as a progressively differentiating surface vesicle with an associated system of neurones, the function of which was to filter and modulate exogenous stimuli; later, a similar service was to be performed vis-à-vis endogenous stimuli; still later, Federn (1952) was to give expression to these ideas in his concept of the external and internal ego boundaries. The *substantive ego* must, of course, be differentiated from the concept of *early ego functions*, the latter serving as modulators of stimulus thresholds, and hence, as archaic protective devices. If one chooses to define *ego* in terms of these protective devices, then all later psychoanalytic work, such as that of Mahler and her colleagues (1975) which establishes the mothering figure as the basic stimulus barrier, clearly likewise affirms the primary object-seeking function of the early ego.

2. LIBIDO IS A FUNCTION OF THE EGO. This statement represents a syncretic proposition which is more confusing than revealing

as it confounds dynamic, structural, and economic considerations. There appears to be little basis for attempting to redefine *libido* as an ego function rather than retaining it as a term representing a synthetic object-seeking drive, and hence, a form of energy that promotes object affiliation. In fact, Fairbairn's statement constitutes a reductionism very similar to many of Melanie Klein's formulations that failed properly to differentiate defensive-representational (introjective) from autonomous (incorporative) processes. Such reductionism may be seen to result from Fairbairn's attempt to jettison classical structural concepts while attempting to retain certain dynamic and economic ones. The issue is made plain in his fourth claim, to the effect that "there is no such thing as an 'id.'"

3. THERE IS NO DEATH INSTINCT; AND AGGRESSION IS A REACTION TO FRUSTRATION OR DEPRIVATION. In large measure, this claim is moot, as few contemporary psychoanalysts would dispute it. It represents a departure from the view of aggression as expressive of an innate death instinct, as set forth and developed by Freud (1920, 1923) and further elaborated by Melanie Klein (1933, 1935).

4. SINCE LIBIDO IS A FUNCTION OF THE EGO AND AGGRESSION IS A REACTION TO FRUSTRATION OR DEPRIVATION, THERE IS NO SUCH THING AS AN "ID." Here, matters become more complicated. Anyone who has observed neonates must have noted their proneness to unmodulated neurovegetative discharge ("affecto-motor storms"), which becomes "damped down" only upon the ministrations of a mothering figure. Indeed, the turbulent infant's "magic gestures" are directed toward both the reduction of exogenous stimulation and the modulation of instinctual (drive) tension, and he will accept these willy-nilly if they are offered to him. That they can be offered only by an "object," that is, by an "external" instrumentality by which the original "aim" of drive reduction is achieved, does not "prove" the primacy of object over aim insofar as the infant is unable to differentiate

"self" from "object." It may therefore be said that accepting the primacy of object over aim is unnecessary for the acceptance of the great body of Fairbairn's clinical and theoretical contributions.

5. THE EGO, AND THEREFORE THE LIBIDO, IS FUNDAMENTALLY OBJECT-SEEKING. In view of the commentary immediately preceding, little more need be said in respect to this claim.

6. THE EARLIEST AND ORIGINAL FORM OF ANXIETY, AS EXPERIENCED BY THE CHILD, IS SEPARATION-ANXIETY. With this claim, supported as it is by the impressive work of other investigators (Bowlby 1960a,b, 1962, Mahler 1952, 1968, Mahler et al. 1975, Spitz 1957, 1959, 1965), Fairbairn is on solid ground indeed. The subject of separation anxiety, however, requires further elaboration within an object-relations context.

In classical terms, a major component of separation anxiety is, of course, instinctual anxiety. Such concepts as "fear of engulfment" or "fear of fusion," the terror experienced at the prospect of or in the wake of "ego fragmentation," "fear of loss of ego boundaries," "fear of self-dissolution," "fear of death," "aphanisis," and the like, in a metaphorical sense reflect the signal anxiety that appears upon the imminent or actual irruption of unconscious content into the territory of the ego (Freud 1926). The prototype of such irruption is to be found in the state of protopathic or endogenous overstimulation (implied in the phrase "affecto-motor storms") to which the infant is constantly subjected in the absence of "good enough mothering" (Winnicott 1951, 1960). The state of primal ego trauma, as it were, reflects a condition of dangerous overstimulation. In the infant, such a condition may indeed kill and at best conduces to significant inhibition and distortion of further ego development; in the older person, it conduces to psychosis with its ensuing fragmentation and paralysis of the ego's coping and defensive functions.

A second component of separation anxiety reflects a greater degree of endopsychic structuralization, viz., superego anxiety (guilt) (Freud 1923). Here the ego faces extinction at the hands of the superego on two fronts: it may be left, bereft of libidinal investment by the ego-ideal aspect of the superego, and it may become the object of the latter's sadistic (aggressive) assault; both in turn describe the dynamics of melancholia (Freud 1917b). It was Fairbairn's merit to perceive the complex phenomena associated with the splitting defense as directed against the frustrating ("bad") object in order to account for the schizoid phenomena which lie at the base of the separation anxiety, to which he rightly attributes prime importance for any understanding of psychopathology.

7. INTERNALIZATION OF THE OBJECT IS A DEFENSIVE MEASURE ORIGINALLY ADOPTED BY THE CHILD TO DEAL WITH HIS ORIGINAL OBJECT (THE MOTHER AND HER BREAST) IN SO FAR AS IT IS UN-SATISFYING. In this formulation, Fairbairn rests firmly upon the antecedent work of Freud and Abraham on the relationship between object loss and melancholia. Originally, Abraham (1912) described depressed individuals' feelings of inner impoverishment, inability to love, and "badness," and their related need to project aggression (hate) onto others; and later (1916) he postulated the melancholic's regression to oral cannibalism where the "lost" object is devoured. Freud (1917b) subsequently described the melancholic's regression from object love to narcissistic identification with the lost object, and Rado (1928) portrayed a split introjection of a "good-bad" lost object as the basis of depression. Thus one can presume upon the infant's "logic" that the equation *lost = bad = unsatisfying = rejecting = frustrating* conveys a pervasive preverbal experience of abandonment, and consequently the infant proceeds powerfully to introject the abandoning ("bad") object. Fairbairn's idea that the introjected bad object is next split into two parts—a rejecting object (R.O.) and an exciting object (E.O.)—finds precedent in Freud's, Abraham's, and Rado's earlier postulations that the introjected object undergoes splitting, albeit the resulting products were accorded a greater degree of complexity by Fairbairn.

Of importance here is Fairbairn's imprecise use of terminology. Clearly, the split-off "objects" he writes about are part-objects, just as was the "original" breast of which they constitute introjective precipitates. What emerges from these considerations is a reminder of Melanie Klein's (1935) doubtless correct view that the persistence of (split-off) part-objects, and hence, the failure to constitute a whole-object, precludes the working through of object loss, and hence, precludes negotiation of the depressive position. One can now begin to understand the relationship among persistent reliance upon splitting, persistence of part-object relations, failure of depressive working through, and inhibition or failure of separation-individuation (chapter 3).

8. INTERNALIZATION OF THE OBJECT IS NOT JUST A PRODUCT OF A FANTASY OF INCORPORATING THE OBJECT ORALLY, BUT IS A DISTINCT PSYCHOLOGICAL PROCSSS. Although this statement has numerous implications, I will discuss only two which seem most relevant here.

First of all, Fairbairn takes pains to avoid the error inherent in failure to differentiate representational (introjective) from non-representational (incorporative) entities and processes. By the phrase "distinct psychological process," Fairbairn refers to the representational characteristics of the "objects" about which he writes and not to their "real" or concrete properties; thus, he attempts to avoid confounding "taking in" with introjection, and "putting out" with projection.

Second, in accordance with the operation of the pleasure principle (Freud 1911a), the infant will spit out what tastes unpleasant and will swallow (incorporate) what tastes pleasant. Both unpleasant and pleasant oral stimuli (potential food items) leave an accretion of memory traces in the infant which forms the bases for the later elaboration of the (symbolic) defensive functions of, respectively, projection and introjection. One may assume that a major feature of failure of good enough mothering consists precisely in subjecting the infant to a preponderance of unpleasant (negative) oral stimuli; consequently there occurs a major build-up of negative memory traces which must be gotten rid of, as it were. The riddance mechanism is, of course, projection, as a result of the untrammeled operation of which the infant proceeds to "construct" a basically hostile (persecutory) environment. The pervasive mistrust that typifies psychotic and borderline personalities may be traced to this source (chapters 1, 3, and 5).

Fairbairn's developing views regarding the significance of early introjective and projective mechanisms found expression in his evolving ideas about which object, good or bad, was primally introjected. Earlier (1944), he had postulated the primal introjection of the bad object whose function was to "remove" and exert internal mastery over an external persecutor. Later (1951a), he adopted the view that the primally introjected object was neither "all good" nor "all bad" but was, rather, preambivalent in nature. Here one finds a significant expression of his implied view that representational and defensive functions are inextricably interrelated. As there could be no endopsychic or mental representations without associated introjective-projective defenses, his assertion that "internalization . . . is a distinct psychological process" follows.

9. TWO ASPECTS OF THE INTERNALIZED OBJECT, VIZ., ITS EXCITING AND ITS FRUSTRATING ASPECTS, ARE SPLIT OFF FROM THE MAIN CORE OF THE OBJECT AND REPRESSED BY THE EGO.

10. THUS THERE COME TO BE CONSTITUTED TWO REPRESSED INTERNAL OBJECTS, VIZ., THE EXCITING (OR LIBIDINAL) OBJECT AND THE REJECTING (OR ANTILIBIDINAL) OBJECT.

11. THE MAIN CORE OF THE INTERNALIZED OBJECT, WHICH IS NOT REPRESSED, IS DESCRIBED AS THE IDEAL OBJECT OR EGO IDEAL.

12. OWING TO THE FACT THAT THE EXCITING (LIBIDINAL) AND REJECTING (ANTILIBIDINAL) OBJECTS ARE BOTH CATHECTED BY THE ORIGINAL EGO, THESE OBJECTS CARRY INTO REPRESSION WITH THEM PARTS OF THE EGO BY WHICH THEY ARE CATHECTED, LEAVING THE

CENTRAL CORE OF THE EGO (CENTRAL EGO) UNREPRESSED, BUT
ACTING AS THE AGENT OF REPRESSION.

13. THE RESULTING INTERNAL SITUATION IS ONE IN WHICH THE
ORIGINAL EGO IS SPLIT INTO THREE EGOS—A CENTRAL (CONSCIOUS)
EGO ATTACHED TO THE IDEAL OBJECT (EGO-IDEAL), A REPRESSED
LIBIDINAL EGO ATTACHED TO THE EXCITING (OR LIBIDINAL) OBJECT,
AND A REPRESSED ANTILIBIDINAL EGO ATTACHED TO THE REJECTING
(OR ANTILIBIDINAL) OBJECT.

With these five statements, Fairbairn begins to construct an
endopsychic structure and a theory of object relations as well.

First, Fairbairn's split internalized object, comprising the
exciting object (E.O.) and the rejecting object (R.O.), constitutes the bad object that excites and frustrates. As already noted,
these various "objects" are in fact *part-object-representations* derived from the build-up of positively and negatively valent
memory traces, the last, in turn, derived from the vicissitudes of
the mother-infant feeding interaction. What is striking in these
five claims (9–13) is the essential claim for the existence of what
can only be construed as an "original" whole-object, subsequently split into an E.O., an R.O., and an ideal object (I.O.). If
that is not enough, there also exists ab initio an "original ego"
that correspondingly undergoes splitting into a libidinal ego
(L.E.), an antilibidinal ego (Anti-L.E.), and a central ego (C.E.).
Clearly, the implication of these statements to the effect that
some sort of whole-self- and whole-object-representations exist
ab initio is at variance with Fairbairn's view of the late oral stage
of infantile dependence (Fairbairn 1941, Pruyser 1975).

The theoretical difficulties that stem from claims 9 through
13 arise because Fairbairn views repression and splitting as
essentially the same, which allows him to jettison those structural considerations that do not suit his theorizing while retaining those topographic ones that do; thus, what is repressed is
consigned to the "unconscious" while at the same time "there
is no such thing as an 'id.'" What is more, he postulates a
central ego as the agency of repression, into which the E.O. and

the R.O. "carry" the other two egos. Thus, the E.O. and the R.O. are also agents of repression and Fairbairn ends up with not one but three repressive agents, namely, the C.E., the E.O., and the R.O. But since the E.O. and the R.O. are themselves part-object-representations, the question arises, and remains unanswered, how part-object-representations bring about repression. And, in accordance with Fairbairn's view that repression and splitting are essentially the same, there remains the unsettingly conclusion that split-off part-representations engender their own splitting!

Indeed, clinical experience with borderline personalities and with psychotics (chapters 2–3, and Masterson 1976) amply demonstrates that something akin to Fairbairn's postuled E.O.-L.E. and R.O.-Anti-L.E. alliances does in fact exist and is not repressed; rather, their associated representations and affects are often strikingly available to consciousness, as would be expected in the case of splitting (Freud 1940).

These difficulties may, in part, be resolved if one sets aside Fairbairn's confounding of repression and splitting and resorts to what is now known as representational development (Jacobson 1954a, 1964, Kernberg 1966, 1972a). If Fairbairn's concept of the split internalized bad object is correct, one may view the E.O. and the R.O. as part-object-representations, both admittedly "bad" but of different affective valence. As these part-objects become internalized on the basis of very early mother-infant interactions, the corresponding part-self-representations, to which one may provisionally apply Fairbairn's terms L.E. and Anti-L.E., become affiliated with or assimilated to them, thereby generating two polar opposite representation-affect complexes which remain separate as a consequence of splitting (Kernberg 1966). Thus, the E.O. and the R.O. do not "carry into repression" their respectively associated L.E. and Anti-L.E.; rather, their affiliation or association is based upon libidinal ties, a consideration which Fairbairn (1944) takes pains to spell out.

It follows from these considerations (as well as generally [Freud 1915b]) that repression has not yet made its appearance at the very early time when Fairbairn attributes the internalization and splitting of the primal object to the infant. Indeed, the onset of normal repression is directly related to the beginning of whole-object relations (chapters 3 and 5); and, in turn, the attainment of whole-object relations entails the achievement of a significant degree of self-object differentiation and the end of reliance upon splitting and magic hallucination.

Prior to the inception of whole-object relations (Melanie Klein's depressive position), "self" and "object" are undifferentiated and nothing is foreign to the archaic ego which is, as it were, overstocked with a welter of primitive and ambivalent representations and affects. When early object-representations come to be perceived as alien, that is, as nonself, so too are those representations and affects that will become the objects of repression; the developing ego comes to differentiate itself from "outside objects" and, concomitantly, from those endopsychic contents that will become repressed into the unconscious (chapter 1). Thus, progressive ego growth, which entails progressive "self-object" differentiation, generates two analogous ego-alien territories—an "internal" territory (the Ucs) and an "external" territory (the object world).

In the light of these considerations, the "internal situation" can be schematized as follows:

Part-object representation	*Associated affect*	*Part-self representation*
E.O. _____	Pleasant	_____ L.E.
R.O._____	Unpleasant	_____ Anti-L.E.

According to this view, it becomes necessary to revise several of Fairbairn's ideas regarding early endopsychic structure: (a) the E.O.-L.E. and R.O.-Anti-L.E. alliances are not repressed; (b) there is no significant differentiation of the two representational components of the respective alliances. Rather, according to what is now known of infantile development, part-self- and part-object-representations remain in decreasing degree mutually undifferentiated through the first three years of life (chapters 2,

3, and 5, as well as Mahler et al. 1975); and (c) the associated affects (drive derivatives) that "bind" the E.O.-L.E. and R.O.-Anti-L.E. alliances together cannot be purely libidinal in nature. As I will show, clinical experience dictates otherwise.

Fairbairn's third "alliance," that of the central ego (C.E.) and the ideal object or ego ideal (I.O.), must now be examined. Fairbairn writes of an "original ego" and an "original object" (the latter implying the mother and her breast) as if the former were a unitary or whole mental structure and the latter were a whole-object. In effect he postulates that the "original object" undergoes internalization and subsequent splitting into the dyadic bad object and the I.O. In the 1951 addendum to his 1944 "Endopsychic Structure" paper, he describes the I.O. "as 'the ego ideal' rather than 'the super-ego'" (pp. 135–136), while in his 1949 paper he clearly considers the I.O. as the superego which provides "the basis for the establishment of moral values" (pp. 159–160fn). In reaching this last conclusion, Fairbairn formulates a conception of the I.O. strikingly similar to that set forth below. His conception of the C.E. "as comprising preconscious and conscious, as well as unconscious, elements" (1944, p. 104) clearly establishes the C.E. as analogous to Freud's (1923) concept of the ego.

In connection with these considerations, however, a serious objection must now be raised. Fairbairn (1941) describes the infant's object relations during the late oral stage of infantile dependence with the phrase "mother-with-a-breast" (p. 41), pointing out that the infant perceives the maternal whole-object as if it were a part-object, and there is no reason to doubt the correctness of this view. As previously noted, however, it does not square with his implication that some sort of "original" whole-object exists from the beginning.

14. THIS INTERNAL SITUATION REPRESENTS A BASIC SCHIZOID POSITION WHICH IS MORE FUNDAMENTAL THAN THE DEPRESSIVE POSITION DESCRIBED BY MELANIE KLEIN. In part, one may account for this claim on the basis of the difference between Melanie Klein's

and Fairbairn's earlier views of the nature of the primally introjected object. Melanie Klein had postulated the primal introjection of a good "object" with the subsequent introjection of a bad "object" as a consequence of the primal object's (the breast's) frustrating aspects. On the other hand, Fairbairn (1944) could not account for how a split internalized object (whose existence had become evident to him clinically) could come into being unless the splitting constituted a defense directed against a bad object. He wrote, "it is always 'bad' objects that are internalized in the first instance, since it is difficult to find any adequate motive for the internalization of objects which are satisfying and 'good.' Thus it would be a pointless procedure on the part of the infant to internalize the breast of a mother with whom he had already had a perfect relationship" (p. 93fn). Here Fairbairn strongly implies that (symbolic) representations can only arise from defensive operations; but, while this insight is important, it neglects the fact that "good" (i.e., "positive," libidinal, gratifying) representations, derived from the accretion of their corresponding, antecedent memory traces, arise spontaneously as a consequence of good mothering; his later view of a preambivalent or mixed good-bad primal object is compatible with that fact. I suggest that the preambivalent object that Fairbairn later concluded underwent primal introjection constitutes the representational precursor or anlage of the good-bad whole-object that later comes into existence during the period of the depressive position, whereupon splitting comes to be replaced by repression in the classical sense.

Granting the correctness of this suggestion, and in view of the representational and defensive complexity with which Fairbairn endows the vicissitudes of very early mother-infant interaction, then his conclusion that the "basic schizoid position" is "more fundamental than" Melanie Klein's depressive position appears warranted.

15. THE ANTILIBIDINAL EGO, IN VIRTUE OF ITS ATTACHMENT TO THE REJECTING (ANTILIBIDINAL) OBJECT, ADOPTS AN UNCOMPROMISINGLY

HOSTILE ATTITUDE TO THE LIBIDINAL EGO, AND THUS HAS THE EFFECT
OF POWERFULLY REINFORCING THE REPRESSION OF THE LIBIDINAL EGO
BY THE CENTRAL EGO.

16. WHAT FREUD DESCRIBED AS THE "SUPEREGO" IS REALLY A
COMPLEX STRUCTURE COMPRISING (A) THE IDEAL OBJECT OR EGO
IDEAL, (B) THE ANTILIBIDINAL EGO, AND (C) THE REJECTING (OR
ANTILIBIDINAL OBJECT. In his paper on endopsychic structure
(1944), Fairbairn describes the L.E. as comparable to the
(conscious) C.E., but differing from the C.E. in, among other
respects, "its more infantile character" and its "smaller measure
of adaptation to reality" (p. 106). He further states that the L.E.
"corresponds . . . to Freud's 'id' " but proceeds to qualify that
statement by pointing out that the L.E. is "not . . . a mere
reservoir of instinctual impulses, but . . . a dynamic structure"
(p. 106). In the light of present knowledge, it may be said that
Fairbairn was groping toward a dynamic-representational charac-
terization of the L.E. in the sense of "self-as-object" (Rinsley
1962). Thus, one may view the L.E. as comparable to Freud's
(purified) pleasure ego, and also as a complex part-self-representation linked affectively to a corresponding part-object-
representation, the E.O. The "id impulses" striving toward
discharge ("pleasure gain") then become linked to pleasurable
(positive, libidinally valent) memory traces, which proceed to
evolve into a part-self-representation; this part-self-representation
in turn becomes assimilated to or affiliated with a corresponding
part-object-representation. These two part-representations—in
this case the L.E.-E.O. "alliance"—together with their associated
libidinal affect, comprise a triadic structure (Kernberg 1966)
which Masterson and I (chapter 2) have termed an *object-relations
part-unit*.

Similarly, under conditions of frustration, "id impulses"
striving toward discharge become linked to unpleasant (negative,
aggressively valent) memory traces and proceed to evolve into a
part-self-representation; this part-self-representation in turn becomes assimilated to or affiliated with a corresponding part-

object-representation. These two part-representations—in this case the Anti-L.E.-R.O. "alliance"—together with their associated aggressive affect, comprise a second triadic structure or *object relations part-unit.*

Fairbairn's third or C.E.-I.O. "alliance" becomes even more complex when it is examined closely in this context. Clearly, the C.E. constitutes the "residue of the undivided ego" or the residue of the "original" ego. But nowhere does Fairbairn explain the nature of such an ego; neither does he explain the nature of the putative (original) object from which are subsequently split the E.O., the R.O., and the I.O. However, a close reading of his statements about the C.E. and the I.O. leaves no doubt that the C.E. corresponds to Freud's reality ego. As this is the case, then the I.O. (which Fairbairn also terms the ego ideal) must have the qualities associated with being "real," and hence, "external" in Federn's sense (1952). I shall discuss and attempt to resolve these issues later.

The following generalizations may now be extracted from the preceding discussion of claims 15 and 16: (a) both the E.O. and the R.O. are bad ("rejected") part-object-representations; correspondingly, their affiliated L.E. and Anti-L.E. are bad part-self-representations; (b) the I.O. and the C.E. comprise good ("accepted") representations that bear a powerful relation to reality; and (c) the superego is composed of both good (accepted) and bad (rejected) representational-affective components; the former reflect and reinforce the individual's striving toward reality, while the latter reflect and reinforce the individual's narcissism and are uncompromisingly persecutory in nature.

17. THESE CONSIDERATIONS FORM THE BASIS OF A THEORY OF THE PERSONALITY CONCEIVED IN TERMS OF OBJECT-RELATIONS, IN CONTRAST TO ONE CONCEIVED IN TERMS OF INSTINCTS AND THEIR VICISSITUDES. In view of the foregoing discussion, this statement must necessarily be regarded as incorrect as it sets out a dichotomy of "instinct" and "object" that is misleading and that does damage to Fairbairn's own profound clinical insights. What is

now known of the development of object relations reflects the essentially unitary nature of dynamics, structure, and representation, which may be separated only for heuristic purposes.

APPLICATIONS TO BORDERLINE DISORDERS

The Intertranslatability of "Egos" and "Representations"

Fairbairn's view of endopsychic structure is squarely within the self-as-object tradition as contrasted with the self-as-process tradition with which classical metapsychology has been associated (Rinsley 1962). Thus his various egos and objects are in fact representations; hence they are accessible to the patient's and the analyst's preconscious and conscious awareness.

It becomes possible, therefore, to analogize Fairbairn's split internalized bad object with the part-object-representations associated with the split object-relations unit (SORU) (see chapter 2). Fairbairn's R.O. is thus comparable to the part-object-representation associated with the withdrawing (rejecting) part-unit, while his E.O. is comparable to the part-object-representation associated with the rewarding part-unit. Both are "bad" because they are derived from the internalization of the infant's interaction with a "not-good-enough-mother," whose profoundly ambivalent mothering leads the infant to develop a "false self" (Winnicott 1960). The false self comes into existence in relation to the split-off E.O. and the split-off R.O., the former perceived as rewarding passivity at the expense of growth, and hence, as ultimately frustrating, and the latter perceived as profoundly persecutory in nature.

The false self, with its as-if or pseudocomplementary characteristics, emerges as the L.E. and the Anti-L.E., which together constitute the infant's part-self-representations as they come into respective association with the E.O. and the R.O. In the case of the borderline individual, these part-self- and part-object-representations have become only partly differentiated, while in the case of the psychotic they have remained undifferentiated (chapters 3 and 5, as well as Kernberg 1972a).*

The subject of repression must now be reconsidered. Fairbairn (1943) objected to Freud's concept of repression as a defense against "intolerably guilty impulses" and "intolerably unpleasant memories"; rather, he considered repression as a defense against "intolerably bad internalized objects" (p. 62), and, since he viewed repression and splitting as essentially the same, splitting became a defense against bad objects. But splitting serves as a defense only where there is a persistence of part-object relations and becomes replaced by repression (as viewed in the classical sense) in the case of more mature personalities, that is, neurotic and essentially healthy individuals in whom self- and object-representations have become differentiated.

It is not surprising, therefore, that Fairbairn confounds repression with splitting. For while splitting certainly serves as the defensive precursor of repression, it continues to operate significantly only in the case of pre-Oedipally fixated personalities, that is, those incapable of whole-object relations. When such patients come to analysis, Oedipal issues and the defense invariably associated with them, namely, repression, constitute epiphenomena. This is not to say that the precursory splitting defense will not be found to be operative among neurotics if the analysis is pushed ever more deeply into archaic material, or if pre-Oedipal "interpretations" are freely or preferentially offered to the patient, thereby allowing regression to proceed well beyond what is required. From these considerations one may reasonably

---

*In a recent paper, Masterson (1979) presents a somewhat different definition of the false self. According to him, and in accordance with the view set forth in chapter 2, the false self comprises a postulated "alliance" between the rewarding part-unit and the "pathological ego," the latter corresponding to Freud's purified pleasure ego. However, if the part-self-representation associated with the rewarding part-unit corresponds with Fairbairn's L.E., and the L.E. in turn corresponds with Freud's pleasure ego, there is no need to postulate any such "alliance."

conclude that the "schizoid factors" (that is, manifestations of the splitting defense) that Fairbairn encountered in his analytical work, to which he was so clinically sensitive and from which he drew his basic inferences regarding endopsychic structure, typify individuals with what has since come to be termed *borderline personality* or *disorder*.

Fairbairn's effort to relate his endopsychic structures to classical ones must also be mentioned. As noted, the L.E. may be compared to Freud's purified pleasure ego, while the C.E. may be compared to Freud's reality ego (Freud 1911a), the former possessing the characteristics of a part-self-representation and the latter possessing the characteristics of a whole-self-representation. So far as Freud's superego is concerned, matters are even more complex. To quote Fairbairn (1944):

> Actually, the 'super-ego' corresponds not so much to the . . . 'antilibidinal ego'* as to a compound of this structure and its associated object. . . . At the same time, the 'antilibidinal ego' is unlike the 'super-ego' in that it is . . . devoid of all moral significance. . . . it seems to me impossible to offer any satisfactory psychological explanation of guilt in the absence of the super-ego; but the super-ego must be regarded as originating at a higher level of mental organization than that at which the antilibidinal ego operates. Exactly how the activities of these two structures are related must in the meantime remain an open question [pp. 106–107].

Thus, the harsh, sadistic aspect of the superego comprises, for Fairbairn, a composite structure made up of the part-object-representation associated with the rejecting SORU part-unit (that is, the R.O.) and its corresponding part-self-representation (that is, the Anti-L.E.). Indeed, the sadistic component of the classical superego is composed of the same rejecting SORU part-unit that

---

*I have taken the liberty of replacing Fairbairn's original term "internal saboteur," which he used in this passage, with his later, more satisfactory term "antilibidinal ego."

is discovered clinically in the borderline patient's SORU; and the associated affect turns out to be the abandonment depression with its components of instinctual and superego anxiety (chapter 2).

So far as the moral component of the superego is concerned, a solution to Fairbairn's "open question" may now be suggested. It has already been noted that the healthy ORU is comparable to Fairbairn's C.E.-I.O. alliance, and that the I.O. (which in the therapeutic transference assumes the form of the maternal [parental] image which "rewards" efforts toward separation-individuation) comprises the form of a reality-oriented, whole-self-representation. Thus, the moral component of the superego consists of whole-self- and whole-object-representations, based upon reality and determining standards and guidelines accessible to consciousness. Where the C.E.-I.O. alliance preponderates, "ego" and "superego" come into mutual compliance and, insofar as the C.E. and the I.O. are whole-representations, significant separation-individuation has occured, "lost" objects have been mourned, and the superego has become their repository (Freud 1923).

SUMMARY

It is not surprising that those analysts who found classical, self-as-process metapsychology unsuited to their taste were prone to view endopsychic structures as vivid representations, nor is it surprising that they readily perceived prerepressive defenses in their patients as an expression of their perception of those defenses within themselves. One such analyst was Sullivan. Another, as we have just seen, was Fairbairn, whose profound contributions to our understanding of schizoid phenomena and of endopsychic structure may be expected to have a lasting and growing impact on psychoanalytic thought. Yet another is Federn, himself endowed with extraordinary self-sensitivity (Weiss 1960), and whose contributions to a metapsychological phenomenology proceeded from his interest in schizophrenia. Federn's contributions are discussed in chapter 1.

CHAPTER 5

A REVIEW OF
ETIOLOGY, DYNAMICS,
AND TREATMENT

This chapter continues to develop the concept of borderline psychopathology discussed in Chapters 2 and 3, a concept based on object-relations considerations. Special attention is given to the critical failure of separation-individuation, and consequent split object-relations unit (SORU), in borderline personalities. All inferences and conclusions are based on extensive clinical experience comprising the analytic treatment of borderline adolescents in combined individual and residential treatment, intensive analytically oriented casework, and family therapy with borderline adolescents and their families (Masterson 1972a,b, 1973, 1974, 1975, Rinsley 1965, 1967a,b, 1971a,b, 1974a), and analytic treatment of borderline adults (Masterson 1976). Common to all the treated cases were the following:

1. The mothers of borderline adolescents and adults were themselves found to be suffering from various degrees of borderline disorder.
2. The mothers of future borderline adolescents and adults typically took pride in and found significant gratification from their infants' dependency during the normal autistic-presymbiotic

phase of postnatal life, i.e., from birth through the second post-natal month. Beginning during the differentiation subphase and extending throughout the ensuing subphases of the separation-individuation phase, however, their responses to their developing infant took on a stereotypic and predictable pattern, i.e., they in various ways reinforced the infant's passivity by "rewarding" the latter's passive-dependent clinging behavior and, again in various ways, withdrew from, rejected or actively "punished" the infant whenever the infant displayed more actively aggressive, exploratory coping activity. Typically the borderline mother, embarked upon raising a future borderline child and adult, exuded happy satisfaction when asked about her experiences with her neonate, only to lapse into frowning, emotional blandness, or disdain when discussing her progressively more active infant during the latter half of the first postnatal year and beyond. Direct experience in observing the mothering patterns of young borderline mothers in a child development nursery amply confirmed the inferences drawn from the treatment of older borderline patients and their families.

3. In contrast to the borderline mother, who enjoyed her infant's abject dependency but who later consistently thwarted the latter's innate drive toward separation-individuation, the psychotic mother (including mothers who raised children diagnosed in adolescence and adulthood as suffering from schizophrenic illness) responded almost ab initio to her newborn infant with dysphoria, perplexity, confusion, or outright denial of his significance or even his existence; indeed, there was no joy in motherhood for these young women, who could only respond to their infants by depersonifying them into transitional or fetish-like objects (Rinsley 1971a).

4. The particular variety of mother-infant interaction which proves to be etiologic for the later development of borderline disorder—reward for passive-dependency, rejection (withdrawal of libidinal supplies) in the wake of aggressive assertiveness—in fact represents one variety of such depersonification (appersona-

tion) of the infant (chapter 11). The mother of the future border-line individual deals with him essentially as she was herself dealt with during this critical period by her own mother; she recapitulates a mode of mother-infant interaction which reflects the persistence of her own archaic separation anxiety; she perceives her infant as, alternatively, "all good" or "all bad," the former when he clings dependently to her, the latter when he makes efforts to separate from her; when he functions as her "all good" baby, the mother "feels good," satiated, and gratified; when he functions as her "all bad" object, she feels enraged and depressed. In thus serving as the projective repository of the mother's own complexly overdetermined and chronically reinforced conflict over separation-individuation, the infant comes to be "something other than what he really is"—there is no interactional and developmental goodness of fit, as it were, between mother and infant; the mother is unable to serve as the "maternal beacon" (Mahler et al. 1975) who increasingly supports the child's innate drive toward separation-individuation; the "good enough mothering" of which Winnicott (1951, 1960) has so sensitively written is pervasively lacking.

5. The ambivalence-ridden mother-infant interactional pattern—reward for dependency, withdrawal and rejection in the wake of aggressive assertiveness—in turn becomes powerfully introjected by the infant, and serves as the basis for the evolution of what Masterson and I (chapter 2) have termed the *split object-relations unit* (SORU) of the borderline. The latter, in accordance with Kernberg's (1966) formulations, comprises a triadic affective-representational structure, analogous to Fairbairn's (1951b) "split internalized bad object," which is pathognomonic for borderline personality organization. The SORU, in turn, consists of two part-units—the withdrawing or rejecting (aggressively valent) part-unit and the rewarding (libidinally valent) part-unit—which are specifically introjectively related to the two major themes of the infant's interaction with his borderline mother. (See Table 2–1, p. 39) for a detailed description of the part-units.)

THE CONSEQUENCES OF THE
PERSISTENCE OF THE SORU

The persistence of the SORU leads, in turn, to a number of interrelated and fateful consequences for the developing infant and child:

1. From the standpoint of defenses, the normal archaic infantile splitting mechanism is reinforced and maintained; "good" (libidinal, gratifying, positively valent) and "bad" (aggressive, negatively valent) representations and affects are, as it were, kept apart so that the self and the object world continue to be viewed persistently as either "all good" or "all bad." When the self-representations are perceived in the "all good" mode, reinforcement and fixation of the infant's archaic infantile-megalomania (infantile grandiosity) ensue, with further retrenchment of the individual's primary narcissism; when the self-representations are perceived in the "all bad" mode, intense, depressive self-derogation regularly result, with associated feelings of emptiness, uselessness, evil, and destructiveness. When object-representations are perceived in the "all good" mode, the result is a manifestation of pathological idealization reflective of the projection of components of the infantile ego ideal, in part to ward off awareness of the alternative "all bad" mode of perceiving object-representations, in which "external" objects are sensed and responded to as dangerous persecutors.

2. As a consequence of pathological inhibition of the interrelated processes of desymbiotization and separation-individuation, self-images (self-representations) and object-images (object-representations) remain in a state of partial or incomplete differentiation; in simpler language, self and object remain in significant measure perceptually fused together, leading to a persistent condition of transitivism. As "self" and "object" remain perceptually, cognitively, and affectively interchangeable, continued impetus is provided for the maintenance of primitive defense mechanisms, specifically introjection and projection, primary identification, denial (disavowal) and magic and nega-

tive hallucination (scotomatization), all of which exemplify the basic splitting defense.

3. The state of incomplete self-object differentiation, expressive of the persistent "symbiotic dual unity" (Mahler et al. 1975), reflects the significant arrest of the child's progress toward the attainment of whole-object relations and the achievement of object constancy (Fraiberg 1969). The stage of late orality ("mother-with-breast": Fairbairn 1941) is never fully traversed; hence whole-objects (persons) continue to be perceived and dealt with as part-objects (e.g., as bodily parts, such as breasts or genitalia). Recognitory memory is not properly replaced by evocative memory, and the growing child's transition from sensorimotor to early operational thought does not come about (Piaget 1937), leaving prominent residues of autistic ideation ("thought disorder") as contaminants of what would otherwise have emerged as developed abstract-categorical (circular-operational) thinking during adolescence.

4. As progress toward whole-object relations is thwarted, and since such relations are essential for the occurrence of depressive working through (Klein 1935, 1940, 1946), the child continues to be developmentally arrested at the depressive position. As a consequence, the child (and later, the borderline adult) never achieves the capacity to mourn, with the result that later separations and losses are never worked through and "lost" objects remain powerfully introjected so that their counterparts in reality are superficially switched, exchanged, or quickly "replaced."

5. Following Kernberg (1966), part-self- and part-object-representations remain in significant measure "undepersonified" ("unassimilated," "unmetabolized"), a condition which ensures the persistence of the images associated with these respective representations in a notably concrete or "real" form. These "real" images, in fact, comprise primitive ego and superego forerunners which, in accordance with the borderline individual's transitivistic condition, "pass in and out," as it were, by means of introjection (introjective identification) and projection (projective identification). As a result, they fail to be normally internalized,

and hence, fail to contribute to the evolution of progressively smoothly operative defensive, adaptational, and representational functions (chapter 1). In addition, the affects (consciously perceived, instinctual drive representations) associated with these unassimilated image-representations likewise fail in normal internalization; they remain unbound and un-deinstinctualized, and hence, unsublimated, repetitively and unaccountably subjecting the borderline individual to episodic, periodic emotional buffetings which puzzle, confuse, frighten, and depress him.

6. Normal developmental phase-specificity is seriously deficient in the case of borderline individuals (Kut Rosenfeld and Sprince 1963). Progress through the established sequence of sphincter dominance is more apparent than real so that later anal (ambivalent) and phallic-Oedipal resolutions never adequately occur, and the defenses and object relations otherwise associated with them continue to subserve the overweening pressure of oral-narcissistic needs. The last, in turn, continue to find expression in the part-object nature of the borderline individual's relationships: progress toward mature genitality, with the subsumption of infantile partial aims under genital primacy, is thwarted and the individual remains essentially polymorphous-perverse and sadomasochistic.

7. Ego growth remains stunted. The dearth of neutralized energy associated with the SORU brings about an arrest of the transformation of the pleasure ego into the reality ego with associated failure of the development of normal repression (Freud 1911a). Of signal importance, in this respect, is the evolution of a powerful alliance, as it were, between the (infantile) pleasure ego and the rewarding part-unit component of the SORU which contributes so heavily to the clinical symptomatology of the borderline personality.* Whenever the individual perceives the prospect of loss or rejection or, paradoxically, of fulfillment or success, the withdrawing (rejecting) part-unit

---

*In accordance with Fairbairn's terminology, the libidinal ego (L.E.) is analogous to the pleasure ego. See p. 93 *supra*.

becomes activated, with its powerful charge of felt abandonment depression; the rewarding part-unit thereupon becomes activated in turn, leading to a wide spectrum of maladaptive and self-defeating behavior ("failure script") aimed at achieving the "good" feeling, which reflects the underlying fantasy of, and wish for, symbiotic reunion.

These internal vicissitudes, as it were, constitute the essentials of the fundamental etiology of the narcissistic problem which lies close to the core of borderline symptomatology, as first described clinically by Freud (1916) and reviewed recently by Kris (1976). The borderline individual comes to treatment with an enormous block to the satisfaction of passive-libidinal wishes; he feels himself to be defective or flawed (Balint 1968), actively exhorts but is fearful of the satisfaction of his needs, enviously demands to be loved, stubbornly and repetitively attempts the avoidance of pain at high cost to himself, and feels that the world owes him the very supplies he ultimately despairs of ever receiving.

8. A final consequence of the persistence of the SORU is the evolution of a particular variety of ego function, first characterized as "borderline empathy" by Krohn (1974) and further studied by Carter and Rinsley (chapter 6). As already noted, the borderline mother depersonifies her future borderline child in such fashion as to render him a projective repository of her own narcissistic needs rather than a growing individual in his own right. As a consequence, the child soon develops a pseudo-complementarity with the mother based upon his persistent symbiotic tie to her, and, in particular, in relation to her primitive ego and superego forerunners as she comes to project these willy-nilly into him. It is, after all, these forerunners to which the infant perforce comes early to respond, in order to ensure the flow of vital narcissistic supplies and to stave off the terrifying abandonment with which the mother threatens him should he proceed toward separation-individuation. The result is the evolution of a "hypertrophied" sensori-perceptual ego function directed toward the early detection of the latter fearsome possibility, which manifests itself in later life as the borderline

individual's "uncanny" ability to detect and sense the attitudes and motives of others in relation to himself. This hypertrophied sensori-perceptual ego function thus comes to appear and serve, in effect, as a "distant early warning system," a sensitively tuned scanning or reconnoitering capacity which imparts an unmistakable if not always floridly paranoid quality to the borderline individual's interpersonal relationships.*

SYMPTOMATIC AND DIAGNOSTIC CONSIDERATIONS

Although borderline symptomatology had been recognized and described since the latter third of the last century (Rosse 1887), it remained for Grinker and his colleagues (1968, 1977) to set forth a combined clinical and factor-controlled account of the borderline syndrome. Their careful study of a small group of adult borderline patients yielded the following characteristics which, they concluded, typified borderline personalities: (1) significant impairment of the individual's sense of identity; (2) significant impairment of the capacity to develop and maintain meaningful object relationships; (3) various degrees of impairment of the sense of reality, with associated coping and adaptive impairment; (4) the presence of undue degrees of aggression (hostility) and of underlying or overt depression; and (5) in some cases, pronounced anaclitic clinging, abject dependency, and pseudocomplementarity in interpersonal relations.

Based upon these formulations, the following condensed description may be said to apply:

---

*As noted in chapter 6, there exists growing evidence that this unmodulated scanning or reconnoitering function reflects ongoing, generalized autonomic over-reactivity in both borderlines and psychotics, resulting in turn in various degrees of impairment of higher cognitive and perceptual functions and of cognitive-affective integration. It is probable that its etiology is to be found in early patterns of inadequate mothering with failure to "tone down" the infant's normal affecto-motor storms. The early work of Bergman and Escalona (1949) is relevant in this regard.

Borderline Personality

Individuals with borderline personality present a protean, often multisymptomatic clinical picture resulting from incomplete separation-individuation; they may at various times present symptoms indicative of psychosis, neurosis, and personality disorder; they often report episodes of ideational confusion; complaints of feeling empty, "phony," and unauthentic are common; their attitudes and feelings are often unstable, unpredictable, and quixotic, and are manifested against a background of pervasive underlying or overt hostility and depression; their actions are often impulsive and unpredictable; they exhibit shallow, often shifting, interpersonal relationships and unstable occupational histories; subjective complaints of boredom, anxiety, depersonalization, and anhedonia are common; there is often a history of alcohol and/or drug overuse and abuse; a paranoid oversensitivity and depressive vulnerability to real and imagined personal slights, separations and losses, and, paradoxically, to actual or anticipated successes is frequent; although thought organization may be superficially or spontaneously coherent, more vigorous examination will often reveal the presence of "latent," underlying or covert thought disorder.

PSYCHOTIC-LIKE SUBTYPE. These individuals display significant impairment of their self-identity and sense of reality; their behavior is often highly inappropriate and maladaptive; their attitude toward others is marked by pervasive hostility and negativism; marked underlying depression is typical and transient; and more prolonged psychotic episodes are not uncommon.

AS-IF SUBTYPE. As-if borderlines typically appear as overcompliant or pseudocompliant, their interpersonal relationships as pseudocomplementary, pseudointimate, and pseudohostile; although self-identity and the sense of reality appear intact and behavior appropriate and adaptive, they tend to "blend in," to assume the features and qualities of others or of situations in which they find themselves.

ANACLITIC-HYSTERIFORM SUBTYPE. These individuals present with exhibitionistic, provocative, and seductive features; affect is labile, anxiety and depression typical, and interpersonal relationships are characterized by importuning helplessness and anaclitic clinging.

PLEOMORPHIC SUBTYPE. Those borderline individuals not readily described by the preceding subtypes may be classified here. As a group, they present mixed, multisymptomatic "neurotic" features and symptoms ("pseudoneurotic"); the use of somatization is frequent and "psychosomatic" symptoms are common.

Viewed from a phenomenological or descriptive standpoint, borderline symptomatology may be seen to fall midway, as it were, between psychosis on the one hand and psychoneurosis on the other. Viewed from a developmental standpoint, borderline psychopathology is conceived as ensuing from a specific developmental arrest or fixation between the extremes of pervasive failure of self-object differentiation (psychosis) on the one hand and its essential achievement (neurosis) on the other (chapter 3). The recognition of an object-relations basis for the diagnosis *borderline* thus contributes significantly to the resolution of a number of problems long associated with the nosology and clinical understanding of borderline psychopathology:

It allows resolution of the controversy concerning whether or not borderline individuals are "really psychotic" or "really neurotic."

It represents a significant step toward establishment of the relationship between antecedent developmental arrest and later clinical diagnosis.

It establishes the diagnosis *borderline* as a definitive nosologic category rather than as an omnibus wastebasket classification into which may be dumped an otherwise motley group of seriously disturbed individuals whose symptomatology fails to conform neatly to other "established" diagnostic slots.

As such, and as an intermediary diagnostic link between psychotic and psychoneurotic syndromes, it contributes to a more definitive differential diagnosis of the latter.

Finally, as noted below, it allows for the rational development of therapeutic methodology and technique for borderline individuals, based upon an in-depth understanding of their particular variety of internal object relations.

THERAPEUTIC CONSIDERATIONS

Kernberg (1975) has presented a succinct review of contributions to the theory and technique of psychotherapy of borderline patients, and any discussion of psychotherapeutic work with borderlines could well begin with his conclusion that they fare best with a "modified" exploratory approach, in contrast to their relatively poorer response to both classical psychoanalysis and predominantly or exclusively "supportive" techniques. Indeed, optimal psychotherapeutic technique with borderline adults is seen closely to resemble the multifaceted approach which proves effective in the case of adolescents (Rinsley 1965, 1974a), which includes confrontation of negative transference material, the reinforcement of the positive transference to promote identification with the therapist, and, when tolerable for the patient, the use of genetic-dynamic exploration and analysis of transference. The key is, of course, sedulous avoidance of methodological or technical rigidity; the analyst or therapist must be ever prepared to sense the patient's anxiety tolerance from moment to moment and from hour to hour and to respond flexibly in accordance with it. The often near-kaleidoscopic shifts of therapeutic transference which appear during therapeutic process with borderlines reflect their concomitant variations in ego strength; obviously, one does not attempt to analyze a patient who has temporarily regressed into a psychotic condition. By the same token, misplaced efforts at suppressive "support" during periods when the patient is capable of in-depth work are regularly perceived as rejections or abandonments and responded to with bouts of negativism and hostility, the origin of which remains otherwise obscure to the well-intentioned therapist.

The knotty problems associated with the psychoanalytic treatment of borderline individuals arise, as Kris (1976) has pointed out, from the early pre-Oedipal, preverbal nature of the developmental arrest or fixation which gives rise to their symptomatology, including the protean features of their therapeutic transferences. There is, within treatment, no unfolding of the classical transference neurosis as expressive of the underlying infantile neurosis with its endopsychic conflict between instinctual expression and its repressive inhibition. Inasmuch as the basic fixation ("flaw": Balint 1968) long antedates the communicative use of words, interpretations conveyed in secondary-process language, especially those having to do with the transference, often serve no useful therapeutic purpose; insofar as considerable borderline symptomatology is alloplastic and subjectively experienced by the patient as ego-syntonic, the suffering that would be experienced if the "acting out" were thoroughly inhibited is warded off, and the borderline expends considerable effort in maintaining such a stance, in particular, vis-à-vis the therapist's efforts toward him. Furthermore, the narcissistic components of what some have termed the borderline's "psychotic transference" evoke correspondingly powerful, narcissistic countertransference experiences and responses in relation to which the therapeutic effort is likely to founder. Indeed, Freud's (1916) early and sensitive description of just these features of analytic work with the "exceptions" reflected in the feeling of futility which they had induced in him as he struggled to overcome the powerful resistances which they in effect articulated.

The failure of the classically recumbent position in the treatment of borderlines may in part be traced to their experience of loss of contact, i.e., extinguishment of the analyst's object-image and their fear of their own passive-libidinal aims; by the same token, persistently "supportive" psychotherapy, with reassurance and emphasis upon the here-and-now, is generally perceived by borderlines as an effort to shut them up, derived in turn from the therapist's countertransferentially reactivated fusion anxiety, which the borderline's hypersensitive scanning-reconnoitering mechanism detects as evidence of intended or imminent abandonment. Contrariwise, in the hands of a skilled therapist, the vis-à-vis position tends to minimize these factors, permitting both parties more or less continuously to monitor and assess each other's responses, and optimizing the therapist's need to modulate and exert control over regressive experiences which are notably prone to develop during those periods in which the patient is particularly, if dangerously, accessible to in-depth work.

Detailed exposition of psychotherapeutic technique with borderline patients has been set forth by Masterson and Rinsley (chapter 2) and Rinsley (chapter 3) and, comprehensively, by Masterson (1976), the principles of which I will now briefly summarize.

Since, as has been noted, the borderline individual is effectively devoid of insight into the essentially maladaptive nature and effects of his symptomatic behavior and, indeed, usually experiences it as ego-syntonic, early on the therapist is required to make active, even intrusive, efforts to assist the patient to inhibit and control such behavior. In some cases, hospitalization, with the full array of "external" controls, is required to preclude acting out, while in others with rather better endogenous controls over motility, the authoritative nature of the therapist's personality and communications will, for the time being, suffice. Technically, therefore, the therapist begins treatment with the aim of confronting and clarifying the symptomatic behavior, thereby to begin the effort of rendering it progressively ego-dystonic in the patient's eyes. At the same time, the patient begins therapy with the long-overdetermined need to persist in his symptomatic behavior because it causes him to "feel good," expressive of the alliance between the rewarding part-unit and the pleasure ego (Fairbairn's L.E.).

Faced with the therapist's repeated confrontations of his symptomatic behavior as maladaptive and deleterious to himself and to others, the patient now proceeds to attempt to inhibit or control it, based in large measure upon his early identification with and need for supplies from the therapist. The attempts will, however, repeatedly fail as in their wake the withdrawing (rejecting) part-unit becomes activated, leading to burgeoning resistance based upon the patient's projection of the withdrawing part-unit into the therapist, followed in turn by reactivation of the rewarding part-unit with ensuing acting out by the (affiliated) pleasure ego (L.E.).

A fragment from the opening phase of therapy of a 34-year-old borderline man is illustrative:

> (*Effort at control*) God knows I've tried to control myself . . . whenever I got frustrated in my work I wanted to go out and shack up with the first hooker I could find, but I didn't. . . .
> (*Activation of the withdrawing part-unit*) I got to thinking what a mess I'm in . . . and what a prick you are . . . you want me to screw up, I know it . . . you play a "macho" game with me to see who's the bigger man, who's "got it" (*note the phallic reference, left uninterpreted at this point*) . . . so I say, to hell with you!
> (*Later in the hour*)
> (*Activation of the rewarding part-unit*) So you know what I did? I went to a bar and had a few beers and I picked up this broad . . . she was really old and disgusting . . . and we had a few beers and I spent the night with her, oral sex and everything . . . how about that? (*Note oral-genital indicator of impaired phase-specificity and obvious maternal-incestuous implications.*)

After many months of confrontive and carefully titrated interpretive work, including circular waxing and waning of resistance through the reactivated part-units with ensuing acting out, further confrontations, etc., the patient gradually came to the realization that the problem resided within himself and not within the therapist or in the heretofore persecutory world-at-large:

> I guess I've been putting it on everybody but myself . . . you (therapist) too . . . I guess I want everything or nothing . . . like I was a baby or a little kid, but it scares me (*fear of passive-libidinal stance*). I feel so empty, and like there's a grown-up part of me (*healthy object-relations unit,* cf. below) and a baby, both in the same "me" . . . crazy!

By means of gradually more frequent, occasionally sustained exploratory efforts directed toward determining and elucidating the historical antecedents and determinants of the patient's SORU and the behavior expressive of it, the therapist has brought the patient to a beginning awareness of the etiology of his illness:

> You know, I guess I wanted my mother all the time, but I never got enough . . . she always told me everything would work out, everything would be just fine . . . she even took me home from school when I was faking being sick and let me sleep in bed with her.

The patient had early come to view his father as unloving, unrewarding, unaccepting of him, aloof, emotionally cold, and withholding of praise: "It was my old man I really hated . . . he hated me, he was jealous of my relationship with my mother. He told me I'd never amount to anything, I'd wind up a bum, a hippy."

Considerable work now followed, devoted to analysis of the patient's evident splitting of his mother into the idealized, loving "all good" object-representation and the rejecting, withdrawing, punitive "all bad" object-representation which he had come to displace on to the person of his father; the denouement came with his realization of the basis for the split:

> Yeah, I see it now . . . wow! It was my mother who really didn't want me to grow up, to leave her . . . you know I almost said "smother" for "mother" . . . and I blamed my father all the time. I guess he was part of it, though . . . he did his "no-grow" number with her too.
>
> (And in the transference)

You know, I thought you'd do the same as she did . . . you'd put me down or tell me I was no good, that I'd never get better . . . or else hand me some crap that everything would be all right.

The patient was now aware of his redoubtable need to project the SORU into his therapist and to conform his behavior to whichever of the two part-units, withdrawing or rewarding, he had reposed in the latter. Thus:

I used to get furious at you when I'd do what you wanted . . . I just knew you wouldn't be satisfied no matter what I did, so then I'd screw up just to prove it . . .
(*Again*)
I guess that's how I tried to keep myself from getting bet- ter . . . it meant I'd lose you, like my mother . . . if I grew up I'd have to leave her . . .

Analysis of the patient's polymorphous-perverse sexual behav- ior revealed it to comprise both a defense against castration at the hands of the "all bad" father and a regressive persistence of the effects of the "all good" mother's long-standing and occa- sionally near-blatant seductiveness, the latter at times involving the mother's masturbatory manipulation of the patient's genitals during his baths prior to his entrance into primary school at the age of six years. Of notable significance was the patient's revelation, after a half year of therapy, that he could only be sexually potent if he "felt nothing" for the woman; conversely, the beginning of positive ("loving") feelings witnessed a near- total loss of erectile potency with a regression into polymorphous perversity, the latter often responded to by the woman's loss of interest and, not rarely, by her disgust; thus, the impotency served the interrelated functions of preserving the symbiotic tie to the borderline mother and warding off her "real" rivals.

Thus, as therapy proceeded, the necessary exposure and con- frontation of the patient's SORU and its behavioral effects could combine with increasingly frequent, more "classical" analysis of unconscious determinants. As the patient had proceeded to project his primary-narcissistic infantile-grandiosity into the therapist, and thereby to "cede" it to him and "give it up," he assumed ever-greater degrees of psychological-mindedness; hence, he was increasingly accessible to in-depth analytic work.

As has elsewhere been pointed out (chapters 2 and 3, as well as Masterson 1976), early and ongoing therapeutic work with the SORU, if successful, leads the patient toward the awareness and understanding that *both* the withdrawing and the rewarding part-units are pathological ("bad"). As this awareness proceeds, the pathogenic effects of the long-persistent pleasure ego (L.E.) fall away, and its alliance with the rewarding part-unit becomes progressively vitiated, thereby liberating the long-inhibited reality ego (C.E.), which draws increasingly upon the reservoir of un-neutralized aggressive and libidinal energies similarly "liberated" from the two part-units as the abandonment depression under-goes resolution. This resolution, in turn, signals the inception of, and the working-through attendant upon, true mourning, which likewise signifies the inception of whole-object relations and the ultimate relinquishment of the depressive position.

The transferential antecedent for the inception and completion of this therapeutic work is the generation of a new, "healthy" object-relations unit (see Table 3-1, p. 71).

After 2½ years of treatment, the patient had indeed moved through quasi-independence toward mature dependence by means of "exteriorization" of his SORU onto the therapist within the therapeutic transference (Fairbairn 1941), followed by its "re-interiorization," as it were. He could thus say: "I guess I've always had "good" and "bad" in me . . . just like you . . . like everybody else. I was afraid to let you see it so I had to screw up . . . boy, what a mess I was. . . !" The patient had now found steady employment and was experiencing tender feelings toward women without loss of his potency; his use of the splitting defense had largely fallen away; he was no longer an "exception."

SUMMARY

This chapter reviews the developmental arrest underlying the etiology of borderline psychopathology, specifically failure of separation-individuation, including the effects of the latter upon psychosexual development and its particular distortion of object relationships. A diagnostic nosology of borderline disorders is proposed. Finally, brief excerpts from an adult case in analytical treatment are presented to illustrate points of theory.

CHAPTER 6

VICISSITUDES OF EMPATHY

This chapter attempts to delineate and illustrate an unusual, almost "extrasensory" form of perception and communication observed in individuals with borderline personality organization (Krohn 1974). Such individuals display a pseudo-empathic sensitivity to the primitive affective states of others and are also exquisitely sensitive to subtle, preverbal "messages" from those to whom they are emotionally close, specifically those with whom they have a symbioticlike relationship. The traumatic early development of borderline individuals is a consequence of having been reared by borderline parents (chapters 2 and 3, as well as Masterson 1972a,b) such that a pathogenic fixation occurs during the late symbiotic to early separation-individuation phases (Mahler et al. 1975). This juncture in the infant's psycho-social development is characterized by an unstable internal sense of self which requires continual confirmation by the (symbiotic) mother, mutual sensitivity to nonverbal cuing between mother and child, lack of separation of self and object, and lack of integration of "good" and "bad" experiences into whole-object experiences and relations (Kernberg 1972a). Pathologic persistence of this state of affairs leads to the development of an overly intense awareness of the environment as the child seeks confirmation of his nascent sense of self and even more assiduously seeks to avoid "dangerous" experiences which are perceived to threaten it. As manifested in the borderline adolescent and adult, this

---

Dr. Linnea Carter was the senior author of this chapter in its original version.

awareness appears in the form of a unique ability to empathize with others, but in fact represents a particular manifestation of the persistence of projective-introjective defensive operations (Shapiro 1974).

Individuals with borderline personality organization (borderline syndrome) display shifting extremes of mood, mutually conflicting and contradictory personality traits, and serious difficulties in interpersonal relations (Kernberg 1975). They often appear for psychiatric help with complaints of vague but pervasive confusion, mistrust and lack of understanding of the motives of others, and alternating feelings of well-being and despondency. Impaired anxiety tolerance, poor control of impulses, and repeated or chronic occupational failure (Fast 1975) are frequent symptoms. Very often, young people whose performance begins to fail at the junior high school level fall into this diagnostic category (Rinsley 1972); they often become involved with illicit drugs, which conveys the appearance of group affiliation, or else they may be "loners" who eschew even the appearance of close relationships. In their experience, other people are either "all good" or "all bad" as they proceed to idealize those from whom they anticipate supplies and treat with disdain those from whom they expect little or nothing; these states can alternate with stunning, almost kaleidoscopic rapidity.

The subjective experience of the borderline individual is that of an unpredictable and irregularly changing world. He sees his heroes develop feet of clay as he repeatedly idealizes them and is inevitably disappointed; tiny frustrations assume the dimensions of catastrophies, with ensuing eruptions of disproportionately strong affects, often rage. The borderline is sometimes aware of, but frequently unconcerned about, the inconsistency of his subjective feelings and his sense of discontinuity, which he may characterize as his being "phony" or having a "façade." He is often overalert to nuances of change in his environment and to others' minutest reactions to him; but while he is often uncannily sensitive to the latter, they mystify him and are perceived as justifications of his worst fears of what others will indeed think of him, and his own responses in turn may be dysphoric, unpredictable, and perplexing.

GENETIC AND STRUCTURAL CONSIDERATIONS

Any understanding of the dynamics and significance of the distorted "empathy" of the borderline individual requires a consideration of the etiology of borderline personality organization, and specifically of the traumatic fixation basic to it. The latter may in turn be understood in terms of what Rinsley (chapter 11 and 1971a) has termed *depersonification*, which refers to a mode of parent-child interaction within the context of which the developing infant or child is perceived and dealt with by his parenting figures as something or someone other than what he really is. Thus, the child who is consistently perceived as "bad" serves as repository for the parents' disowned and projected "bad" feelings and self-percepts, as in the case of a youngster born out of wedlock who symbolizes the "badness" of the parents' sexual impulses. Again, the parent may require repeated vicarious gratification of aggressive wishes and needs by subtly condoning the child's untoward aggressive behavior, a pattern which is common among delinquent youth (Johnson 1949, Johnson and Szurek 1952) who are, in effect, valued for their "negative" or antisocial characteristics and actions. The child may be consistently and pathologically overvalued for "positive" traits or characteristics such as physical beauty, intelligence, or athletic prowess, or else perceived as "perfect" or blameless, the personification of the parents' projected ego ideal.

The major patterns of depersonification of the child are several. Thus, the child may be viewed as an inanimate object, a "thing," such as a toy or doll, or as a projected part or organ of the parent; or as a parent figure by parents who were themselves deprived of adequate parenting and who yearn for someone to provide them with purpose, organization, limit setting, and decision making; or as a spouse, which represents a notably sexualized variety of adultomorphization. Again, the parent may depersonify the child into a sibling, a pattern typical for families in which grandparents play a significantly pathogenic role, as in the case of a mother with a weak husband or no husband whose own mother treats her and the grandchild as siblings; the mother is thus seen to compete with her own child for supplies from the grandmother and relates to her child as a peer, thereby depriving the latter of age-appropriate limit setting, controls, and discipline (Jones 1913).

Whatever the particular pattern of depersonification, the result is to distort the child's evolving identity and sense of himself as a whole or integrated person (Ackerman 1962, Lidz et al. 1965, Rinsley 1971a). In effect, the mother of such a child requires and utilizes him in order to generate a feeling of completeness within herself, thereby relieving her own sense of personal discontinuity and feeling of emptiness. As the developing infant of such a borderline mother seeks a reliable trustworthy mothering experience, he finds it not in stable maternal ego functions but in primitive ego and superego forerunners (Krohn 1974), and it is in relation to these that he develops his unusual sensitivity. Because in such cases the mother does not respond to her infant's "real" needs, but rather to him as a projective repository of *her* needs, she experiences polarized joy or rage as her needs are respectively gratified or frustrated within the mother-infant relationship. For example, a mother who needs a chronically dependent, clinging child to make reparation for her impaired sense of mastery and maternalism will respond joyously to his expressed need for nurturance, and with irritation, anger, or rage at other times (chapter 2); conversely, the mother who chronically anticipates and needs an aggressive child is attentive to him when he is actively asserting himself and will ignore him when he is docile or compliant.

The child destined to develop a borderline personality lacks a sense of self-continuity. Whenever he acts in such fashion as not to fulfill the role his borderline mother has set out for him, specifically, to remain passive, clinging, and underassertive, she withdraws her supplies—her nurturance, approval, and affirmation of him (Fliess 1961).* He is, in effect, psychically abandoned when he expresses an individuality which the mother cannot accept (chapters 2 and 3, as well as Masterson 1972a,b). This psychical abandonment of the infant in the face of his otherwise normal aggressiveness results in a particular form of developmental arrest which is basic to the etiology of borderline personality organization (see chapter 5).

It must be remembered, of course, that the child of a borderline mother accumulates experiences outside the sphere of the pathologically introjected push-pull relationship with her which contribute to the growth of the reality-principle-orientated part of the ego as the latter pursues its split-off, attenuated course toward what degree of separation-individuation it is able to effect (chapter 2). However, the relative dearth of available neutralized energy, associated with the persistent splitting defense, further contributes to the arrest in the transformation of the pleasure ego (L.E.) into the reality ego (C.E.), so that the former, with its alternating "good" and "bad" self-object representations, remains predominant. At this point in development, not only have self-images not separated from object-images, but the latter retain a concretistic affinity for the "real" objects which they represent, i.e., they remain undepersonified or unmetabolized (Kernberg 1966).

The self of the borderline individual, such as it loosely coalesces, is thus seen to comprise: an idealized, infantile-grandiose part-self-representation associated with a rewarding part-object-representation, *plus* a helpless, devalued part-self-representation which rages against a sadistic, persecutory, frustrating, and rejecting part-object-representation, *plus* an "embattled"

---

*Fliess (1961) has referred to such withdrawal as, in effect, leading to what he terms *abolishment* of the child, which, in transactional-analytic terms corresponds to the imperative admonition, *"Don't be!"*

healthy self-object-representation which strives unobtrusively toward reality (see Table 2-1, p. 39, and Table 3-1, p. 71). These are, inter alia, essentially isolated from each other by the continued operation of the splitting defense. When the "bad" part-self–part-object representation becomes activated by disappointments, frustrations, disillusionment, or the "threat" of success, there is no recourse to a reliable core of good introjects (chapter 1). Under these circumstances, the "all-good" part-self–part-object representation becomes activated, leading to the acting out of regressive, infantile-narcissistic forms of behavior which symbolically express the underlying fantasies of reunion with the symbiotic maternal part-object. The following case illustration clearly reveals such behavior.

Case Illustration

Anne B. was a 12½-year-old Caucasian, Protestant, seventh-grade student who was admitted to an adolescent inpatient service after several runaways and suicidal attempts. She was described as "a tyrant at home," with unpredictable outbursts of rage, a supercilious attitude, no friends, and a personality characterized as "abrasive." On admission, she complained of anger toward and abandonment by her mother, as well as of needing help and feeling confused: "I don't know what comes first . . . everything is all rushing at me at once . . . If only I could get it sorted. . . ." The admitting psychiatrist found her overalert, suspicious and vague; her associations were classically loose, circumstantial, and tangential; she denied hallucinations and neither expressed nor admitted to delusions. When challenged on statements which were clearly autistic, she managed to pull her thinking together and present her ideas logically.

Anne was the middle of her mother's three children, one from each of the first three of her total of five marriages, the last two of which had produced no children. The mother, Mrs. E., was herself born out of wedlock and put up for adoption by her natural mother; some nine months later her maternal grandmother (Anne's great-grandmother) located her in a foundling home, took her into her own home and a year later adopted her. Mrs. E.'s natural mother had been married twice and had had three other children, one of whom did not survive; the other two had been institutionalized with blindness and profound mental retardation. Mrs. E.'s mother had never told her anything about her natural father or the circumstances of her birth. Mrs. E.'s maternal grandmother (also her adoptive mother) had been married and divorced three times, and had had one child, now deceased. Until she was 12 years of age, Mrs. E. had thought that her natural mother was her sister.

Encouraged by Anne's grandmother, Mrs. E. married Mr. A. when she was 14 years old; five years later her first child, Jane, was born; shortly thereafter the couple got a divorce. Mrs. E. later told all of her daughters that Mr. A. had died, but during the course of the family therapy during Anne's hospitalization, she revealed that Mr. A. was indeed alive and that she had "made a deal" with him never to contact her or Jane. Mrs. E. now reported that this marriage had been unhappy and traumatic as she had discovered that Mr. A. had polymorphous-perverse sexual needs: he had been a practicing bisexual outside the marriage and had committed numerous perverse sexual acts with her.

Mrs. E. described Mr. B., her second husband and Anne's natural father, as "the one great love of my life." Having impregnated her with Anne, he initially refused marriage and demanded that she have an abortion; when it had become too late for that, he insisted that the baby be put up for adoption. Approximately a month after Anne's birth, Mrs. E. convinced Mr. B. to marry her and allow her to keep Anne. The marriage was short-lived, with Mr. B. deserting his family, following which Mrs. E. made three suicide attempts and was hospitalized for severe depression. The maternal grandmother now reappeared, took Jane and Anne into her home and threatened to have them legally taken away from Mrs. E. unless she agreed to the grandmother's wishes. When Mrs. E. agreed, the grandmother took her home from the hospital (thereby recapitulating with Mrs. E., Jane, and Anne what had happened years before with Mrs. E. herself).

When she was 23 years old, Mrs. E. married Mr. C., her third husband, who died two years later of cancer. A third daughter, Barbara, was born of this marriage and Mrs. E. was pregnant with her fourth child at the time of Mr. C.'s death. She voluntarily aborted the unborn child after having concluded that it would be too difficult to raise four children without a husband.

Three years later, when she was 26 years old, Mrs. E. married Mr. D. This marriage lasted seven years, and allegedly broke up after a brother of Mr. D. attempted to molest Jane and Anne sexually; Anne told Mrs. E., and when Mr. D. refused to talk about the incident with his brother or to take any further action, Mrs. E. left him, taking the children with her. It was not long after this divorce that Anne's behavior began to be a source of irritation and consternation to Mrs. E. Anne was later removed from the home and placed in a group-care facility, where she was reported to be "unmanageable." A few months after Anne's admission to the hospital, the mother married her fifth husband, Mr. E.; this marriage has lasted for over three years to the present time.

Mrs. E. is an exceedingly attractive, youthful-appearing 37-year-old woman who could almost pass as Anne's sibling; she exudes a fragile, tragic, clinging air of helplessness; the clinical impression is that of a borderline personality of a predominantly infantile type with an enormous need for externally applied organization and controls.* When this family had originally come to the attention of social service agencies in their moderate-sized town, Mrs. E. was reported to have had marked difficulties in assuming the maternal role, setting no limits for the girls and

---

*Mrs. E.'s serial marriages, expressive of her need to "replace" lost objects without normal depressive working through (mourning) of the losses, is typical of borderline personalities.

finding herself helpless to interrupt the chaotic behavior which Anne was displaying and inducing in the other children. In addition, Jane, Anne, and Mrs. E. would often interchange clothing, with Mrs. E. often dressing in teenage garb. To further complicate Anne's impaired sense of identity, Mrs. E. had decided, following her divorce from Mr. D., that she and the three girls would resume use of the name "C." as their surnames, and it was only after some of these enormously confused and confusing matters came to light during Anne's hospitalization that she elected to use "B.," her legal paternal surname.

Anne had believed for many years that she was "special" to her mother and even when their interactions had been intensely hostile she believed that it was because her mother cared more for her than for her sisters; on the other hand, Anne at times believed strongly that her mother's imputed "special" care for her in fact meant that the mother harbored a specific hatred for her. The youngest daughter, Barbara, had indeed been named after Mrs. E., and Anne had for some years carried on "secret" homoerotic relations with Barbara, during which she fantasized having homosexual relations with Mrs. E.

From this tangled intergenerational web, the family therapy process was nonetheless able to distill the basis for an understanding of some of the factors which had indeed caused Anne to be "special" to her mother. Like Mrs. E., Anne had been conceived and born out of wedlock and had been abandoned by her parents (Mrs. E. literally had been abandoned by both grandparents and Anne had been rejected by her father while her mother had been hospitalized). Nonetheless, despite (or perhaps because of) Mr. B.'s rejection of her as well, Mrs. E. continued to idealize him as her one true love, and Anne became her substitute for him. Anne was thus depersonified as someone to and by means of whom Mrs. E. could make reparation for the traumas and deprivation she herself had experienced during childhood, by projecting her needs and her own diffuse identity into Anne. Anne also became a phallic object for Mrs. E., thereby in part replacing her father; she experienced Mrs. E.'s preoccupation with her as a sexual seduction and became obsessed with sexual fantasies about Mrs. E. (Later, during her hospitalization, Anne expressed her deep-seated fear that she was a lesbian.) Having been depersonified as an injured facsimile of Mrs. E., as the latter's phallic object, and later as the mother's pseudosibling, Anne proceeded to evolve a singularly incohesive, deficient identity; she expressed her feeling of emptiness and of her symbiotic tie with Mrs. E. in repeated allegations: "If she disappears, I disappear . . . I'm a nothing. . . ." Her impaired object constancy was displayed in her fear that Mrs. E. would disappear if she, Anne, remained hospitalized, later stating that if she grew up, Mrs. E. would evaporate in a hissing cloud of sulfurous fumes, much like the Wicked Witch in *The Wizard of Oz* after Dorothy accidentally doused her with water.

Anne was a bright girl who could easily express herself articulately (her admission WISC scores were: Verbal IQ = 119, Performance IQ = 121, Full-Scale IQ = 122). On thematic tests she described maternal figures as pretentious and affectively cold, scolding, and disapproving; on the other hand, one was required to please them; however, *if the child made a decision on its own, the mother would die.* Anne perceived herself as evil and destructive; incapable of giving or accepting love, she nonetheless had a "need to have someone . . . aware of me."

Her hospital room had a terrazzo floor, and she likened herself to the tiny fragments of stone, picking out one which symbolized her "goodness" while the countless thousands of others symbolized her "badness"—a tiny, huddled, insignificant piece of "goodness" surrounded by a sea of persecutors, an arresting portrayal of her projective view of herself and her world. During this time her animistic view of the world emerged —she stated that if she looked long enough at inanimate objects she could bring them to life.

Anne spent considerable time ruminating concerning her fears of inadequacy and death, and her alternating feelings that she was superior to everyone else or utterly worthless. She could remark, "my mother's problem is *my* problem," but could not comprehend how this was so, preferring to maintain her "ideal object" by (grandiosely) assuming the burden of the latter's pathology.

On the ward, Anne assumed an aloof, superior attitude toward her adolescent ward mates, relating to them in an aggressively provocative, abrasive manner which quickly and repeatedly elicited a hostile response, or at least distance. She appeared mystified by the peer relationships she saw around her and justified her inability to participate in them by rationalizing that she was indeed "above all that." Nonetheless, Anne was exceedingly sensitive to slights and minor rejections, to which she traditionally responded with overt hostility or despondency; she would then state that she felt worthless.

At times Anne professed belief in extrasensory perception and reincarnation, claimed clairvoyant powers, and reported experiences of precognition of dangerous and lethal events; these beliefs in turn made her feel powerful and dangerous, but also at the mercy of the magical powers of others.

Anne was expert in the use of projective identification in dealing with the staff; she was extraordinarily sensitive to certain feelings in her ward physician and the nurses and childcare workers; for example, at times when her ward physician or her individual psychotherapist would introspectively uncover mild (countertransference) feelings of irritation, frustration, and discouragement in themselves, Anne would hurl forth a provocative comment, such as, "You hate all of us! You get your kicks by restricting us!" She was able to detect, but would then grossly exaggerate, the affective quality of the countertransference, as if unable to believe or comprehend that affects could be tempered or modulated in others, instead of remaining "raw" and primitive as were her own (Krohn 1974). Indeed, such remarks appeared designed to elicit angry, restrictive negative responses, therewith to justify her accusations and reaffirm her view of the world as retaliatory and persecutory. Again, Anne proved to be similarly sensitive to latent, positive feelings in her ward physician and her therapist, during which times she would proceed to take advantage of the situation by commenting on how much better she was, how much more insight she had, and how these were due to the working relationship she had with the individual in question. The almost uncanny manner by which Anne was able to intuit staff members' feelings toward her (which were well below the latter's conscious awareness) required the most sedulous and sensitive attention to one's subjective, affect-laden responses to her, lest she almost literally orchestrate the latter or "play" upon them. It should be emphasized that her projective identifications occurred in connection with an empathiclike "tuning in" to latent affective states already present in the staff member(s), and not de novo.

At numerous times during her hospitalization, Anne seemed at the point of integrating her "all good" and "all bad" representations, and she was indeed able to verbalize her considerable intellectual understanding of them. However, she would repeatedly "dash" the staff's hopes that she was indeed solidly progressing toward this goal by acting out in self-destructive ways, such as breaking her eyeglass lenses and ingesting the shards, attempting to starve herself, etc., as though to act out the two "sides" of her split endopsychic structure while undergoing little internal change. For example, Anne had been on a somewhat limited caloric intake for weight control; she wished to please and imitate the slender female ward physician (a clear maternal transference figure) and would voluntarily forego fattening snacks; however, she began secretly disposing of her food until her "diet" had become a hostile caricature of giving the doctor what Anne perceived she wanted. She then reversed her behavior, as it were, and entered a period of bulimia, during which she attempted to scavenge in the garbage for extra food. When confronted with these apparently contradictory actions, she glibly "explained" that she ate when she felt empty and did not eat when she felt angry, thereby sidestepping the challenge to her splitting defense.

In a typically as-if fashion, Anne utilized her sensitivity to others to simulate the stance or behavior she perceived was wanted of her, and during much of her treatment this led her to present herself as the "good patient" who was gaining insight, complying with structure, etc., thereby enabling herself to remain essentially unchanged (Rinsley 1971b, Rinsley and Inge 1961). As in the above example, she would attempt to please the idealized ward physician, thereby activating the "good" part-self–part-object representation; but when the arduousness of the task or some fancied slight disillusioned her, the "bad" part-self–part-object representation became activated, so that she "spoiled" her effort or else actively attempted to hurt herself.

After two years, during which Anne seemed to be slowly progressing through vigorous interpretive work, the staff decided to reduce her overall residential program so that fewer people were involved with her, with a view toward simplifying and facilitating the staff's ability to deal therapeutically with her manipulative staff-splitting (Rinsley 1971b).

Anne was infuriated by her return to room status which, she argued, represented an intolerable staff intrusion into her control of her own life, which she proceeded counterphobically to enhance by setting her own limits: she placed a 4 × 8-foot pallet on her room floor and refused to move from it except to go to the toilet; she ate there, slept there, and attempted to spend the entire day sitting there, at times attempting to curl up into a small "ball" in the corner, all of which was duly taken up in the family therapy hours with Mrs. E. and Mr. E.

At one point the family therapist announced that she would be away the following week and that there would be no family meeting. Upon the family therapist's return two weeks later, it was discovered that a bizarre incident had taken place. Four days after the last visit, Mrs. E. had undergone a period of depersonalization (brought on, as she later explained, by a frightening feeling of distance and separation from Anne): alone at her place of employment, Mrs. E. had tied herself up with a rope and then freed herself sufficiently to call the police, reporting that she had been bound by a black male intruder who had also stolen a small amount of coinage from the company's cash drawer (the money was later found by the police in an adjacent lavatory, and appparently no questions were raised concerning the veracity of Mrs. E.'s story). On returning home after her "ordeal," Mrs. E. revealed the actual facts to no one; she arranged to sleep on her bedroom floor, ostensibly because of muscular stiffness and strain. This situation persisted for three days, following which Mrs. E. returned to her bed on the afternoon of the third day.

Uncannily, Anne decided to return to *her* bed on the afternoon of the same day! At the time both had returned to bed, some 120 miles of distance separated them and there had been no vis-à-vis telephone or written communications between them. The common denominator, however, was that their actions had taken place when they ordinarily would have been meeting with the family therapist, had the latter not been out of town.

Later analysis of this incident provided considerable impetus for Anne's further exploration and understanding of her pathological link to Mrs. E. Upon learning of the incident, Anne's inclination was to reactivate the "bad" part-representations, to assume the powerfully evil position that her angry withdrawal within her room had caused Mrs. E.'s strange, masochistic behavior, a mimicking of Anne's sleeping on the floor. For her part, Mrs. E. was seen to have responded to the therapeutic curtailment of Anne's residential program almost exactly as had Anne, namely as an unwarranted intrusion (rape and theft fantasies centering upon her place of employment) by Anne's ward staff (some of whom were black—note the "black intruder").

Anne had long been acutely aware that she had a "façade" behind which she had felt "empty" and had been more than dimly aware of a feeling of chronic disappointment that her inner state had gone unrecognized by others; she was perpetually unable to distinguish between the idealized, "all good" object which ultimately let her down and any manifestation of a "real," good experience with a reliable, predictable object. After she had gotten over her anger at being "controlled," she became aware that the feedback from her ward and the more extended residential environment did not match her "façade," but rather, that the staff did indeed understand the emptiness which lay behind it. The foregoing two years of interpretive work within the context of an environment which provided graded, predictable, "external" controls witnessed her increasing ability to resolve the discrepancies among her ideally "good" self, her despicably "bad" self, and her weak but "real" self. As her sense of self was consolidating, her affinity for the symbiotic mother diminished, threatening the symbiotic mother-daughter tie, culminating in Mrs. E.'s "last ditch" attempt to identify regressively with Anne and thereby to maintain control over her, as expressed in the bizarre office incident. This time, however, the regressive pull with Mrs. E.'s action exerted failed to re-activate Anne's "bad" part-self–part-object representation; in fact, Anne found the incident so bizarre as to catalyze her awareness of her mother's illness, and her growing sense of separateness from it. She had indeed begun to individuate as her subsequent, successful clinical course demonstrated.*

SUMMARY

Anne's case illustrates the mutual sensitivity of a borderline mother and daughter, including the function of "empathy" in maintaining their symbiotic tie. Persistent from the developmental period of nonverbal communication, this exquisite sensitivity, as manifested in borderline personalities, reflects and expresses a unique "tuning in," as it were, to the affective

---

*After 3½ years of intensive residential treatment, Anne was ready for discharge as an essentially neurotic adolescent and for continued analytic treatment as an outpatient.

experiences of others, but devoid of a capacity for understanding cause or circumstances (Shapiro 1974). In the case of healthy infantile development, mother and infant are, reciprocally, empathically "in tune": the mother effectively responds to and meets the developing infant's needs as basically distinct from her own—she deals with him "where he is" and experiences pleasure not only in his obvious dependence on her but also in his beginning the protracted process of differentiating from her (Winnicott 1949).

Normal empathy is a natural outgrowth of a successful symbiotic phase in which an adequate mother recognizes and respects her infant as a developing individual; normal empathy also requires the successful resolution of the separation-individuation phase, such that the developing child comes to recognize that others are whole-objects who are different from him but who are reliable and predictable in their responses to him and his behavior (chapter 3). The neurotic or healthy nonborderline individual experiences empathy as he perceives another's feelings, recognizing that he is capable of feeling similarly in similar circumstances, and using a recapitulation of his own feelings as a basis for the congruence (Shapiro 1974). By contrast, the borderline individual needs his excruciating awareness as a "distinct early warning system" in order to anticipate the unpredictability —and hence, danger—he projects, induces, and perceives in his surroundings.

A major aspect of therapeutic technique with borderline patients concerns the management of the therapeutic transference, such that *both* the "good" and the "bad" split part-representational structures are confronted and interpreted by the therapist as the patient projects them (chapter 2). A significant stumbling block in the way of this work has to do with the therapist's proneness to view and interpret the patient's primitive thoughts and feelings about him exclusively as projections and displacements, and thereby to neglect or ignore the patient's use of this particular form of "empathy" as a scanning or reconnoitering ego function which has enabled him to survive in a world he perceives as kaleidoscopic and threatening.* Under such circumstances, that is, when the confrontative-interpretive process ignores the accurate part of his perceptions, the patient feels attacked and thereupon reactivates the "bad" part-self– part-object representation, continuing the cycle of derogation-idealization which typifies borderline transference.

The borderline individual becomes, as it were, a slave to his awareness, not utilizing his sensitivity selectively, but rather, cumbersomely and excessively in the most innocuous situations. An effective therapeutic approach recognizes the survival importance of this sensitivity, including the ever-present nucleus of the patient's perceptions which are in fact accurate; such an approach witnesses a growing alliance between the therapist's ego and the reality-orientated part of the patient's ego as basic for the effective interpretation of the patient's hypersensitivity to "all good" and "all bad" object relations and representations (chapter 2).

---

*There exists considerable and growing evidence that this unmodulated scanning and reconnoitering function is a result of ongoing, generalized autonomic over-reactivity in both borderlines and psychotics, resulting in turn in various degrees of dissemblance of higher cognitive and perceptual functions, and of cognitive-affective integration. It is probable that its etiology is to be found in patterns of early, inadequate mothering with failure to "tone down" the infant's normal affecto-motor storms.

CHAPTER 7

ALTERED STATES
OF CONSCIOUSNESS
AND GLOSSOLALIA

In this chapter, an attempt is made to examine possible relationships among nonpharmacologic self-induced altered states of consciousness (ASC), the relaxation response (Benson et al. 1974, 1977), and specifically the phenomenon of glossolalia, within a neurophysiologic and developmental context and with reference to the dynamics and psychosocial etiology of borderline psychopathology.

SOCIAL TRENDS AND BORDERLINE PHENOMENA

Of significance is the fact that the borderline concept reached its full prominence during the turbulent decade of the 1960s. That period was marked by this country's ever-deepening involvement in the armed conflict in Southeast Asia; the assassinations of John F. Kennedy and Martin Luther King, Jr.; the emergence of a mounting student rebellion, typified in the extreme by violent

---

Dr. Joel O. Brende was the senior coauthor of this chapter in its original version.

underground groups such as the Weathermen; the so-called drug subculture; the burning of major cities; the full thrust of the civil rights movement; the disaffection with traditional forms of religion with a concomitant decline in church attendance; the burgeoning divorce and illegitimate birth rates; the proclaimed defection by youth and young adults from traditional values and morals, epitomized by the so-called Playboy Philosophy which, in effect, extolled subjective hedonism; the appearance of the so-called women's liberation movement, with its often militant feminism and its associated "unisex" philosophy; the pervasive mistrust of authority figures who, like God, had been "demythologized," reflected in a proliferating civil litigiousness and a resurgent antielitism and egalitarianism. "Minority activism" assumed a variety of forms, while all varieties and manifestations of discrimination and inequality were to be expunged from society by legislative action or judicial decree. Szasz (1961, 1965) proclaimed that mental illness was a "myth" subserving society's need to imprison nonconformists and other undesirables in mental hospitals without due process of law, while other activist writers, such as Herbert Marcuse (1955) and Norman O. Brown (1959) claimed that, in effect, people became sick only because an oppressive, archaic social patriarchy made them so, and Laing (1967) declared that "madness" and "sanity" were ultimately indistinguishable. "Hard" and "acid" rock music became the aural shibboleths of adolescents, accompanied by an ongoing series of terpsichorean inventions with the "partners" standing at a distance while posturing and gesticulating.

During this period, the "generation gap" and the expanding use of illicit drugs appeared to reflect the increasing mutual alienation of children and parents, the former turning in increasing numbers to a burgeoning welter of alienated adults, including self-appointed "gurus," who exhorted them to "turn on, tune in, and drop out," not infrequently in drug-suffused communes where they could seek asylum in group pseudomutuality. The failure of parental authority found concomitant expression in the public schools, where a growing number of educational practices, including "child-centered" curricula, "open" classrooms, ungraded classes, "social" promotions, and purposeful grade inflation produced increasing numbers of "graduates" who could not adequately read, write, or reckon and who could only mistrust the adult parental and pedagogic surrogates responsible for their predicament.

The disturbed, identity-diffuse adolescents who emerged from such confused families and classrooms could readily confound freedom and license. Many proceeded into a "new wave" of "sexual liberation" while others, in reaction to it, embraced a resurgent asceticism with its renunciation of marriage and parenting. A host of arcane culture-alien "religions," many based upon Eastern mystical imports, made their appearance as alternatives to traditional institutional religion which had since become "demythologized," secularized, and popularized, and many young people embraced them in the vain hope of achieving a sense of identity and acceptance which they had never achieved at home, in school or in church; indeed, a substantial number of them exhibited patterns of thought, affect, and behavior typical for borderline disorder. Small wonder, then, that the 1960s could be termed the *decade of the borderline*, the period of the "new narcissism" (Johnson 1977).

ALTERED STATES OF CONSCIOUSNESS

Both generally and within this sociocultural context, the burgeoning Western interest in nonpharmacologic self-induced altered states of consciousness (ASC) invites discussion, especially in view of their alleged benefits for physical and mental health. Such altered states of consciousness, variously described by numerous authors, are presumed to have in common what Hess (1957) has termed the *trophotropic response* and Benson (1975) the *relaxation response*.

Gellhorn (1967) has described the trophotropic response as an acetylcholine-mediated physiologic activity originating within the limbic system, more specifically, within the anterior hypothalamus. He considers that the trophotropic response occurs as a rebound from adrenergically induced fight-flight activity, as originally described by Cannon (1929) and termed by Hess (1957) the *ergotropic response*, considered basic for defense and survival. In contrast to the latter, which is regulated by the posterior hypothalamus and activates sympathetic pathways, the trophotropic response activates parasympathetic pathways; it leads to a reduction in autonomic, skeletal-muscular, and metabolic activity, thereby "protecting" the organism from stress while promoting restorative functions; in addition, it is associated with decreased cerebral cortical activity and reduced activity of the reticular activating system (Gellhorn and Kiely 1972), and hence, with various degrees of drowsiness or states of under-alertness and underarousal.

The practice of one well-investigated relaxation technique, transcendental meditation (TM), has been found to enhance the trophotropic response, leading to decreased oxygen consumption and carbon dioxide elimination, reduced cardiac and respiratory rates, and increased galvanic skin resistance (Wallace 1970). The trophotropic response associated with changes in subjective mental states has been accorded various names, such as deep trance, tranquility, dream state, etc.

Certain ASC have also been found to be associated with the ergotropic response, including an EEG arousal pattern. Olds and Milner (1954) demonstrated that artificially induced activation of the posterior hypothalamus can be associated with pleasurable activity and subjective states. Schacter and Singer (1962) found that the ergotropic response can be associated with either the fight-flight response or with a hyperphoric (euphoric) response, depending on the social context, and Fischer (1971) has described a pleasurable, hyperphoric, aroused ergotropic state associated with inhibition of willed motor activity and oneiric hallucinatory experiences. Indeed, Gellhorn and Kiely (1972) have stated that such pleasurable, aroused, hyperphoric states, including those otherwise known as "peak" or "mystical" experiences, "ecstasy" and the like, which may be encompassed by the general term, ASC, represent combinations of ergotropism and tropho-tropism. ASC have also been described as follows (Group for the Advancement of Psychiatry 1976, Tart 1969): dissolution of boundaries separating the self from the external world, accompanied by feelings of fusion with the environment, the universe, God, etc., and of power and grandiosity; perceptual alterations and distortions, including time sense and one's own bodily image; and oversuggestibility, reflecting an enhanced tendency to accept the instructions and expectations of others in leadership roles. Although anxiety over potential loss of identity or control may precede these experiences, the subject often experiences a paradoxical gain through an associated or ensuing sense of heightened control of fantasy, feelings, or action. The state of "boundarylessness" or fusion has been reported during contemplative meditation, in which the subject concentrates awareness on an external object without thinking about it (Deikman 1966); again, the use of TM has been described as leading to "increased empathy," representative of the ability to experience the dissolution of subject-object boundaries (Lesh 1970). In particular, the state of boundarylessness or fusion, together with the subject's oversuggestible dependency on, or sense of surrender to, a significant leadership figure whom the subject endows with omniscience or omnipotence may assume the features of a religious experience, accompanied by feelings of enhanced personal vitality to the point of "ecstasy," as well as by fantasies of rebirth.

While ASC have been induced by such modalities as relaxation, biofeedback, hypnosis, autogenic training, and hallucinogenic drugs, and indeed may occur spontaneously, the mentation or utterance of repetitive chantlike sounds or of sounds simulating intelligible speech has more recently been found to serve as a reliable self-induction technique (Benson et al. 1974, Glueck and Stroebel 1975, Wallace 1970). The mantra is a well-known example. Originally a word or phrase recited or sung by devout Hindus, the mantra is used by Eastern religious devotees and increasingly by Occidental transcendental meditators to induce the meditative state, which is an ASC. As traditionally used in TM, the mantra is not employed for group chanting; nor is it a commonly known word or phrase; rather, it is "chosen" by the guru or teacher, supposedly to "fit" the personality of the new student of TM. Many teachers of TM emphasize that the mantra should be the meditator's unique possession, to be revealed to no one (Glueck and Stroebel 1975), an exhortation to secrecy which has caused some to raise questions of cultist charlatanism and quackery. Mantras used by Eastern-inspired meditative and religious groups include such chants as: *Namo naraya naya; Nam myoho renge kwo; Auooommm; One;* etc. Typical of these mantras are their repetitiveness, their content of "words" devoid of intellectual significance and their emphasis on vowel sounds. The expression of vowel sounds, as in the mantra, *Auooommm*, subserves emotional expression (Rousey 1974, Rousey and Moriarty 1965) and right temporal lobe functioning (Milner 1962, Ornstein 1972), as contrasted with consonants, which subserve object-relatedness (Rousey 1974) and left temporal lobe functioning (Shankweiler and Studdert-Kennedy 1967, Studdert-Kennedy and Shankweiler 1970). A meditative state induced by dwelling on the word *One* has been associated with induction of the relaxation response and with the imagery of "mystical" experiences (Benson 1975) and may be postulated to reflect a preponderance of right temporal lobe over left temporal lobe functioning.

BRAIN WAVE ACCOMPANIMENTS TO ASC

Brain wave accompaniments and responses to ASC have been of considerable and growing interest to investigators. Alpha and theta brain wave production has indeed been described as the "royal road to serenity" (Maulsby 1971) and to creativity (Brown 1970). Brain wave patterning can be modified by biofeedback, hypnosis, autogenic training, meditation, and yoga. Alpha waves, with a normal frequency of 8–13 Hz, become well-established in humans by 8–11 years of age; they emanate from the occipital cortex in resting subjects; their activity is increased in subjects not engaged in information processing and when attention shifts to auditory stimuli (Durup and Fessard 1936) and is usually blocked when attention shifts to visual stimuli, at which time faster beta frequencies appear (20–35 Hz), typically associated with externally directed problem-solving activity.

Brown (1974) noted that subjects utilizing biofeedback or meditation in an effort to increase alpha wave activity described associated feelings of relaxed attentiveness and a heightened awareness of inner thoughts and feelings; as a result of regular practice, they were able to produce more low-frequency (slow), high-amplitude alpha waves which might continue after the eyes opened. Benson et al. (1974) observed that meditators who had successfully learned the relaxation response utilizing a mantra displayed a regular increase in the intensity and synchronization of slow (5–8 Hz) alpha waves combined with intermittent theta wave activity (4–7 Hz). The combination of higher-amplitude alpha and theta waves in adults has been associated with feelings of unreality (Brown 1974), rich fantasy production (Fischer 1971), and intuitive problem-solving ability. Since theta waves constitute the predominant pattern of the EEG in two-year-old children, meditation could be construed as conducive to controlled regression to the imagery and affective state of the child who has not yet completed separation-individuation (Mahler et al. 1975) and who remains symbiotic to a degree. Indeed, subjects trained in alpha-theta wave production sometimes report "oceanic" feelings of fusion with the universe, God, etc., as well as the increased "empathy" and dissolution of subject-object boundaries described by Lesh (1970).

The subject of cerebral hemispherical lateralization of function is of notable importance in relation to these considerations. Sperry (1968) advanced the view that the two hemispheres function differently in respect to mode of consciousness and awareness, but interact harmoniously in the normal individual with intact corpus callosum. Ornstein (1972) regarded non-dominant hemispheric functioning as predominantly intuitive, spatial, receptive, tonal, and holistic; Kimura (1973) associated it with the production of vowel-predominant sounds. By contrast, dominant hemispheric functioning was regarded as predominantly analytic, linear, active, verbal, and organizational (Ornstein 1972), and was associated with the production of mixed vowel-consonant syllables (Kimura 1973).

According to Ornstein (1972) and Galin and Ornstein (1972), alpha wave production is observed in dominant hemisphere EEG leads when nondominant hemispheric functioning is predominant. Glueck and Stroebel (1975) observed that mantra-induced meditation, particularly when an "assigned" mantra was used, increased occipital alpha wave production, initially in dominant hemisphere EEG leads, which suggests that such meditation initially activates the nondominant hemisphere; this is followed by the production of low-frequency, high-amplitude alpha waves which sweep forward to the frontal areas, which then appear in the nondominant EEG leads in 1–2 mins., and which are followed in turn by trains of mixed theta and alpha activity alternating with periods of beta activity. It thus appears that the formation of automatic ideational speech in the form of a mantra not only activates the nondominant hemisphere but also activates the dominant hemispherical speech centers located in the posterior temporal, parietal, and frontal lobes. Association fibers interconnect these speech centers with the rest of the cerebral cortex, as well as with the thalamus, via subcortical pathways (Penfield and Roberts 1959).

The occurrence of rapidly induced, slow-wave alpha synchronization involving both hemispheres may be taken to suggest that mantra-induced meditation facilitates "communication" among the various systems within the brain. Thus, meditators frequently report that they experience thoughts or ideas, which are ordinarily repressed, as entering conscious awareness. In-

deed, Glueck and Stroebel (1975) postulate that during meditation there occurs a greater freedom of exchange between the
cerebral hemispheres such that repressed memories, presumably
stored in the nondominant hemisphere, become accessible to
conscious awareness.

In the case of subjects undergoing psychotherapy, the meditative experience has been reported to facilitate the psychotherapeutic process (Carrington and Ephron 1975, Shafii 1973). In
some cases, however, it arouses considerable anxiety. In a study
of 187 hospitalized psychiatric patients who had been taught TM
while hospitalized, Glueck and Stroebel (1975) found that a
majority had remained actively interested in it but that 17 percent
had stopped meditating regularly and 6 percent had stopped
entirely. They suggested as an explanation for this "dropout"
phenomenon that some meditators lack an adequate repressive
barrier; in such cases meditation, instead of producing a felicitous freeing-up of previously repressed ideas, images, and memories, mobilizes an influx into consciousness of aggressively
charged material accompanied by burgeoning anxiety over threatened loss of control. Instead of producing the hoped-for effects of
anxiety-reduction, muscular relaxation, and autonomic stabilization, meditation threatens to provoke psychotic decompensation in such cases.

Otis (1974) suggests another explanation for the "dropout"
phenomenon. He considers that some meditators appear unable
to experience pleasurable feelings. In view of the fact that
ergotropic arousal can be associated with either the fight-flight
or the hyperphoric response (Schacter and Singer 1962), it is
likely that in the case of those subjects who experience disruptive degrees of anxiety during meditation there is little or no
association of ergotropism with pleasant (positive, hedonic)
images and affects. Such subjects could be viewed as deficient in
"good" internal objects (chapter 1, and Kernberg 1968, Mahler
1968), which would normally have been internalized during the
first trimester of the first postnatal year, a period of meso-
diencephalic and limbic predominance.

SPEECH AND COMMUNICATION:
DEVELOPMENTAL CONSIDERATIONS

During the first six months of the infant's life, the predominant speech elements are vowels (Irwin 1948); during this period, the predominant elements of the infant's psychological life are his drives and associated affective states and responses. Rousey and Moriarty (1965) have proposed that the child's vowel sounds reflect the expression of basic drives and affective states; they further postulate that ego development during the latter six months of the first year correlates with the increasing use of consonants, reflective of left temporal lobe or dominant hemispheric functioning (Shankweiler and Studdert-Kennedy 1967, Studdert-Kennedy and Shankweiler 1970); hence, consonant sounds are taken to reflect mastery of instinctual drives and the capacity for object-relatedness.

The infant, whose beginning sense of self evolves through the normal separation-individuation process, has by six months of age begun to communicate with mother by means of vowels and "soft" consonants such as, h, l, m, n, p, t, w, and y, including the sound pattern, ma-ma-ma (Brazelton 1969), which is taken to mark the beginning of language as it communicates need and reflects the use of symbolism (Rousey 1974). It will be noted that the period in which these developments occur coincides with the latter half of the early oral (oral-incorporative) and the beginning of the late oral (oral-aggressive, oral-sadistic) stages of psychosexual development, and with Mahler's symbiotic phase and early differentiation subphase.

During the second six months of the infant's life, the number of consonants increases to include the "hard" sounds, b, d, f, g, and k, exemplified by the sound pattern, ba-ba-ba, coincident with the late oral stage and with Mahler's differentiation and early practicing subphases. The later-emergent consonant sounds, r, s, sh, and zh (zh as in azure), coincide with the classical anal stage and with Mahler's later practicing and rapprochement subphases.

AUTOMATIC SPEECH AND SOUND PRODUCTION: GLOSSOLALIA

Many individuals who gravitate toward or seek meditative experiences do so to allay, or seek relief from, feelings of inner meaninglessness and emptiness, "inner disunity," and alienation and detachment both from their own subjective experiences and from other persons. Such a self-perception is common among borderline personalities (chapters 5 and 6). Those meditators who rely on vowel-exclusive mantras utilize mentated or uttered vocalizations and speech sounds which originate in the non-dominant (nonverbal) cerebral hemisphere (Chaney and Webster 1966, Milner 1962); hence, they may be viewed as examples of instinctual or drive-related *affective communication*. By contrast, meditators who use mantras composed of a mixture of vowels and consonants, associated with the dominant (verbal) cerebral hemisphere (Kimura 1973) may be considered as engaging in *object-related communication*.

Examples of the latter would include the Tibetan Buddhist mantra, *Om mani padme hūm* (Blofeld 1977), which contains a predonderance of "soft" consonants which characterize the vocalizations of the young infant and a similar but shorter mantra, *One* (Benson et al. 1974), reportedly accompanied by "good feelings" suggestive of mother-infant relatedness. The so-called Jesus Prayer, mentated or recited aloud ("Lord Jesus Christ, Son of God, have mercy on us!"), is a well-known mantra used by Eastern and Occidental devotees, in some cases with yogic accompaniments such as concentration on the breath and heartbeat, to induce a sense of inner unity (Blofeld 1977) and to achieve a mystical state, defined as a loving union with a supernatural object (Group for the Advancement of Psychiatry 1976); it is composed of vowels and "rapprochement subphase" consonants. Glossolalia, also known as "speaking in tongues," may be considered to be both an ASC-inducing technique and an example of object-related communication associated with the ergotropic state (Goodman 1972); indeed, glossolalists characterize it as "joyful" and "ecstatic" (Brende 1974, Harper 1965, Horton 1966, Kelsey 1964, Synan 1975). Glossolalic speech is unintelligible; it allows for the activation of both cerebral hemispheres by means of vowel-predominant sounds (nondominant hemisphere) and mixed vowel-consonant syllables (dominant hemisphere) (Kimura 1973).

The glossolalia-related ASC constitutes a significant feature of the experience which Pentecostalists call "being filled with the Holy Spirit," as described within Christian tradition in the New Testament Book of Acts (Acts 2, 3, 4) and based upon Old Testament antecedents (Isaiah 28:11,12) (Kildahl 1972). A modern revival of this phenomenon took place in 1900–1901 in Topeka, Kansas (Horton 1966, Kelsey 1964, Kildahl 1972, Stagg et al. 1967) with an ensuing gradual—and, within the past 15 years, accelerating—mushrooming of interest and involvement in it to the point of significant infiltration of "neopentecostalism" (also called the "charismatic movement") within nonpentecostal denominations. The more conservative of the latter, including the Presbyterian, Lutheran, Episcopalian, and Roman Catholic Churches, now either tolerate small subgroups of glossolalists or embrace the movement as authentic. Estimates of the worldwide prevalence of glossolalia include 36 Pentecostal bodies with approximately 1½ million members plus 23 other Pentecostal organizations reporting no statistics as of 1955 (Bloch-Hoell 1964), with a doubtless multifold increase since that time.

Glossolalic utterances generally display a preponderance of vowel sounds initiated by consonants; the following is a typical example of glossolalic speech: *Iana kanna, saree saree kanai, karai akanna kanai karai yahai, oh saramai, saramoiyai iana kanna.* This affective object-related language was actually uttered effortlessly by a housewife washing dishes in her kitchen during an approximately ten-minute period, accompanied by a sense of contentment and well-being similar to that reported by practitioners of mantra-induced meditation (Kildahl 1972).

The following example of glossolalic speech was analyzed in accordance with Rousey's principles: *Baia sheea leea batagadalia bashia tada katadalium.*

The main consonant sounds were *h, g, b, t,* and *d.* There is an occasional *sh* sound . . . and . . . numerous vowel sounds. Of note is the fact that there are no double consonant combinations. . . . The intonation pattern is repetitive, rhythmic, and melodic. . . . There is a preponderance of oral consonant sounds . . . and vowels. There is little indication of any advanced ego development or psychosexual development beyond the oral period. . . . The repetitive, rhythmic, and melodic pattern is suggestive of the self-stimulation seen in many infants. The recorded speech seems to reflect the ego state seen in a normal child who uses sounds in his own unique way to express feelings during the last half of the first year of life. The sounds are emotionally derived verbalizations without rational meaning but provide a sense of gratification. Perhaps the gratification obtained by a one-year-old child when . . . engaging in baby talk is to develop awareness of himself, test his ego boundaries . . . and the responses of the parent on whom he is totally dependent. Thus, it appears possible that the early affect states and memory traces of irrational verbalizations are . . . recalled by the successful attempt to "speak in tongues" [Brende 1974].

Richardson (1973) has reviewed research studies directed toward a psychological interpretation of glossolalia, including the work of investigators who regard it as a symptomatic expression of psychopathology; he concludes, largely on methodological grounds, that the evidence for the latter is inconclusive. Richardson does, however, concede its possibility, quoting Vivier (1960),

Dynamically [glossolalics] can be considered as a group of people who, psychologically speaking, have had a poor beginning in life. This has been reflected by their difficulty in adjustment in the home situation in infancy and later childhood . . . they have been torn by insecurity, conflict, tension, and emotional difficulties.

Being troubled by doubt and fear, anxiety and stress, they have turned from the culturally accepted traditional, orthodox, and formalized, to something that held out for them the unorthodox, the supernatural; to an environment of sensitiveness for emotional feelings and a group of people bound with the same purpose and clinging to each other for support.

To date there has been little reported work devoted to an understanding of the effect of glossolalia on personality functioning. Lovekin and Malony (1977) concluded that glossolalia exerted no significant integrative effect on 51 Roman Catholic and Episcopalian nonpatient adult subjects. Wilkerson (1963), however, reported that it had a therapeutic effect in symptomatic hard-core drug users and Brende (1974) reported beneficial effects of glossolalia in four hospitalized adolescents, the case of one of whom is reported below in greater detail.

Brende's (1974) four inpatient adolescents met the historical-developmental, familial, and individual symptomatic criteria for the diagnosis of borderline disorder (Masterson 1972b, 1976). All had suffered from significant separation-individuation failure based upon a lack of early and ongoing stable parenting; all presented with primarily behavioral symptoms, including drug abuse, waywardness, sexual promiscuity, and gross maladaptiveness, and all lacked the capacity for meaningful interpersonal relationships. All four reported their experiences with glossolalia in terms of powerful and magical feelings, feeling "good," feeling "loved," and, most significantly, *feeling in control* to a greater degree than was reported by meditators utilizing more passive techniques based upon the relaxation response.

All four adolescents had learned to speak in tongues following exposure to a Pentecostal movement known as *The Way* (Wierville 1967). They described, at that time, giving up conscious control of intelligible speech and abandoning themselves to the motor activity of speaking, to sound production per se, to the spontaneous ideas which came to mind, and to their feelings; they viewed their glossolalia as a sign of power and of "being special," conferred on them by being "filled with the Holy Spirit." Unlike other types of meditators, they were uninterested in relaxation as such, but rather actively sought something "special"—the love and power of the Spirit. They reported that the glossolalia-related hyperphoria they had experienced was similar to that associated with taking drugs, but that the grandiose feelings associated with drug taking seemed, with glossolalia, under full—or at least better—control. After six months of practicing glossolalia, the associated internalized "good" feelings appeared to have become stabilized, and all four had ceased its practice after six to nine months.

Case Illustration

An example of the effect of glossolalia on the course of treatment is the case of Lisa, a 16-year-old adolescent girl who was admitted to the hospital with a diagnosis of depressive reaction in a schizoid personality and who was clearly diagnosable as a borderline adolescent utilizing Masterson's criteria (1972b). Lisa was the product of a normal birth and was described as developing normally during her first year. Her mother, described as an immature woman, became an alcoholic and sexually promiscuous after divorcing Lisa's father when Lisa was eight years old, abandoning the child to be shuttled among relatives during the ensuing five years, including a final brief period with the natural father and a stepmother. Lisa "hated" the stepmother and mistrusted her father, and at age 13 began running away, feeling strong needs for affection and closeness which led her into sexual promiscuity.

At the time of admission, Lisa was described as extremely anxious and depressed; she stated that she was worthless and displayed profound mistrust of others, including the staff, who she stated would be "against" her. Her sensorium was clear and there was no evidence of sensoriperceptual losses or distortions. Her WISC scores placed her in the average range of intelligence. Her thought processes displayed obsessiveness, concretism, associative looseness, and tangentiality, their content characterized by topical vagueness and by overdetermined persecutory and nihilistic ideas bordering on, but never reaching, delusional proportions. Her depressed affect alternated with blandness and with an inappropriate, childlike sweetness which transparently covered pervasive underlying hostility. Numerous sadomasochistic fantasies included a preoccupation with blood, gore, and violence, and with herself as recipient of violent assault by others. She was terrified of abandonment, which she had attempted to deal with by counterphobic efforts to run away, only to be "found" by others as proof that they cared for her, and by assuming the role of the masochistic, injustice-collecting victim in her heterosexual relations with peer boys. On the ward, her behavior alternated between the extremes of anaclitic-symbiotic clinging to staff and peers and sadomasochistic techniques for provoking their hostility and rejection.

Lisa's exposure to glossolalia occurred several months after her admission as a result of attending meetings of "The Way" movement while on temporary leave from the hospital. The friends who had invited her to one of these meetings encouraged her to try speaking in tongues, which she did despite considerable initial apprehensiveness; nevertheless, she soon found herself uttering a few strange words and sounds which then blossomed into a freely spoken "language." During this experience, she felt a sense of awe and an emotional peak followed by a feeling of inner vitality, which she later described as being "filled with the Holy Spirit," and which she took as evidence of God's authenticity and of her new-found special relationship with Him.

Lisa's enthusiasm for glossolalia persisted and within four months she appeared significantly improved; however, she then began to withdraw from others and her depression returned; this was followed by her leaving the hospital against advice and reverting to her former dependent, sadomasochistic relationship with a boyfriend. Following an arrest by the police in another state five months later, she resumed speaking in tongues and was returned to the hospital, where she was warmly received by the staff and her former ward mates.

During this second phase of hospitalization, which began ten months after she had first practiced glossolalia, Lisa's behavior was characterized by striking polarities, including alternating feelings of rage and helplessness, dependency versus "separating," holding back versus giving, and "good" versus "bad" feelings, all indicative of her efforts to work through the splitting defense of the borderline adolescent (Masterson 1975). During periods of possession by the "Holy Spirit" or of feelings of symbiotic reunion with her "good God," she found it difficult to trust staff and ward mates, including the chaplain, and she referred to the hospital as "the Devil's playground"; at these times, she appeared actively psychotic. At other times, she attempted to proselytize other patients, exhorting them to speak in tongues as she did. Her extreme preoccupation with and dependence on "God" became a source of irritation to others, who felt that she therewith kept them at a distance. Indeed, Lisa could be seen as clinging to these experiences as if God and the Holy Spirit were serving her as symbolic parental surrogates and when others implied or urged that she eschew speaking in tongues, she indulged in it all the more.

A brief two months after her readmission, Lisa again left the hospital against advice. This time, she found employment but continued to experience feelings of helplessness and periods of depression. During a subsequent two-year period she maintained intermittent telephone contact with one of the older, experienced psychiatric aides, a maternal woman who had taken a particular interest in Lisa during her hospitalization, whose talks with her provided her with a measure of support. At the end of this period, some three years following her initial experience with glossolalia, Lisa married and has not been heard from since.

Lisa's experience with glossolalia occupied much of her time during her hospitalizations; she could use it repeatedly and at any time to ward off others or to call out for care, "love," and behavioral control. Her glossolalia served her as a form of regressive, affective, and object-seeking communication representative of the "baby talk" which conveys emotion, expresses need, and serves to define and test the early self-object boundary in relation to the symbiotic, omnipotent parental (maternal) surrogate. Her glossolalia and the experiences related to it could also be viewed as examples of regression in the service of the ego (Kildahl 1972, Kris 1952, Shafii 1973), which served as a turning point, enabling her to begin, to some extent, to reinitiate emotional growth and the long-arrested process of separation-individuation within the context of a semistructured milieu which served Lisa as a sort of extended family and with the supportive assistance of a maternal staff member. The introjection of a "good object" in the form of God or the Holy Spirit during episodes of glossolalia appeared to catalyze Lisa's beginning efforts to work through her profound ambivalence, and thereby to begin to resolve the "all good"-"all bad" split within her undifferentiated self-object representations and to begin to differentiate the latter (chapter 3).

Glossolalists generally appear to enact experiences not dissimilar to Lisa's. Although the glossolalic speech may be initiated or terminated at will, there is no rational understanding of its meaning and its utterance evokes joyful, hyperphoric feelings and a sense of power without loss of control. Glossolalists explain the associated sense of inner coherence or unity as a result of union with an externally perceived God or Holy Spirit, akin to feelings which Martin Buber (1958) described as constituting the "I-Thou" experience. In such cases, glossolalia appears to promote the introjection of a "good" (libidinal, positive) self-object representation, characteristic of the level of object-relations development of the symbiotic infant and the adult psychotic (chapter 3), but experienced only temporarily by the glossolalist who harbors no major psychopathology.

SUMMARY

Our exploration of the relationship among altered states of consciousness (ASC), the relaxation response, and especially glossolalia, and their significance for the dynamics and etiology of borderline psychopathology, yielded the following inferences, conclusions, and hypotheses:

1. Benson and his coworkers (1974, 1977) have convincingly demonstrated that the relaxation response underlies the ASC which accompanies certain forms of meditation, particularly those which may be grouped under the TM rubric.

2. The brain wave accompaniments to ASC, particularly those evoked by biofeedback and meditation, suggest the occurrence of dedifferentiation of dominant and nondominant cerebral hemispherical functioning with both neurophysiologic and associated experiential regression to a developmental level prior to self-object differentiation and the achievement of object constancy.

3. Analysis of speech elements common to mentated or spoken mantras used by practitioners of TM and to glossolalic sound production according to the method of Rousey (1974) reveals significant similarities between the two, which are reflective of infantile affective and object-related communication characteristic of sound production at that developmental level.

4. Although adequate studies of the physiologic and brain wave accompaniments of glossolalia have not been reported, subjective reports of glossolalists and analysis of glossolalic sound production strongly support Goodman's conclusion (1972) that the glossolalic phenomenon represents an ergotropically related ASC. Available evidence further supports the view that achievement of the glossolalia-induced ASC engenders developmental regression to an infantile level prior to self-object differentiation and the attainment of object constancy, and concomitant and associated neurophysiological regression reflective of a state of cerebral hemispherical dedifferentiation and subsequent reintegration.

5. In view of the fact that developmental arrest or fixation at a level prior to self-object differentiation and the achievement of object constancy forms the basis for the etiology of borderline

and psychotic psychopathology (chapter 3), one would expect to find a disproportionate number of borderline individuals drawn toward or actively engaged in glossolalia, an inference which is supported by the findings of Vivier (1960).

6. Finally, by the same token, glossolalia could be viewed as having a possible role, along with other modalities and under carefully monitored conditions, in the treatment of some cases of borderline and psychotic disorders, and excerpts from a clinical case are presented in support of that possibility.

CHAPTER 8

OBJECT CONSTANCY

In this chapter, object inconstancy, especially as it relates to the narcissistic personality, and object impermanency, especially as it relates to the borderline personality, are studied and compared. Object constancy may be defined in terms of cognitive-perceptual (mnemonic) and affective (emotional) parameters (Fraiberg 1969) and is correctly understood to encompass both (A. Freud 1960, 1968). The mnemonic component has to do with the capacity to summon up a consistent inner image or representation, that is, to have evolved from reliance on recognitory memory to the capacity for evocative memory (Beres 1968, Hartmann 1952, 1956a), a transformation that probably begins during the last trimester of the first postnatal year (Spitz 1957), is well underway toward the end of the second year (Metcalf and Spitz 1978), and is completed toward the latter half of the third year (Mahler 1965b, 1968, Mahler et al. 1975). The affective or emotional component is expressed in the growing child's libidinal tie to, or emotional bonding with, the mother, which has its inception in the symbiotic phase (1–6 months), is marked by the normal (stranger) anxiety at 8 months (Spitz 1957), and is well developed by the middle of the second year, at roughly 18 months (Nagera 1966).

Object constancy is not to be confused with *object permanency*, a term originating with Piaget (1937). Object permanency has to do with the growing infant's perceptual ability to differentiate "external" objects from his manipulation of them, to perceive them as existing independent of him per se. In accordance with the results of Piaget's two-barrier displacement procedure, object permanency ordinarily develops when the child is about 18 months old. The evolution of the infant's emotional (libidinal) tie to the mother and his achievement of object permanency cannot, of course, be regarded as fortuitous; failure of the former is doubtless related to failure of the latter (Pine 1974a, Schafer 1968). The implication is that failure to generate the maternal libidinal bond would result in the developing infant's failure to appropriately traverse the later stages of sensori-motor cognition, with all that this further implies for the later achievement of preoperational, concrete operational, and circular operational (abstract-categorical) thought.

It is not superfluous to point out that there exists a significant correspondence between the infant's build-up of object-representations and self-representations; for the infant to be able to perceive objects, including animate and human ones, as a part from his infantile-grandiose construction of them, he must have a self, albeit a primitive one. Thus, the infant has made a passage, as it were, from the monadic, autoerotic, and primarily narcissistic position to and into the sphere of two-person (better, two-object) psychology, the arena of Balint's (1968) "basic fault."

MEMORY TRACES AND OBJECTS

The following discussion will be addressed to the vicissitudes and effects of the infant's primitive perceptual experiences during the first six postnatal months; this period comprises Mahler's phases of absolute autism (0–1 month) and symbiosis (1–6 months) and corresponds with the classical early oral (oral-receptive, oral-incorporative) stage of psychosexual development.

During this period, the infant's world is organized in accordance with both the pleasure principle (Freud 1911a), a prototypically "all good"-"all bad" surround, and the pristine part-object percepts in terms of which the primary feeding part-object (breast) is apprehended as "good" if it feeds and satisfies and "bad" if it does not. The infant already possesses the capacity to differentiate presented food items in terms of whether they taste "good" (e.g., a dilute sugar solution placed on the infant's tongue), and hence, are swallowed or whether they taste "bad" (e.g., a dilute hydrochloric acid solution placed on the infant's tongue), and hence, are spit out. It is assumed that the "good" food item, the so-called good breast (part-object) and the mother's positive (that is, libidinalized) attitude toward the feeding experience, as reflected in the subtle cues associated with her neuromuscular state at the time, together comprise a manifold of perceptual experiences that catalyze mother-infant bonding and proceed concomitantly to lay down positive (libidinal) memory traces in the infant. Conversely, the "bad" food item, the so-called bad breast (part-object) and a maternal attitude of perplexity, undue anxiety, depression, and hence, rejection comprise a manifold of perceptual experiences that either inhibit or distort normal mother-infant bonding and proceed concomitantly to lay down negative (aggression-laden) memory traces in the infant. Highly significant is the fact that the former, positive feeding experience, including its components of holding and cuddling, puts temporarily to rest the infant's visceral-autonomic affecto-motor storms, is conducive to healthy digestive-assimilative functioning and leads to repose. By the same token, the latter, negative feeding experience maintains the infant's state of heightened inner tension, including visceral-autonomic lability that disrupts the bonding relationship, resulting in an angry, over-irritable and suboptimally nourished infant (chapter 4).

It follows that predominantly negative feeding-bonding experiences during the phase of absolute autism, that is during the autoerotic period, may be expected adversely to affect the generation and quality of the infantile self-object, as the latter proceeds to condense with the inception of the symbiotic phase approximately one month after birth. A build-up of predomi-

nantly negative memory traces thus yields a predominantly negative self-object that has a number of pejorative effects on the
infant's ensuing development.

If unmodified as a result of later restitutive mothering or
therapeutic intervention, the negative self-object evolves into
the growing child's predominant self-percept. Its persistence
overdetermines the continued assimilation into it of predominantly negative (aggressively valent) sensori-perceptual experiences, thereby consolidating the accretion of early memory
traces, and hence, of self-object experiences and representations
that will ultimately emerge in the form of a diffuse or "negative"
identity (Erikson 1956, 1963).

The persistent, negative self-object has the further effect of
arresting or fixating the developing infant's object relations at
the symbiotic phase, thereby inhibiting his progress through the
subsequent differentiation, practicing, and rapprochement subphases of separation-individuation, and hence, thwarting the
process of desymbiotization (Mahler, Pine, and Bergman 1975).
It is as if the otherwise healthy increment of exploratory motility
that accompanies the infant's entrance into the separation-
individuation phase threatens to loose the powerful "raw" aggression associated with the negative self-object, an occurrence
that must be inhibited lest what there is of the positive self-
object ("good breast") is annihilated. It should be remembered
that the healthy growth process during this period is comprised
of repetitive cycles of regressive self-object refusion and differ-
ferentiation in the wake of efforts toward desymbiotization
(Jacobson 1954a, b, c, 1957, 1964, 1971); hence the persistent
(negative) self-object represents a failure of the latter.

Although only larvally within the sphere of two-person psychology, the persistent, negative self-object forms the basis for
the ensuing development of the *basic fault* (Balint 1968) that is
derived from a failure of "good enough mothering" or adequate
"holding" (Khan 1963, Modell 1963, 1968, 1975, Winnicott
1950–55, 1951, 1960) and that is representative of an essential
failure of goodness of fit, mutual cuing, or communicative

matching between mother and infant. As a consequence, the infant's entrance into and developmental use of transitional experience (Winnicott 1951) are inhibited, and transitional objects assume the features of fetishes (Dickes 1978).

The persistent, negative self-object has the further effect of overdetermining the primitive splitting defense by arresting or fixating the infant's development at the level of magic-hallucination. This state of affairs augurs ill for the child's later transition from reliance on splitting to normal repression, for his generation of whole-object relations, and for his eventual working through of the depressive position with the resultant acquisition of the capacity to mourn. Persistent magic-hallucination within the context of the predominantly negative self-object, with its compensatory function of creating a longed-for, need-satisfying feeding object—that is, a good enough maternal part-object—fixates the infant at the point at which differentiation of the self-created and objectively reappearing maternal figures (object permanency) fails adequately to develop. This fixation inhibits the latter development of reality testing.* An additional, related effect is protracted infantile-megalomania, expressed in part through feelings of entitlement, that is, that one may indeed command need-satisfaction by means of the motoric expression of magic-hallucination, i.e., magic gestures.

The reverberations of these early infantile experiences find evident expression in the history and presenting symptomatology of adult psychotics, as well as adults who suffer from borderline personality disorder. The borderline adult experiences relationships in terms of whether they "provide" and "gratify" or whether they "withhold" and "deny." His ideation is characterized by "soft" or "hard" thought disorder, which is governed

---

*The relationship among fetishism, splitting, and impaired reality testing was originally perceived by Freud (1905, 1927, 1940b). In ambivalently attributing a penis to a woman, the male fetishist, deviant as to both aim and object, confounds the penis and the breast much as does the "hysterical" female for whom a penis in the vagina is psychically equivalent to a nipple in the baby's mouth. Cf. Fairbairn's (1941) *hysterical transitional mechanism*.

by the ever-present pull toward either-or, black-and-white, autistic-preoperational thinking. He feels that he is "bad," that something is vaguely or indefinably wrong with him, that he does not really know who or even what he is. His grandiosity leads him into positions that reflect a pervasive sense of entitlement; via a repertoire of quasi-communicative metaphors and magic-gestural actions, he believes he can command the hostile, ungratifying environment to provide for his needs. His combination of egoism and readily frustrated dependency leads him into a seemingly endless array of short-lived and/or unstable relationships; he passes from one person to the next as if changing tires on his automobile. His sexual relations are usually characterized by deviation as to aim (e.g., sadomasochism) and as to object (i.e., anomalous sexual object "choice") and are fundamentally polymorphous-perverse. His personality generally reflects a proneness to addiction, which may involve drug abuse or may mean relating to others much as if they represented pharmacologic agents capable of easing tension, providing "highs," and the like.

FIXATION AT THE LEVEL OF THE DYAD

Psychoanalytic stage theory has taught us that the developing child traverses three major sphincter-related periods during the preschool years; and further, that these sphincters serve as developmental anchor points, as it were, which are related to wider and deeper aspects of nascent object relations (Erikson 1963, Rinsley 1981). No later than the first trimester of the first postnatal year, dyadic (two-person) psychology has its inception in the context of the mother-infant symbiosis. By the end of the classical oral-incorporative (oral-dependent) stage, the infant has already begun the process of separation-individuation from the "symbiotic dual unity," which will result in progressive self- and object-differentiation and which will lead to the later "rapprochement crisis'' (16–26 months) that heralds the inception of true object constancy at about three years of age. Triadic (three-person) Oedipal psychology begins with the child's entrance into the on-the-way-to-object-constancy phase at roughly 30 months of age. To Spitz's (1957) original three "organizers of the psyche," namely, the 3-months smiling response, the 8-months stranger anxiety and the acquisition of communicative speech (the "No!" response), is now added a fourth, the Oedipal constellation (Kaplan 1980).

Developmental arrest or deviation at the level of the dyad thus signifies the persistence of the negative self-object. In "oral" terms, it signifies a preponderance of negative feeding and bonding experiences. In "anal" terms, it signifies an impairment of the capacity for mastery and for exercising impact on others and on the surround. In "phallic" (Oedipal) terms, it signifies an inability to achieve adequate triadic object relations (the father-mother-child complex of differentiated representations), and hence, an inability to differentiate the male object from the female object; and inasmuch as impaired gender-related object differentiation has its counterpart in gender-related self-differentiation, the latter remains essentially unclear.

As noted, borderline individuals complain that they do not really know who they are; nor are they clear about their gender. The result is persistent, partialistic, polymorphous-perverse sexuality, in some cases conveyed by gender-appropriate but excessive sexuality that serves as a defense against the underlying confusion of self- and gender identity and role.

The infusion of triadic-Oedipal object relations with dyadic, predominantly anal-stage object relations in these cases thus severely contaminates the gender-related issues common to the former with issues of impact, control, and mastery common to the latter.* One major effect of this contamination (the so-called pre-Oedipal Oedipus) finds expression in the strongly sado-

---

*Ovesey's cogent distinction between homosexuality and pseudohomosexuality (1969) comes to mind in this connection.

masochistic features that typify the individual's later, emergent sexuality, in which issues of dominance and submission override and ultimately vitiate the capacity for intimacy or, in more classical terms, the achievement of genitality. Evident in such cases is the deployment of defenses against the unrequited and fearsome wish for symbiotic reunion and refusion, conveyed in both the regressive polymorphous-perversity that signifies a return to pristine sphincter equipotentiality and the reliance on obsessional, affect-isolative, primarily cognitive defenses, including ritualisms and undoing, directed toward scotomatizing or disavowing that wish.

An example is the husband who abuses his wife, whether by physical or verbal assault, when she does not keep the house "just so," keep the children quiet, etc. Analysis of such a case generally reveals several levels of pathological interaction: sexual intimacy with the wife signifies incestuous relations with the mother; the "mother-wife" is, however, a (breast) part-object toward which primitive rage is directed when it is perceived as a split-off, "bad," ungratifying part-object that fails to relieve tension, preclude annoyances, and the like; again, at an even deeper level, intimacy symbolizes the terrifying yet ardently wished-for symbiotic reunion against which the rage serves as a defense. In such cases, the sadomasochistic components are not difficult to perceive.

Kohut's contributions to the psychology of the self and to the psychology of narcissism (1971, 1977), are grounded on a larval two-person psychology (the self-object). Kohut applies his views and his psychoanalytic technique to that group of patients he considers to be suffering from narcissistic personality disorder, which is characterized by the persistence of what he terms *stable*, *cohesive self-objects*. These individuals maintain a sundered self (or, better, self-object representation), comprising a *grandiose self* and an *idealized parental image*, both of which become evident in the so-called mirroring transference during the course of treatment. In such cases, the self-object may be viewed as a manifestation of a pathologically persistent maternal introject

(Rinsley 1980a), in relation to which the individual may indeed achieve occupational and intellectual goals, but at the expense of seriously impaired object relationships.

By contrast, individuals suffering from borderline and psychotic disorders suffer from the persistence of *fragmented, unstable self-objects,* that is, from endopsychic self-object representations that are prone to regressive reanimation or revivification (Jacobson 1954a,b,c, 1964, Kernberg 1966) and to willy-nilly reliance upon introjective-projective defenses (Rinsley 1980a). In such cases, the individual is prone to the disruptive effects of *abandonment depression,* whether in his general behavior or in the context of the therapeutic transference (chapters 2–5, as well as Masterson 1974, 1975, 1976).

OBJECT INCONSTANCY AND OBJECT IMPERMANENCY: CLINICAL EXPRESSION

The inability to consistently summon up internal representations or images of others, whether eidetic or not, comprises the clinical expression of *object impermanency*, which reflects a failure to have progressed beyond reliance on recognitory memory; at best, it signifies the persistence of fragmented, unstable self-objects that typify the psychotic and the borderline personality, the latter in particular when approaching psychotic levels of experience. If such summoning up is indeed possible, but the representations or images so generated prove to be essentially devoid of libidinal affect or ungratifying, then one speaks of *object inconstancy*, which reflects the persistence of stable, cohesive self-objects that typify the narcissistic personality. In keeping with the view of Anna Freud (1960, 1968), object constancy implies an affective (libidinal) investment in the object which reinforces the evocative recall of the object-representation or object-image; by the same token, without such affective reinforcement, the object-representation may be extinguished; or, at best, its evocative recall will comprise little more than a regressive revivification of the sought-after inanimate object (as in the case of the 18-month-old infant).

Clinical experience with both borderline personalities and narcissistic personalities leads one to the conclusion that the borderline individual suffers the symptomatic ravages of object impermanency whereas the more purely narcissistic personality suffers from the effects of object inconstancy. The impairment of internalized object relations, common to both disorders and reflected in the split object-relations unit, subjects both types of personalities to *abandonment depression* (chapters 2, 3, 5, and 9, as well as Rinsley 1980a).

The borderline individual's "all good"-"all bad" self- and world view, grounded in the persistent, pristine splitting defense, is further reflected in a pattern of shifting, unstable affective and interpersonal relationships that in turn convey the persistence of fragmented, unstable self-objects. As noted, the hallmark of these self-objects (really part self-objects) is the individual's reliance on primitive projective and introjective defenses by means of which the archaic, revivified ("demetabolized": Kernberg 1966) self- and object-representations, with their charges of unneutralized ("raw") instinct, readily traverse the porous ego boundary, thereby passing "in and out," as it were. Associated with the untrammeled operation of these defenses is the individual's episodic descent into frankly psychotic experience ("micropsychosis"), with its accompaniments of dysphoria (mood disorder) and impaired abstract-categorical ideation (thought disorder), which typify the more regression-prone borderline personality. Significant impairment or failure of evocative recall in these cases signals the frightening extinguishment of stable, reliable, "good enough" mental representations, accompanied by the resurgence of the aforementioned, frighteningly revivified "bad" mental representations. The inability to summon up or evoke "good" mental representations further results in what might be termed *fantasy deficiency*, with its associated inability to anticipate and plan ahead. The resultant impaired frustration tolerance leads to the impulsivity that characterizes much of the behavior of borderline individuals. A related phenomenon, *alexithymia*, comprises both fantasy deficiency and the inability to describe or discuss one's feelings; it is common among patients who suffer from psychosomatic disorders (Nemiah and Sifneos 1970, Sifneos 1973, 1975).

The developmental pathogenesis of borderline disorder has been traced to a depersonifying "push-pull" mother-infant relationship in which the child receives libidinal reinforcement for passive-dependent, anaclitic behavior, that is, for remaining symbiotic, and is threatened with the loss of libidinal supplies, and hence, with rejection or abandonment, for any efforts toward separation-individuation (chapters 2–5 and 11, as well as Masterson 1974, 1975, 1976, Rinsley 1980a). The child's development is arrested at the level of partial self-object differentiation (see chapter 2).

In accordance with the concept of the diagnostic-developmental spectrum or continuum (Adler 1981, Rinsley 1980a, 1981), the narcissistic personality is viewed as representing a "higher level" borderline personality. In addition, the narcissistic personality is viewed as closer to the "neurotic border" (Grinker and Werble 1977, Grinker et al. 1968, Ornstein 1974). As noted, the pathological self-object (pathogenic maternal introject) of the narcissistic personality is much less susceptible to the vicissitudes of projective-introjective defenses than is the pathological self-object of the borderline personality. It is as if the mother of the former had sanctioned a spurious separation-individuation; that is, *the narcissistic individual appears to have desymbiotized* while clinging, as it were, to the idealized maternal part-object-representation that, in association with the corresponding part-self-representation, has generated what Kohut has termed the *grandiose self*. Metaphorically, the maternal message appears to have been, "You may go through the motions of separation-individuation, and hence, you may achieve, but only if everything you accomplish is in relation to me." The effects of this injunction on the narcissistic individual's interpersonal relationships are evident in the complementary maternal injunction that amounts to a preclusion of whole-object relationships; thus, although the narcissist's interpersonal relationships are ordinarily not as unstable as those of the borderline, they are permeated with a failure of empathy, exploitativeness, and emotional aloofness.

Kernberg's (1980c) paper, "Regression in Leaders," describes these and related characteristics in the talented, ambitious narcissist who rises to leadership responsibilities with devastating effects on others and on the organization for which he or she works in a supervisory or executive position.

The object inconstancy of the narcissistic personality signifies a failure or deficiency in the affective-libidinal cathexis of otherwise mnemonically evocable object-representations or object-images; unlike the borderline individual, the narcissistic person's capacity for evocative recall is relatively intact. Again, in contrast to the borderline personality, the narcissistic personality suffers no deficiency of preparatory, or even creative, fantasy; however, such fantasy is essentially devoid of affective-libidinal investment, and hence, ultimately, of humaneness.

The Nazi holocaust brought to public view a host of basically emotionally aloof (schizoid), unspeakably sadistic persons such as Josef Goebbels and Adolf Eichmann, architects of the Jewish "final solution," who were otherwise intelligent or even gifted and who, in true as-if fashion, could be engaging and even charming when their ends suited such behavior. Until his latter-day deterioration, Hitler himself, an organizational and charismatic genius, was one of the world's greatest and most evil leaders. The files of history are replete with a host of essentially narcissistic personalities, ranging from outstanding personages such as Alexander the Great to lesser ones such as the American mobster, Alphonse Capone; such personalities are both gifted and immeasurably egomaniacal.

Other examples are the immensely successful, affluent captain of industry or the leading intellectual, whose relationships are shrewdly and skillfully exploitative; family members are viewed as a coterie of indentured servants who exist only to serve the narcissist. Narcissists show little interest in their spouses, and their children display a high incidence of emotional disorder, including delinquency.

A Comment on Pathogenesis: Evocative Recall

The criterion here set forth that is assumed to distinguish the borderline personality from the narcissistic personality, namely, the capacity for evocative memory in the latter and its impairment or deficiency in the former, deserves further comment. It should be noted that Spitz (1957) relates the infant's 8-months (stranger) anxiety to at least a larval capacity for evocative recall at that time (Fraiberg 1969) and that some ten months later the infant has achieved object permanency (Piaget 1937). Again, full object constancy, developed toward the latter half of the third postnatal year (Mahler 1965b, 1968, Mahler et al. 1975), signifies the child's capacity to evoke a stable, reliable inner representation or image of the absent mother.

It is necessary, therefore, to attempt to account for the apparent dissociation of affective-libidinal cathexis from the evocable mental representation or image in the case of the narcissistic personality. An important clue is the narcissistic personality's notable degree of obsessional character organization, with its abundant reliance on affect-isolative defenses. The narcissist's ideas and images are essentially bereft of affective investment, which has been replaced by pseudoaffect. Where has the real affect gone? The answer in part appears to lie in different depersonifying or appersonative mother-infant interactional patterns that respectively characterize emergent borderline and narcissistic personalities (chapter 11). Whereas the future borderline personality is threatened with a cut-off of essential libidinal supplies, that is, with abandonment, if he pursues separation-individuation, the future narcissistic personality is so threatened only if separation-individuation compromises the integrity of the symbiotic self-object (i.e., the tenaciously introjected pathogenic maternal part-object). In this latter case, an obsessional character organization develops as a defense against the regressive wish for symbiotic reunion or refusion. Basic to this character organization is the prematurely evolving capacity for evocative image recall, which is dissociated from the affect linked to the pathogenic maternal introject. The result is an apparently coherent, "adultomorphic" *false self* (Winnicott 1960). Fairbairn (1941) offers further insight into such internalized object relations with his obsessional transitional mechanism, by means of which both the "good object" and the "bad object" are introjected (chapter 1). In terms of the depersonification (appersonation) that typifies the mother-infant relationship in these cases, one may conceive of the generation of a false self by means of a premature, idealizing introjective generation of a spurious whole-object ("good" + "bad") that remains essentially undifferentiated from its correspondingly spurious whole-self ("good" + "bad").

THE TRANSITION FROM MAGIC TO FANTASY: A FURTHER COMMENT ON ENTITLEMENT

Magic hallucination and magic gestures characterize the world of the primarily narcissistic infant; their original function is to command the flow of need-satisfying supplies from the pristine part-object (breast); hence, they reflect the very earliest part-object relations. As the infant enters the second postnatal year, the function of language will come to serve the same magical purpose: the infant will invest his expanding vocabulary with magical significance (word magic). Overvaluation of words and thought is characteristic of the classical obsessional personality and the narcissistic personality, and finds more primitive expression in the symptomatology and utterances of psychotics and borderline personalities.

The achievement of object permanency at approximately 18 months of age represents the result of what the psychoanalyst terms *internalization*. As McDevitt (1980) points out,

> At the end of the practicing subphase and the beginning of the rapprochement subphase (between 12 and 18 months) we see a more active type of imitation in which the child takes more initiative . . . The model now used by the junior toddler for his imitations and beginning identifications consists of mental representations of the behavior patterns of the love object. As Piaget . . . has pointed out, deferred imitations and symbolic play, as well as verbal evocation of the mother in her absence, indicate that behavior has become detached from its previous motoric context and now rests on representation in thought [pp. 137–138].

The term *transitional* aptly applies to this momentous shift from purely sensorimotor to early preoperational functioning. In Winnicott's sense (1951), it signifies the generation of that creative "space" in which representational manipulation of self and "outside" may occur within the realm of pure fantasy while, at the same time, the reality of both is preserved. In Fairbairn's sense (1941), it signifies the "dichotomy and exteriorization of the object" by means of which the "external object" is progressively endowed with the characteristics of reality, and self and object thus come to be differentiated.

The healthy person with at least average intelligence expresses the achievement of his transition from magic to fantasy in terms of preparatory or anticipatory fantasy that signifies the capacity for delay of drive discharge (frustration tolerance), which is a prerequisite for appropriate planning. The gifted individual also expresses it through fantasy-generated creative play, from which emerge the scientific and artistic achievements of culture. The borderline individual never adequately manages the transition, while the narcissistic personality does so only in a context of emotional asepsis and at the fearful price of impaired internal and external object relations.

A most significant symptomatic manifestation of a failed or impaired transition from magic to fantasy among borderline and narcissistic personalities is their sense of entitlement, the conviction that "the world owes me a living." Entitlement is described in the DSM-III (1980), under Narcissistic Personality Disorder, as follows: "expectation of special favors without assuming reciprocal responsibilities, e.g., surprise and anger that people will not do what is wanted." Frustration of the sense of entitlement among borderline personalities is prone to produce reactive rage, abject despair, or retaliatory aggression, which may be verbal (devaluation) or physical; among narcissistic personalities, such frustration evokes much milder degrees of chagrin, depression, or retaliation; common to both are feelings of rejection (abandonment).

Gestural and word magic—specifically, the infantile wish that others should intuit the unexpressed or metaphorical meaning behind one's words or acts and should divine one's needs without having to be told—are basic to the sense of entitlement.

Among the more severe schizotypal borderline personalities, the sense of entitlement merges into "magical thinking, e.g., superstitiousness, clairvoyance, telepathy, sixth sense, 'others can feel my feelings,' and 'ideas of reference'" (DSM-III 1980). Among those deteriorating toward psychosis, the next regressive step is characterized by the appearance of frank delusions, both nihilistic and persecutory, and of illusory, hallucinatory, and somatic delusional experiences.

SUMMARY

The foregoing discussion has addressed the interrelated phenomena of object permanency and object constancy, with particular attention to the impact of their impairment on the development of internal object relations—especially insofar as they are conducive to the persistence of the primitive self-object.

In keeping with the concept of the developmental spectrum or continuum (Adler 1981, Rinsley 1980a and chapter 9), the view advanced here is that the narcissistic personality is a less primitively organized variety of the borderline personality, since disordered internal object relations, and the pathogenic "push-pull" mother-infant relationship that gives rise to them, are characteristic of both personality types.

CHAPTER 9

DYNAMIC AND
DEVELOPMENTAL ISSUES

This chapter elaborates on and extends the view that border-line psychopathology comprises a congeries of disorders of intermediate severity along a spectrum or continuum between the psychoses and the psychoneuroses, a view that has gradually gained acceptance on the basis of a growing number of recent studies (chapter 3, and Ornstein 1974, Stone 1980). In accordance with this view, borderline psychopathology, considered both symptomatically and developmentally, is seen to represent a group of "stably unstable" (Schmideberg 1947) personality trait disorders ranging from syndromes "at the psychotic border," including the so-called hysteroid dysphorics, to those "at the neurotic border" (Grinker and Werble 1977, Grinker et al. 1968, Klein 1977, Liebowitz and Klein 1979), including the narcissistic personalities described and treated by Kohut (1971, 1977). The following inferences and conclusions may be drawn from the results of these studies:

1. The term *borderline* no longer refers to an omnibus category of ill-characterized and ill-classified forms of psychopathology (DSM-III 1980).

2. The question of whether borderline individuals are "really psychotic" or "really neurotic" has become irrelevant.

3. Some clinicians (Giovacchini 1979) have questioned the veridicality of neurosis (psychoneurosis) as a genus of psycho-

pathology based on Oedipal-triadic determinants; indeed, the diagnostic category of neurosis finally found its way into the DSM-III (1980) as an afterthought.

4. Advances in understanding the developmental pathogenesis and dynamics of borderline disorders have materially added to an understanding of their psychotherapeutic and psychopharmacologic responsiveness (chapter 11, and Rinsley 1980a).

5. Those investigators concerned with the heredo-constitutional (genetic) basis of mental disorder have succeeded in demonstrating suggestive if not yet definitive heritability linkages within the families of borderline individuals whose relatives have suffered from the major psychoses, personality disorders, and addictions (Stone 1980).

6. There is evidence that the apparently increased clinical frequency of borderline and narcissistic disorders is related to the upsurge in, and increased public visibility of, manifestly narcissistic life styles during the past 20 years in this country and abroad (chapters 7, 10–11, and Lasch 1978).

7. Some consider that the decline of the nuclear family (Lasch 1977), with its burgeoning of parental perplexity, has led to laissez-faire and libertarian child rearing, and to public educational practices conducive to the forms of identity diffusion and disturbance that typify the personality structure of borderline individuals (chapters 10–11).

THE DEVELOPMENTAL PERSPECTIVE

Of relevance to the concept of borderline disorder as symptomatically and developmentally transitional between the psychoses and the psychoneuroses is the recent revival of the age-old nature-nurture controversy in the form of the diathesis-stress model as applied to schizophrenia (Anthony 1968, Eisenberg 1968, Gottesman 1968, Kety et al. 1968). In accordance with this model, borderline disorder comprises a "spectrum" of syndromes indicative of significant degrees of adaptational-coping impairment of lesser severity than "frank" psychosis; adaptational-coping capacity (or impairment) is viewed as a result of a combination of environmental-experiential determinants and genetic loading specific for the individual. The diathesis-stress model differentiates two subgroups of borderline "spectrum" cases, namely, those who periodically regress into psychotic decompensation (akin to Grinker et al.'s Type 1 borderlines "at the psychotic border") and those who do not (akin to Grinker et al.'s borderlines "at the neurotic border" [Grinker and Werble 1977, Grinker et al. 1968]). The concept of a spectrum or continuum of psychopathology is inherent in the contributions of a number of investigators ranging from the psychodynamic-psychoanalytic (Frosch 1960, 1964, 1970, Knight 1953, 1954, Rado 1956, 1962) to the genetic-biological (Gottesman and Shields 1972, Kety et al. 1968).

Early psychoanalysis contributed a developmental spectrum-like concept of psychopathology in the form of the psychosexual stage theory (Abraham 1916, 1924, Fenichel 1945), presented in terms of a sequence of sphincter dominance. Stage theory represented an amazingly adept attempt to formulate a developmental chronology of the pathogenesis of mental disorder; it related each syndrome to developmental arrest (traumatic fixation) at a particular stage in the patient's preschool years.

A second developmental approach is found in the prolific contributions of Piaget and his associates (1937). Nonpsychoanalytic in nature, and emphasizing the evolution and growth of adaptive-cognitive internal structures, Piagetian findings overlap with a number of convergent psychoanalytic approaches; two of the most significant are ego psychology and self theory (Hartmann 1964) and object-relations theory (Fairbairn 1954, Guntrip 1961, 1968, 1971), with particular reference to the psychology of internal mental representations (Jacobson 1954a,b,c, 1964, Kernberg 1968, 1972a, 1979a,b).

A third developmental approach comprises the seminal observational-psychoanalytic studies of symbiosis and separation-individuation conducted by Mahler and her associates (Mahler et al. 1975). This work, which began with studies of infantile and childhood psychosis (Mahler 1968), has burgeoned into an in-depth extension of classical psychoanalytic stage theory, recast in terms of Mahler's phases of autism, symbiosis, separation-individuation (with its differentiation, practicing, and rapproche-ment subphases), and on-the-way-to-object-constancy (Mahler et al. 1975). In fact, it was Mahler's speculation (1971) that the psychopathology of borderline personalities resulted from de-velopmental arrest that peaked during the rapprochement sub-phase of separation-individuation, a theory later confirmed by Masterson and Rinsley (chapters 2, 3, and 11, as well as Masterson 1973, 1974, 1975, 1976, 1977, Rinsley 1980a).

A partial confluence of these various and interrelated de-velopmental approaches found expression in Ornstein's important paper (1974), which took its departure from Kohut's earlier contributions to the psychodynamics and treatment of narcissistic personalities (1971). Thus, the notion of a psychopathologic spectrum or continuum is supported by pristine, recent, and current psychodynamic-psychoanalytic research, as well as by primarily biological sources, including genetic, nosological and diagnostic findings.

THE SPECTRUM DISORDERS

The following psychopathologies are classified here as spectrum disorders: "reactive" and schizo-affective syndromes, primary affective disorder, paranoid (psychotic) disorders, borderline personality disorder, and narcissistic personalities. All of these disorders share a number of developmental, psychodynamic, and symptomatic features that are expressions of a failure to achieve separation-individuation (Rinsley 1980a). Such failure is due to developmental deviation or arrest that occurred during the pre-Oedipal period, leaving the spectrum-disordered patient *symbiotic* to a degree. Accordingly, spectrum disorders may be said to represent *disorders of the self* (Kohut 1971, 1977).

Core Symptomatology

PERSISTENT SPLITTING. The self-disordered individual perceives himself in relation to "outside" persons and events in accordance with the pleasure principle (Freud 1911a), and with Fairbairn's paranoid and hysterical transitional mechanisms (1941). Thus, both one's self and others are either "all good" or "all bad"; others are "all good" if they appear to accede, satisfy, and provide, and "all bad" if they appear to withhold, deprive, and reject. Thus one sees the sharply contrasting and alternating contradictory attitudes toward important aspects of one's self and others that Kernberg (1967) has described in borderline individuals; these attitudes, in turn, are based on the persistence of the primitive splitting defense (chapter 2).

IMPAIRED SELF-OBJECT DIFFERENTIATION. Associated with the self-disordered individual's "all good"-"all bad" perceptual dichotomy are variable degrees of incomplete self-object differentiation. The porosity or fluidity of the external ego boundary (Federn 1952) in these cases yields various degrees of depersonalization and estrangement, and parallels a similar condition of the internal ego boundary (chapter 1) where unconscious content has ready access to consciousness (failure of repression). As a result, both the territory of the unconscious and that of the "outside" are dealt with through reliance on persistent, primitive defenses (projection, introjection, archaic forms of identification, denial or disavowal, scotomatization, and magic hallucination). These, in turn, drive the individual toward various attempts to appropriate others (including the therapist), ranging from the schizophrenic's bizarre, fragmented efforts to fuse and unite, to the gross and subtle forms of entitlement that typify the borderline and narcissistic personalities. As a result, relationships become vacillating and pseudocomplementary (psychosis, borderline personality) or exploitative (narcissistic personality), and the therapeutic transference is suffused with narcissism (self-object transference [Kohut 1971, 1977]).

INCHOATE SEXUALITY. Self-disordered individuals suffer in various degrees from what classical psychoanalysis describes as the failure to attain genital primacy (genitality), a condition also known as persistent partialism.* It signifies that the sequence of pre-Oedipal and Oedipal stages of psychosexual development has not been traversed successfully (Kut Rosenfeld 1963), such that genital-sexual behavior regressively subserves pre-Oedipal, predominantly oral needs. As a consequence, sexual behavior either assumes the features of polymorphous-perversion or appears healthy but actually serves the need to appropriate and exploit the partner (part-object).

DEPRESSIVE DYSPHORIA. Although overt or underlying depression is symptomatically most evident in the spectrum patient with primary affective or schizo-affective disorder, it characterizes the entire range of self-disordered individuals. This depression may find expression in "pure" form, by means of vital or vegetative equivalents, or through alloplasticity ("acting out," which is common in children and adolescents). It is associated with persistent partialism (v. inf.) and with the subjective phenomenon which Balint (1968) has termed the "basic fault" (Morse 1972).

Persistent partialism (part-object relations) signifies developmental arrest or deviation at the depressive position, and hence, failure of depressive working-through, which is basic to the attainment of whole-object relations (Klein 1935, 1940, 1946). As a consequence, the self-disordered individual never achieves the capacity to mourn, that is, to work through separations and losses; this lack is a powerful contributor to the superficial, and often vacillating and short-lived, nature of the self-disordered person's relationships.

---

*Partialism technically refers to the derivation of sexual stimulation and gratification from a feature, aspect, or part of the partner (part-object) rather than from the partner as a (whole) person or whole-object (Hinsie and Campbell 1970). The feature, aspect, or part is thus dealt with as a fetish. A well-known example is the male sexual athlete ("satyr") for whom sexual intercourse represents a form of masturbation using the partner's vagina instead of his own hand.

"Basic fault" refers to an impairment of primary and secondary narcissism based on defective early mother-infant bonding. It is experienced and conveyed in the abiding feeling that one is in some indefinable way flawed, defective, damaged, or incomplete, that there has long been "something wrong" or "something missing." In everyday terms, it conveys the meaning, "I am (feel) bad." In borderline and narcissistic personalities, this pejorative self-percept and self-concept may be traced to a particular form of internalized object relations, the *split object-relations unit* (SORU) first described by Masterson and Rinsley (chapter 2), and derived from a particular form of pathogenic mother-infant interaction that reaches its peak during the rapprochement subphase of separation-individuation (Rinsley 1980a). Among the psychotic spectrum-disordered patients, the SORU may likewise be detected, although its symptomatic expression is more fragmented in view of the more pervasive effects of the splitting defense in these cases ("fragmented archaic self and self-objects" [Kohut 1971, 1977, Ornstein 1974]).

LABILE EMOTIONALITY. With the exception of some narcissistic personalities and the manic-depressive patient in remission, self-disorderd individuals often puzzle and confuse others, including their therapists, with an array of polar-opposite, often rapidly fluctuating and alternating emotional responses, most notably, overt and passive aggression. Their complaints of feeling "uptight," "mixed-up," "a mess," "in total confusion," and the like reflect an ongoing state of inner tension, often but not invariably recognizable as typical anxiety. This continual inner tension may be traced to the persistent "affecto-motor storms" of the young infant, which were never adequately put to rest through the ministrations of a "good enough mother" (Winnicott 1950–1955, 1951, 1960), leading to a condition of chronic autonomic-vegetative hyperirritability. This condition, in turn, engenders a chronic state of overalert watchfulness, reflected in a persistent "scanning" or "reconnoitering" function conveyed in the seemingly uncanny ability to "read" or divine the unconscious or unexpressed motives of others, including the therapist (chapter 6, and Krohn 1974).

OBJECT INCONSTANCY. Object inconstancy refers to the inability to summon up stable, reliable inner (mental) images or representations of significant others; it conveys the failure to have developed evocative memory as contrasted with more purely recognitory memory (chapter 8, and Fraiberg 1969, Spitz 1957, 1959). The clinician becomes aware of this awesome problem in the self-disordered patient when the patient is unable to remember what the therapist looks like between therapeutic hours or is able to call to mind only a vague or featureless outline of the therapist's face. In other cases, the patient can picture the therapist but either experiences nothing positive or reassuring, or actually feels worse, after doing so.

A notable aspect of object inconstancy is a condition best characterized as "fantasy deficiency." Some borderline individuals appear to suffer from a quantitative dearth of fantasy, while the schizophrenic, as is well known, often experiences a plethora of frighteningly bizarre fantasies. The relationship between waking fantasies ("daydreams") and nocturnal dreams is underscored by the fact that self-disordered patients often report a deficiency of both. Thus, they are unable to utilize waking fantasy to delay drive discharge, to plan and set realistic goals; and they are unable to utilize nocturnal dreams to work through unconscious conflict and integrate it with the here-and-now represented in the day residues. The self-disordered patient's use of terms such as "empty," "meaningless," "hopeless," "confused," "fake," "a facade" and the like to describe his self conveys an inner poverty of imaginative content reflective of the fantasy-deficient condition, as does the often associated inability adequately to differentiate between waking and dreaming experiences, as originally reported by Knight (1953, 1954) in borderline patients.

IMPAIRED ABSTRACT ATTITUDE. Stone (1980) succinctly reviews the problems with cognitive organization common to self-disordered individuals, ranging from the classical thought disorder of the schizophrenic patient through the "soft signs" presented by the borderline-schizotypal subgroup; also included are the monoideic, overdetermined, and frankly delusional forms of thought expressed by patients suffering from primary affective disorder. Whatever their form of expression, these problems reflect various degrees of impairment of what Goldstein (1959a,b) termed "abstract attitude" (concretism); Bleuler's (1911) term "autism" likewise applies in view of the fact that, in these cases, ideation remains variably affect-dominated and stimulus-bound. In Piagetian terms (1937), thought organization remains developmentally arrested at the sensorimotor and preoperational levels in psychosis, and episodically or continuously at the concrete operational level among borderline individuals.

THE DEVELOPMENTAL-DIAGNOSTIC SPECTRUM IN TERMS OF OBJECT RELATIONS

Section D in Figure 9-1 presents a continuum of the major groups of psychopathological syndromes, arranged in accordance with the known chronology of developmental arrest or fixation based on historical and current psychoanalytic data. Section A in the figure presents the classical psychosexual stages in simplified form. Section B presents the phases (autism, symbiosis, separation-individuation, on-the-way-to-object-constancy) and the subphases (differentiation, practicing, rapprochement) of separation-individuation. Section C diagrams the evolution of the developing child's object relations, based on the contributions of Jacobson (1954a,b,c, 1957, 1964, 1971) as described by Kernberg (1970b, 1972a, 1979a, 1980a). The diagram

$$\frac{G \mid B}{\text{S-O} \mid \text{S-O}}$$

symbolizes the infant's "all good"-"all bad" perceptual organization, in the context of fused or undifferentiated self- and

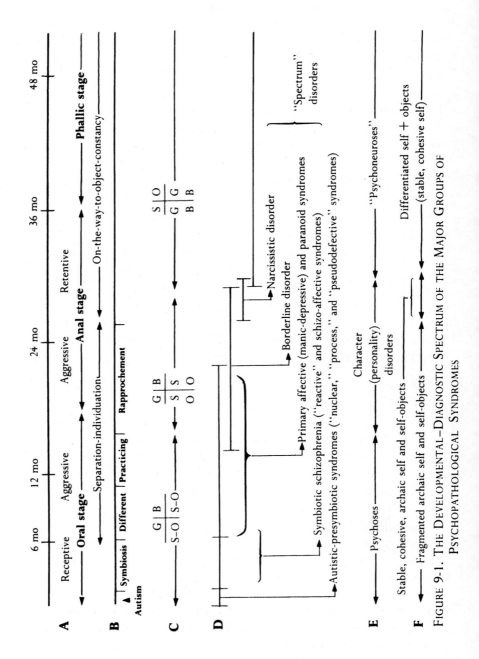

FIGURE 9-1. THE DEVELOPMENTAL–DIAGNOSTIC SPECTRUM OF THE MAJOR GROUPS OF PSYCHOPATHOLOGICAL SYNDROMES

180

object-representations (S-O); it is maintained by the splitting defense and ordinarily continues through the first 16–18 postnatal months. The diagram

$$\frac{G \mid B}{\begin{array}{c|c} S & S \\ O & O \end{array}}$$

symbolizes the persistent "all good"-"all bad" perceptual dichotomy, but in the context of progressively differentiating self- and object-representations; such differentiation roughly coincides with Mahler's rapprochement subphase of separation-individuation (16–26 months old). The diagram

$$\frac{S \mid O}{\begin{array}{c|c} G & G \\ B & B \end{array}}$$

symbolizes the achievement of differentiation of self- and object-representations (self-object differentiation), with the beginning of whole-object relations (good + bad self, good + bad object), and hence, object constancy, the capacity to mourn, and the defense of repression (26–30 months old) (chapter 5, and Rinsley 1980a, Settlage 1980).

The focal significance of the developing child's achievement of self-object differentiation is stated by Kernberg (1980a):

The symbiotic phase of development comes to an end with a gradual differentiation of the self-representation from the object representation, which contributes importantly to the differentiation between the self and the external world . . . two processes make their appearance at the beginning of differentiation. The first is a defensive refusal of the libidinally invested self- and object-representations; this is the earliest protection against painful experiences. When excessively or pathologically maintained, this process gives rise to what will later become psychotic identifications characteristic of symbiotic psychosis of childhood and of affective psychosis and schizophrenia in adulthood . . . [p. 25].

He continues,

> A large majority of patients with borderline personality organization present intrapsychic structural organization and conflicts related to . . . the rapprochement subphase. A small group of borderline patients, however—severely schizoid personalities—present transference developments and regression that seem more related to the differentiation subphase [pp. 27–28].

In revising his original chronology (Kernberg 1972a) of the development of internalized object relations and in particular of the evolution of self-object differentiation, Kernberg (1980a) follows Mahler (1971, 1972a,b) in relating the pathogenesis of most cases of borderline disorder to the rapprochement subphase, a conclusion that is compatible with the findings of Masterson and Rinsley (chapter 2).

Masterson (1977) clearly attributes the origin of schizophrenic psychosis to developmental arrest during the symbiotic phase, the origin of borderline disorder to developmental arrest during the separation-individuation phase, and the origin of psychoneurosis to developmental arrest during the on-the-way-to-object-constancy phase (Mahler's original object-constancy subphase of separation-individuation). Again, borderline disorder is viewed as emergent from a persistent, pathogenic mother-infant interactional pattern that reaches its peak during the rapprochement subphase.

Settlage (1980) comments on the subphase-related etiology of major personality or characterologic pathology, that is, on the nonpsychotic disorders of the self:

> Failure to achieve age-adequate self regulation and ego autonomy during the rapprochement subphase of the separation-individuation process contributes crucially to the pathogenesis of narcissistic and borderline disorders. I have also described the rapprochement subphase . . . and attempted to draw some correlations between it and the psychological formations characteristic of narcissistic personality disorders [p. 98].

Settlage's view that borderline and narcissistic personality disorders have a similar developmental pathogenesis is basically akin to that of Ornstein (1974) and Rinsley (1980a).

Kohut's contributions on self disorders (1971, 1977), although proceeding from a different conceptual framework, nonetheless encompass a developmental perspective. While his view is not anchored to a chronological continuum per se, Kohut uses the concept of progressive self-object differentiation (Fig. 9-1F); impairment of the latter emerges within the self-disordered patient's so-called self-object transference. In accordance with this view, the psychoneuroses are characterized by the attainment of self-object differentiation and a stable, cohesive self, which corresponds with Kernberg's stage 4 in the development of object relations (1972a). Again, the psychoses and borderline personality disorder are characterized by the pathological persistence of fused (symbiotic), partly differentiated or undifferentiated self- and object-representations (self-objects), which correspond with Kernberg's stages 2 and 3 (1972a). These representations are termed *archaic* because, in regressed states, they emerge in vivid and often terrifyingly reanimated form as primitive ego and superego forerunners (chapter 5, and Jacobson 1954a,b,c, 1964, Kernberg 1968); they are termed *fragmented* because they comprise part-objects that "pass in and out," as it were, in accordance with the operation of the primitive splitting defense in any of its various forms (i.e., projection-introjection, projective and introjective identification, pathological idealization, denial or disavowal, scotomatization, or magical hallucination) (chapter 5). Finally, narcissistic personality disorder is characterized by self- and object-representations (self-objects) much less prone to regressive fragmentation despite their archaic nature; hence, the narcissistic personality is considered to represent a "higher level" borderline personality, closer than the latter to the "neurotic border."

Figure 9-1A and D present the concept of classical psychoanalytic stage theory that relates the pathogenesis of primary

affective disorder to developmental arrest during the late oral
and early anal periods, in conformity with the findings of
Abraham (1912). Yerevanian and Akiskal (1979) state: "According to Karl Abraham, individuals prone to psychotic depression are characterized by undue 'oral' traits of dependency coexisting with anankastic or 'anal' personality features." They
cite Chodoff (1972) to the effect that "of the multitude of
conceptualizations about the depressive personality, Abraham's
view had been generally sustained and . . . had enough merits
to warrant further extensions." Corresponding with the chronology of classical stage theory, Mahlerian phase theory allows
the inference that the developmental arrest that underlies primary
affective disorder would be expected to have occurred during
the differentiation, practicing, and early rapprochement subphases of separation-individuation. The developmental contiguity
of borderline and primary affective disorders thus accounts very
well for the dysphoria characteristic of borderline patients "at
the psychotic border" (Grinker et al.'s Type 1 borderlines, and
possibly also Type 2 "core" borderlines [Grinker and Werble
1977, Grinker et al. 1968]), as well as Klein's so-called hysteroid
dysphorics (1975, 1977, Klein and Davis 1969, Liebowitz and
Klein 1979) and the various "character spectrum" and "dysthymic" cases described by Yerevanian and Akiskal (1979).

The developmental contiguity of primary affective and paranoid disorders (Fig. 9-1D) likewise accounts very well for the
frequency of persecutory ideation, not to mention frank paranoid
delusions, among both manic and major-depressed patients
(Akiskal and Puzantian 1979). By the same token, many acutely
psychotic patients with paranoid symptoms, who were often
considered schizophrenic, are now considered to be suffering
from manic disorder (Abrams, Taylor, and Gaztanaga 1974). Of
particular interest and importance is the observation (DSM-III
1980) that individuals with schizotypal, borderline, paranoid,
narcissistic, and histrionic personality disorders, as diagnosed in
accordance with the DSM-III criteria, are considered particularly
vulnerable to *brief reactive psychosis* when under major stress.

These various personality disorders, as well as others (in-fantile, inadequate, antisocial, passive-aggressive, impulse-ridden and polymorphous-perverse), may be viewed as constituting a subspectrum of descriptively distinguishable conditions that share a common developmental etiology and basically similar internal object relations, and hence, are subsumable under the borderline rubric (chapter 3).

As noted above, Kernberg (1980a) chronicles the pathogenesis of affective psychosis and schizophrenia and a particular border-line subgroup of severely schizoid personalities in terms of developmental deviation during the differentiation subphase of separation-individuation. Assuming the correctness of this chronology, it would have to be further assumed that the schizoid personalities to whom Kernberg makes reference suffer from psychotic disorder; in fact, it is likely that Kernberg's subgroup comprises the schizotypal personalities of DSM-III, who are symptomatically and psychodynamically more akin to psychotics than to borderlines. Careful clinical study will reveal some of them to be severely dysphoric.

As presented in Figure 9-1D, patients suffering from symbiotic schizophrenia (Rinsley 1972), including those labeled "reactive" and schizo-affective, have undergone developmental arrest during the symbiotic phase. They constitute another subspectrum of psychotic syndromes, with a continuum ranging from the "more purely schizophrenic" types to those with evident affective symptomatology (Stone 1980). The DSM-III assigns schizo-affective disorder to an omnibus diagnostic category for those cases in which the clinician cannot make a clear-cut differential diagnosis between affective disorder and schizophrenia.

It will be noted that the group designated as autistic-presymbiotic, comprising the so-called nuclear, process, and pseudo-defective schizophrenic syndromes, has been excluded from the group of spectrum disorders as here defined. As presented in Figure 9-1, developmental arrest in these cases antedates the establishment of the primary, undifferentiated self-object built up in the infant as a consequence of pleasurable mother-infant interactions; hence, the arrest occurs during the phase of normal autism, which corresponds with Kernberg's stage 1 (1972a) and is roughly coterminous with the first postnatal month. The ensuing symptomatology has been described elsewhere (Rinsley 1972, 1974a,b).

NATURE–NURTURE AND DIATHESIS–STRESS

Psychoanalytic phase theory admittedly leans heavily on the vicissitudes of the mother-child relationship as fundamental to later personality development, as well as to the pathogenesis of all the psychopathologic syndromes of childhood, adolescence, and adulthood. In trying to understand the nature and outcome of that relationship, we look at the "goodness of fit," mutual cuing, or communicative matching between mother and child from the separation-individuation phase through the preschool years (Mahler et al. 1975). The mother's caretaking during this period is embodied in Winnicott's concept of the "good enough" mother and environment (1950–1955, 1951, 1960). Winnicott's "false self" and Balint's "basic fault" represent related developmental encumbrances that ensue in the wake of impairment or failure of the mother-child goodness of fit during the separation-individuation phase, and doubtless extend back into the antecedent phase of symbiosis. The various self- or spectrum disorders are the result.

Of the various criticisms directed toward psychoanalytic phase theory, two merit serious consideration. The first of these may be construed from Esman's warning (1980) that the emphasis placed on the maternal role in pathogenesis "comes dangerously close to . . . mother-baiting"; he further cautions that certain borderline adolescents appear to have come into the world with "intrinsic deviations in the range of minimal cerebral dysfunction" that made substantial contributions to the admittedly disturbed mother-child relationship. There appears to be increasing general agreement, however, that the genesis of the various disorders of the self is multifactorial, with the role of innate, constitutional, and heredo-congenital determinants assuming increasing importance at the psychotic end of the developmental-diagnostic spectrum, and the role of dyadic-interpersonal, familial, and wider social determinants assuming increasing importance at the psychoneurotic end. The caveat regarding mother-baiting becomes less relevant when we recognize that, regardless of the nature of the pathogenic determinants, their final common pathway is the mother-child relationship.

A second criticism has to do with the tendency to rigidify the various phases and subphases into absolute or near-absolute critical periods that supposedly bear a one-to-one relationship to the various self- or spectrum disorders (Mahler 1971, Mahler and Kaplan 1977). However, few, if any, serious investigators regard either the major developmental phases or the constituent subphases of separation-individuation as sharply delineated chronologically or as invariant in their developmental content, not to mention the widely acknowledged influence of events from antecedent developmental periods ("subphase adequacy" [Mahler 1971, Mahler and Kaplan 1977]).

SUMMARY

Accumulating evidence from diverse studies, including the biological-pharmacological, genetic, and psychodynamic-developmental, points toward the validity of the view that the various psychopathologic syndromes may be arranged along a spectrum or continuum (Fig. 9-1D).

Based on psychoanalytic object-relations concepts, developmental phase theory relates degree of psychopathology, and hence, relative position along the spectrum, to degree of self-object differentiation.

Recent and current literature, as summarized by Stone (1980), allows for the validity of two subspectra, viz., the subspectrum of psychotic disorders that includes the schizophrenic, schizoaffective, primary affective, and paranoid (psychotic) syndromes, and the subspectrum of personality or characterologic disorders. The latter comprises an array of episodically psychotic, psychoticlike, and nonpsychotic syndromes that appear to share common developmental psychodynamics centering on partial self-object differentiation; irrespective of specific symptomatology, therefore, and in contradistinction to the nosology of personality disorders presented in the DSM-III (1980), they are here subsumed under the borderline rubric.

Finally, the pathogenesis of the various disorders or syndromes is considered to be multifactorial, with "diathesis" (genetic loading, heredo-congenital or constitutional determinants) assuming increasing importance among the psychotic and more severe personality disorders, and "stress" (dyadic and triadic parental, wider familial, and social-environmental determinants) assuming increasing importance among the less severe personality disorders and the psychoneuroses.

CHAPTER 10

JUVENILE DELINQUENCY

This chapter explores the role of depersonification, a crucial ingredient in the etiology of the borderline personality, in juvenile delinquency. The term *juvenile delinquency* is derived from the Latin *juvenilis*, meaning young, and *delinquere*, meaning to transgress or fail (*de* + *linquere*, to leave or depart). The term *delinquent* has assumed a latter-day meaning of overdue, unfinished, or incomplete, as in a delinquent record or an unpaid bill. In many jurisdictions, juvenile courts recognize and apply the terms *wayward* (note: Aichhorn's classic *Verwahrloste Jugend*, translated as "Wayward Youth" [1925]) and *miscreant* to youthful offenders: *wayward* means recalcitrant, undisciplined, uncooperative, unresponsive to parental authority and control; *miscreant* means mischievous, evildoing, villainous, or "bad." Since the organization of the first juvenile court in the United States in 1899 in Cook County, Illinois, these terms have been applied variously to designate youthful offenders who have run afoul of the law and been brought to the attention of the court, who are below the statutory age which legally defines adulthood, and who are presumed to lack the capacity for responsibility for their acts. Thus, juvenile delinquents are youths whose acts would have brought arraignment on criminal charges were they adults.

Controversy has marked thinking and research concerning juvenile delinquency ever since the venerable Code of Hammurabi specified harsh punishment for wayward children, and an

Egyptian priest of four thousand years B.C. could lament, "Our earth is degenerate . . . children no longer obey their parents!" (Johnson 1959). A modern example of the controversy is illustrated in the difference between the psychodynamic-clinical and the sociological approaches to the etiology of juvenile delinquency; thus are dichotomized the "sick" delinquents whose antisociality expresses their "underlying" psychopathology, and the "sociologic" or "dyssocial" delinquents whose untoward behavior finds expression in affiliation with group subculture (Hewitt and Jenkins 1946, Schimel 1974, Shaw and McKay 1931, Topping 1943). The controversy is tragicomically portrayed in the well-known Broadway musical, *West Side Story*, in which an adolescent gang member complains that he needs a "shrink" because he needs his "head shrunk," a social worker because he suffers from a "social disease," and punishment because he is just plain "bad."

Modern advances in understanding the juvenile delinquent may be said to have traversed three stages or periods, beginning in the early years of this century with August Aichhorn (1925). Aichhorn taught the necessity to "get inside" the individual offenders, to assist them toward wholesome identifications, to deal with their symptomatic behavior as secondary to the phenomena of their inner life and world. Following Aichhorn, during this halcyon stage, much was achieved in applying psychoanalytic insights to the elucidation of the identifications, defenses, motivations, and actions of wayward youth; indeed, Alexander (1930) could point out the etiologic significance for delinquent behavior of a harsh, self-punitive superego and in a sense could conceptualize antisociality as one variety of masochism.

The second stage of understanding may be said to have had its inception in the pioneering contributions of William Healy and his colleagues in the 1920s, initially in Chicago and later in Boston (Alexander and Healy 1935, Healy and Bronner 1936). They extended psychoanalytic insight into wayward youth and focused on the disturbed family's role in providing inadequate models for juvenile identification, in "scapegoating" selected children and thereby engendering delinquent forms of self-expression. The Healy approach was later to find deeper expression and extension in the contributions of Adelaide Johnson, who could find "superego lacunae" in delinquents resulting from the child's unconsciously compliant "acting out" of the parents' unconscious antisocial impulses and needs (Johnson 1949, 1959, Johnson and Szurek 1952).

The Johnson contribution comprises one variety of work, the more inclusive aspects of which characterize the third stage of understanding of the juvenile delinquent. Pathological acting out of parental needs and impulses by the child gives expression to one form of profound psychological misuse of children, termed *appersonation* or *depersonification*, a phenomenon which has received considerable study in the case of borderline and psychotic children (Rinsley 1971a). Depersonification of a juvenile, whether an infant, toddler, late preschooler, latency child, or adolescent, means that his prime surrogates, whether natural parents or others, perceive and respond to him *as if* he were someone or something other than what he in fact is; the result is to blight or distort the child's evolving identity. Johnson's "superego lacunae" could be understood as reflections of what Winnicott (1951, 1960) was later to identify as a failure of "good enough mothering," with its ineluctable distortion of the child's ego identity based in turn upon a pathogenic parent-child pseudocomplementarity and pseudocompliance. The depersonifying parent, who almost invariably is found to be suffering from psychopathology of at least borderline severity, relies on narcissistic object relations, utilizes primitive mechanisms of defense, and ultimately retards or precludes the child's separation-individuation (chapters 2, 3, 5, and 6, as well as Masterson 1972a,b, 1973, 1974, 1975, 1976).

The depersonification of children has been studied and clarified by many investigators in a variety of contexts and from a variety of disciplines. Among them have been Bateson, an anthropologist with his theory of the disjunctive double bind (Bateson 1972, Bateson et al. 1968); Lidz, who has illumined the familial basis of schizophrenia (Lidz et al. 1965, 1968); Wynne and Singer on the intergenerational transmission of irrationality (Singer and Wynne 1965a,b, Wynne 1961, Wynne and Singer 1963a,b); Fliess (1961), who wrote about "abolishment" of the child; Berne (1961), who developed transactional analysis, including the concept of the "crossed transaction"; Mahler, whose epochal studies of separation-individuation have greatly clarified the complexities of the development of object relations and selfhood (Mahler et al. 1975); Masterson, who has contributed fundamental insights into borderline adolescents in particular and borderline disorders in general (chapter 2, and Masterson 1972a,b, 1973, 1974, 1975, 1976) and the leaders in family therapy, including Ackerman (1958, 1967), Jackson (Bateson et al. 1968, Jackson and Weakland 1961), Bowen (1960, 1968), Haley (1963), and Satir (1967, 1972), whose contributions have emphasized the family as an organismic nexus in relation to which individual "illness" and deviation must be assessed.

This voluminous work has, among other things, explicated the characteristics of those families who spawn and raise seriously disturbed children, whether the latter's symptomatology is predominantly autoplastic or alloplastic. From this work we can also conclude that the degree of pathogenicity of such families is in proportion to the degree of their disarticulation from the wider culture of which they are part, which in turn relates to the degree of intrafamilial blurring and obfuscation of age, gender, and intergenerational and functional identities and roles (Rinsley 1971a,b).

There is no need to belabor the point that juvenile delinquency develops as a product of pathogenic or deficient parenting, or that so-called sociological delinquency, both as a diagnosis and a concept, serves the simplistic need to explain away a clinical phenomenon which can only and readily be understood as a result of intensive clinical, individual, and family study. No family, disarticulated from meaningful extrafamilial sources and objects of communication, may be expected to function internally in such fashion as to produce healthy children; as a corollary, parents who are distracted, estranged, and alienated tend to raise distracted, estranged, and alienated children and the children's failure to acculturate reflects a like failure in their parents (Lewis and Balla 1976). Stated in object-relations terms, the family's projection of its "bad objects" into the extra-familial surround is taken up by its children, who proceed to develop a view of the world as a strange and hostile repository of persecutors. At best, these children perceive their environments much as prisoners perceive their prisons—they attempt to out-wit the "system," to vanquish its impact on them by "beating it at its own game"; at worst, they become psychotic or perish.

The plight of these disarticulated families, precarious in even the best of times, is immeasurably worsened during periods of wider social instability and stress, such as this country has been traversing during the past decade and a half. There can be little doubt that the events of this period have had a pervasively pejorative effect upon personal identity and the rearing and education of the young, including the blurring and erosion of traditional roles and folkways. But if these factors have strained the identities and the child-rearing practices of even the healthiest and most stable of families, they have wreaked even greater havoc upon borderline families whose members perceive, amidst the realities of wider sociocultural disorganization, a further justification for their otherwise long-standing mistrust and detachment. Thus the rising juvenile crime rate, the bur-geoning divorce rate, the expanding use of illicit drugs, the loosening of sexual mores, the pervasive mistrust of any and all authority figures with its associated, near-incredible prolifer-ation of civil litigation—all in turn reflect an increasing public reliance upon narcissistic coping mechanisms (Nelson 1977).

Within such a sociocultural context, increasing numbers of families from all socioeconomic strata proceed to defect from their major intergenerational tasks and responsibilities. Lacking ideals, parents cannot serve as ideals for their children; hence they find it impossible to engage with and appropriately dis-cipline the children's natural narcissism. Abdication of parental authority parallels the abdication of parenthood itself, with increasing numbers of both married and unmarried adults who eschew childbearing and child rearing, combined with the apparent paradox of a soaring rate of illegitimate births. Put simply, the adult's message to the child is, "Since I do not know who *I* am, how can I tell you who *you* are or what you might become?"

Delinquent youth are psychosocially deviant, reflecting their failure to acculturate, which in turn is a result of pathogenic parenting by adult surrogates who themselves had never become adequately acculturated. When the wider cultural patterns and folkways become obfuscated and fragmented, there ensues a vicious circle of individual-familial, and cultural determinants of that variety of psychopathology simplistically termed *juvenile delinquency*.

Juvenile delinquency is thus definable and understandable in terms of a nexus of interrelated individual, familial and sociocultural determinants. Irrespective of the specifics of symptomatic behavior or diagnosis, the delinquent is fundamentally egocentric (narcissistic), whether he functions individually or as a member of a narcissistically self-serving peer group.

A BRIEF SOCIAL COMMENT

And what of this "wider social instability and stress," including its manifestations during the period under present discussion? There can be little doubt that the accelerated pace of recent social change ("future shock": Toffler 1970), with its apparent departure from traditional Judaeo-Christian ethics and values, has left increasing numbers of otherwise stable middle-class individuals and families anxious, depressed, and confused.

There has occurred a progressive "demythologization" of numerous American cultural "as-ifs" and a significant remodeling of others. The "myth" of limitless power and natural resources has been exploded. Traditional, organized religion has encountered serious difficulties as ethical and moral standards have, to state it euphemistically, become "liberalized." The public educational establishment, with its shibboleths of the "open" and "child-centered" classrooms, ungraded classes, grade inflation, and "social promotion", has produced a welter of "graduates" who cannot adequately read, write, or reckon. The once avant-garde Playboy Philosophy, since copied in a seemingly endless stream of publications which appeal to prurience, extols a narcissistic "do-your-own-thing" approach to human relations, in which freedom is confounded with license, and pseudomutuality and pseudointimacy are rationalized on the basis that "anything goes" between consenting adults; polymorphous-perversity is offered as an alternative to conjugal heterosexuality, and "gay is good," "unisex" or "open" marriages, and masturbation are supposed to "liberate" the citizenry from the oppressive shackles of conventional, patriarchic morality.

In addition, during this period the American constitutional "as-if"—that "all men are created equal"—has been pressed into service to justify a bewildering array of civil rights rulings and legislation which have dislocated domestic social structure. Shotgun efforts to legislate away any and all forms of discrimination and inequality, reflective of a resurgent egalitarianism and antielitism, have spawned in their wake a proliferating centralized governmental bureaucracy which has progressively curbed creative individualism and has surfeited the land with a growing army of assorted surveyors, assessors, reviewers, and inspectors.

In the wake of these phenomena, there have emerged—as might be expected—an expanding welter of extremists and zealots, each promising a confused and skeptical populace simplistic, demagogic "solutions," each attracting a vocal following composed of alienated pariahs and honestly concerned citizens. Thus, there have been the beatniks, the hippies, and the groupies. Timothy Leary has exhorted youth to "tune in, turn on, and drop out"; women's liberation has leveled the genders; and youthful dissent has turned vicious (e.g., the emergence of underground revolutionary cadres such as the Weathermen). Or it has found expression in a burgeoning array of culture-alien imported and domestic "religions" from which distracted, alienated youth have vainly sought a sense of belonging and identity which their parents and teachers have denied them (Pruyser 1977). Szasz (1974) has told us that mental illness is a "myth," the invention of unwitting or "Strangelovian" doctors bent upon the imprisonment of those people society does not like; a rampantly antipsychiatric and anti-institutional contingent has declared that psychiatrists and other mental health professionals serve in effect as agents of the police power of the state, and that all psychiatric or "mental" hospitals are per se bad for their patients, especially if the latter are in need of civil commitment (Greenhill 1976).

The state of affairs these phenomena reflect represents a notable degree of sociocultural nihilism in relation to which the phenomenology of juvenile delinquency must ultimately be assessed. If society is devoid of standards of sexual morality and conduct, then the lifelong sexual invert is "normal"; if mental illness is indeed a myth, then a deluded, hallucinating paranoid schizophrenic is "healthy"; if acceptable codes of child rearing and of juvenile conduct and deportment have no significance, then juvenile delinquency is an illusion.

Pari passu the failure of healthy parenting and the decline of the family (Voth 1977) has been the enormous growth in the number of extrafamilial helping agencies, ranging from police- and court-related juvenile and child-protective services to full-time residential treatment facilities, to which parents in increasing numbers have ceded the management and control of their children. Indeed, in Great Britain alone, the number of full-time and combined day and full-time residential facilities for children increased by nearly 500 percent between 1957 and 1970 (Barker 1974, p. 17). The high rate of divorce, the expanding number of illegitimate births, and the increase in the number of pregnancies among secondary-school-age adolescents have added vastly to the number of ill-parented children, limited only by a related increase in the rate of abortion as mandated by "liberalized" laws governing the voluntary termination of pregnancy. It could only be expected that a mounting concern for "children's rights" should emerge within such a social context, expressive of a growing apprehension regarding the nature and quality of foster-care parents, agencies, facilities, and institutions into whose care more and more distracted natural parents have managed to consign their children.

There is no need to recount here the host of recent legislative and judicial acts and decisions mandating the civil and constitutional rights of children; indeed, the law has stepped in where parents have feared to tread (Beck and Weiss 1974, Rolfe and MacClintock 1976). The net effect of the extension and application of due process to younger children and to older-age juveniles is, however, to blur the valid distinction between child and adult in both civil and criminal proceedings. Once again, in the case of children's putative "due process" rights, one witnesses a further and ongoing erosion of parental responsibility and, in the wake of soaring juvenile crime, a related, rising tide of public opinion which demands swift, adult-type "justice" for the juvenile offender.

SUMMARY

The irrationalities of the 1960s have begun to recede in the 1970s and several interrelated factors may be considered responsible. First, the Vietnam War ended in 1975, thereby removing the most evident cause célèbre fueling the so-called generation gap with its expression in a strident, minority youth "counterculture." Second, an evidently conservative trend by the nation's highest court has effectively begun to place needed restraint upon much of the activist zealotry which typified the preceding decade. Third, an expected reaction among growing numbers of youth and adults has occurred against the narcissistic ethos of the 1960s: the young are questioning so-called liberated sexuality, there is a rising tide of public opinion in opposition to publicized sexual deviance, there is increasing resistance to legalized abortions, and pornography is receiving an expanding public challenge; traditional church attendance is rising; the myth of the so-called racially balanced classroom increasingly is being seen for what it is as more and more parents and educators are demanding an end to open classrooms and nonsensical curricula and a return to the teaching and learning of literate cognitive skills; and increasing numbers of legislators are rethinking the practice of dumping the seriously and chronically mentally ill into the community, where they are often exploited and where they often receive worse care at higher expense than in the admittedly suboptimal institutions to which they had become inured. Fourth, and perhaps most important of all, is the demographic effect of a verified and ongoing increase of the mean chronological age of the general population; its long-term overall impact in reducing the percentage of juveniles within the population, and hence, the percentage of crimes committed by them, will eventually be enormous.

These evident trends foretell an eventual reduction in the rate of juvenile delinquency and will inevitably enforce a reassessment of the need for, and hence, funding of, the as yet burgeoning number of diagnostic-therapeutic, special educational, correctional, and protective services for psychosocially disturbed juveniles. An associated swing away from shotgun, revolving-door, behavioristic, mass production methods toward more humane, individualized, and in-depth techniques for dealing with them may thus be ardently hoped for and confidently expected.

CHAPTER 11

BORDERLINE AND NARCISSISTIC CHILDREN AND ADOLESCENTS

The diagnosis and treatment of borderline and narcissistic syndromes in children and adolescents remains a much-neglected subject. This chapter reviews the literature in this area and offers specific therapeutic recommendations.

It is well known that the number of individuals with disorders of the self—which arise from pre-Oedipal pathogenesis—has been steadily increasing (Kohut 1971, Woodward and Mark 1978). The trend toward self disorders has been dubbed "the new narcissism" (Nelson 1977, Lasch 1977, 1978); it reflects the extensive psychosocial and cultural changes that emerged most clearly in the 1960s (chapters 7 and 10). A brief review of these changes is offered as background to the present discussion.

While the 1950s seemed to be a superficially untroubled and even smug time in our country, it was also the era of the bomb-scare ethos and highly charged anticommunist witch-hunting. The 1960s, in contrast, witnessed a series of dramatic changes perhaps best characterized as the "demythologization" of long-standing religious, cultural, and familial values. Mental illness was declared a myth; schooling was designed to prepare students to deal with "life" rather than scholarly pursuits. "Equal opportunity" was a new password; all types of sexual contact were deemed normal and healthy, and birth control pills and easily obtained abortions helped to create an ambiance of "anything goes." The feminist movement tried to free women from the shackles of a stifling patriarchalism, and women moved to establish their place in the ranks of the work force. Accompanying these trends was the decline of the traditional family (Lasch 1977, Voth 1977) and the mutual alienation of parents and children. Divorce, illegitimate births, and juvenile crime rates all burgeoned, as did rock music, mind-altering drugs, and arcane, culture-alien, quasi-religious cults.

In sum, the major differences between the traditional pattern of family life and the contemporary pattern that emerged during the 1960s were as follows:

1. Traditionally, sexual intercourse was only sanctioned within marriage and was closely tied to birth and child rearing. In the contemporary pattern, all forms of sexual behavior are accepted as normal and healthy human communication; as a result, sexual activity bears no fundamental relationship to child rearing or family building.

2. Traditionally, the family's basic task was that of transmitting accepted sociocultural values and norms as a basis for the socialization of subsequent generations. In the contemporary pattern, the family no longer serves this function since the new values are subjective and situational.

3. Traditionally, there was a definitive asymmetry in the basic parent-child relationship. The child submitted to the parents' benevolent but firm authority and support, identified with the parents, and accepted their standards of conduct and belief. Parents carefully nurtured the child's developmental needs and capabilities, and aided the child in his quest for emancipation and independence, which eventually led to the child's own marriage and family building. In the contemporary pattern, there is a relative symmetry in the parent-child relationship. Parents are not active participants in the child's ultimate separation-individuation and emancipation, marriage, and family

building—instead, the child's future is viewed as his or her own affair.

4. Traditionally, the basic task of childhood was the child's early separation-individuation from the mother, with whom he had a symbiotic tie. The father played an important supplementary role in this respect, as well as serving as the protector of the family, breadwinner, administrator, and planner. In the contemporary situation, however, the nurturing of children tends to be equally shared between the father and mother, with the parental roles relatively interchangeable.

Families following the evolving contemporary pattern experience a significant degree of identity diffusion, schism, and skew (Lidz et al. 1965, 1968). There are also signs of gender and role confusion, with intergenerational blurring, miscommunication, and incoherence (Bateson 1972, Bateson et al. 1968, Singer and Wynne 1965a,b, Wynne 1961, Wynne and Singer 1963a,b). Of importance to the present discussion is the finding that families of this kind show significant risk for the development of schizophrenic, borderline, and narcissistically fixated children.

PATTERNS OF DEPERSONIFICATION

A study of one hundred families with borderline or narcissistic adolescents in full-time residential treatment (Rinsley 1971a) revealed the following parental misperceptions of the growing child:

Psychotic and Severe Borderline Patterns

1. The child is perceived as an inanimate object, as if he or she were a doll, toy, or machine. Some perceptions are in keeping with science fiction motifs involving robots, androids, and clones.

2. The child is perceived as part of one's own body or bodily functions—as a symbolic representation of the parent's eyes, ears, muscles, genitals, excretions, and the like.

3. The child is perceived as a subhuman animal or monster such as a pet, wolf, vampire, or zombie.

4. The child is perceived as nonexistent ("abolished") (Fliess 1961). Characteristic of some postpartum psychotic mothers, this extreme pattern involves a scotomatization or negative hallucination of the newborn child which may extend into later childhood.

Less Severe Borderline and Narcissistic Patterns

1. The child is perceived as a surrogate parental figure; he or she becomes a superego representation who provides guidance, controls, and limitations for the parent. There is an essential reversal of parent-child roles.

2. The child is perceived as a spouse, which creates an overtly or covertly incestuous relationship.

3. The child is perceived as a sibling, with consequent rivalry and competition, often of a highly destructive nature.

4. The child is perceived as an endlessly infantile or dependent baby, which reflects the parents' need to keep the child from growing up.

There are differences between the borderline and narcissistic patterns of depersonification. In the former, the parental "message" is that if the child grows up, he or she will be abandoned. In the latter, the parental "message" is that the child may grow up, but only if he or she never leaves the parent or centers his or her life on the parent (Rinsley 1980b). In general, parental pathology is a significant factor in the development of all of these childhood and adolescent syndromes. The family structure that helps to produce borderline and narcissistic children is not unlike that leading to the development of schizophrenic children (Bateson et al. 1968, Lidz et al. 1965, 1968). The main features of the borderline family structure include various degrees of disarticulation from the extrafamilial world; an absence of clear-cut lines of authority; confusion of parental executive and nurturing roles; and obfuscation of parental self- and gender identity as well as intergenerational roles and functions. The intergenerational transmission of irrational forms of thinking and relating is of etiological importance (Singer and Wynne 1965a,b, Wynne and Singer 1963a,b).

SCAPEGOATING AND "THE IDENTIFIED PATIENT"

A scapegoat is one who is made to bear the blame for the evil, misdeeds, or sins of others. The word is derived from the Hebrew term for demon; it alludes to an ancient Jewish ceremony in which a goat was sent into the wilderness as a symbolic representative of the sins and guilt of the people. In the literature of medieval witchcraft, the devil was often personified as a goat. A scapegoat is therefore an expiatory object with enormous demonic powers; since it bears the individual and collective sins of others it has the power to reverse the situation and wreak havoc upon the scapegoaters.

Healy and Bronner (1936) applied the concept of the family scapegoat to their work with delinquent youths. Their work was extended by the contributions of Johnson and Szurek (Johnson 1949, 1959, Johnson and Szurek 1952), who viewed what they termed the superego lacunae of delinquents as expressions of the parents' unconscious needs to act out their own disowned aggressive and sexual needs.

The scapegoated child is usually "the identified patient" and his symptomatology will depend on the particular pattern or patterns of his depersonification. His pseudocomplementary false self evolves in intimate connection with the distorted self-identity of the depersonifying parent; because the child cannot repose his infantile-megalomania in this parent, he cannot trust the parent. The unseparated and unindividuated child feels inadequate, impotent, and empty. As the scapegoat, he feels evil and powerful, yet rejected and abandoned; he soon develops a commitment to not growing up. For example, after nearly two years of therapy, an 11-year-old borderline boy related how his mother would come to his bed during his late preschool years and repeatedly read to him from *The Wizard of Oz*. She called her son "my little wizard" and saw him as someone who would ultimately rescue her ("Dorothy") and allow her to grow up.

Another striking example is the 14-year-old borderline girl in intensive residential treatment who idolized Peter Pan, because "he never got old and he lived forever, flying around the big castle." The castle proved to be symbolic for her mother, from whom she had never individuated; she viewed herself as a satellite forever trapped in her mother's field of influence. The mother herself provided the complementary message: "I knew right away when I had her she was just like me. Even when she was a little baby she fought me all the way . . . she just wore me out. She never wanted to grow up . . . just like me!"

THE THREE BASIC TASKS OF CHILDHOOD

To paraphrase Erikson (1963), the three basic tasks of the preschool child may be represented by three metaphors that convey a child's mode of self-experience: "I am" (oral), "I can" (anal), and "I am a boy or girl" (Oedipal). The "I am" metaphor conveys the child's successful differentiation from the mothering figure and development of a sense of self that signifies his or her separateness per se. The "I can" metaphor conveys the child's awareness of his capacity for mastery and control, and his ability to communicate with and have an impact on others and on the world. The "I am a boy or girl" metaphor conveys a major task of the latter half of the preschool years, one that is largely completed on entance into young adulthood. It signifies the consolidation of the child's gender identity—the boy's sense of maleness and masculinity, and the girl's sense of femaleness and femininity. The successful completion of these three basic tasks determines the child's later capacity for healthy object relations, productivity and creativity.

Because the borderline child has never adequately completed the first of these tasks, the ensuing two remain unfinished. The therapist will hear complaints, directly or through symptomatic behavior, that the child does not know who he or she is. There are feelings of boredom and emptiness (Kumin 1978), as well as alienation. The child is gripped by labile emotions that he cannot comprehend. He describes himself as phony, fake, and unreal. Through projection, he perceives others in the same way.

The borderline patient's failure to develop a coherent sense of self leads to a failure to develop a sense of mastery. These patients talk of not being able to do anything, of being a mess, and of having no friends. Their lack of a coherent gender identity is expressed in patterns of infantile polymorphous-perverse sexuality, which consolidate during adolescence.

These self-perceptions of emptiness, powerlessness, and meaninglessness coexist with powerful charges of omnipotence and grandiosity, all of which creates a dynamic and symptomatic paradox for the borderline patient. Borderline individuals are demanding, egocentric, presumptuous, and intimidating as they attempt to extract from a world they perceive as empty and hostile the very supplies they are convinced it lacks or withholds from them. However, this paradox becomes understandable when it is recognized that these patients' mutually conflicting and contradictory perceptions, affects, and actions reflect the endopsychic structure of children between six months and three years of age.

DIAGNOSIS

As noted elsewhere (chapter 3) the differential diagnosis of childhood psychosis and borderline disorders is poorly developed. The nosology presented here views the borderline and narcissistic disorders of children and adults as manifestations of personality or character pathology intermediate between the psychoneuroses and psychoses (chapters 3 and 5, as well as Ornstein 1974). Object-relations theory allows for a gradation of the severer psychopathological syndromes along a continuum based on degree of self-object differentiation and regression (chapters 5 and 9). In the psychoses, self- and object-representations remain partial and fragmented, and regression is the profoundest. In the borderline conditions, there is some differentiation of self- and object-representations, but these are prone to regressive fragmentation, with lapses into psychotic modes of experiencing. In the narcissistic conditions, the partially differentiated self- and object-representations are relatively stable and therefore more resistant to regressive fragmentation. In such conditions, Oedipal themes, reliance on repression, a harsh superego with obsessional manifestations, and the attainment of some degree of whole-object relations convey a "neurotic-lie" picture (Mahler and Kaplan 1977). Common to all three conditions is the inability to work through real and fantasied separations and losses, resulting in a constant vulnerability to the underlying abandonment depression (chapter 2, and Frankel 1977).

Creak's listing of nine characteristics of psychotic children (1963) is helpful here:

1. An inability to relate normally to people.
2. An apparent unawareness of personal identity.
3. Preoccupation with inanimate objects.
4. Sustained resistance to change.
5. Abnormal responses to sensory experience.
6. A tendency to disintegrate into utter confusion.
7. Speech disorders.
8. Motor disturbances.
9. Isolated incidences of fantastic power against a general background of poor achievement.

Chiland and Lebovici (1977) characterized borderline and prepsychotic children in similar terms. They described such preschool children as irritable and manic-hyperactive, with early and intense insomnia, anorexia, and poor emotional contact. In the early latency children there are school phobia, agitation in class, poor impulse control, insensitivity to discipline, negativism, explosive rage, extrafamilial mutism, dysphasia and dyspraxia, bizarre phobias, and psychopathic traits, including extreme cruelty.

Similarly, Engel's (1963) psychological test study of "borderline psychotic" children led her to characterize them in terms of: (1) their overwhelming preoccupation with basic survival; (2) their intense, only partly successful, struggles to maintain full contact with reality; (3) their view of the environment's demands as insurmountable; (4) their significant use of distancing devices, including bizarre fantasies, to ward off others; and (5) their notable vulnerability to inner and outer stimuli (a characteristic also mentioned in Ekstein's description (1966) of borderline children). Engel (1972) made the following distinctions between borderline and psychotic children:

> As the name implies, borderline children are not as sick as psychotic youngsters. Their alienation from reality is not as complete; they struggle to maintain themselves in the face of pathology. Because psychotic and neurotic aspects of their personality coexist and alternate . . . their treatment offers particular challenges and problems [p. 138 fn].

Prior to the pioneering work of Masterson (1972b, 1973, 1974, 1975), the diagnosis of borderline adolescents was likewise beset with difficulty. These patients were seen as suffering from severe neurosis, ego and superego defects, and developmental arrest (Easson 1969). Their pathology was categorized as a character disorder, a neurosis, pseudopsychopathic schizophrenia (Bender 1959), an adjustment reaction of adolescence, and as delinquency or a behavior disorder. Masterson's description of the borderline adolescent's presenting symptomatology (1972b) included: boredom, restlessness, difficulty in concentration, hypochrondriasis, and excessive sexual and physical activity. These difficulties often led to stealing, drinking, drug abuse, promiscuity, running away, slovenly dress, and dyssocial peer affiliation.

Goldstein and Jones (1977) delineated four major behavioral-symptomatic groups of adolescents with borderline disorders. In Group I, aggressive-antisocial, they included patients showing poorly controlled, impulsive, "activing-out" behavior. There was some degree of inner tension or subjective distress subordinate to aggressive patterns which appeared in many areas of functioning—family, school, peer relations, and society. Group II included active family conflict; these adolescents were defiant toward parental figures and belligerent and antagonistic in the family setting. However, there was little display of aggressiveness or rebelliousness outside the family. These patients often exhibited signs of inner distress and turmoil including anxiety and somatic complaints. Group III, passive-negative, was characterized by negativism, sullenness, and indirect forms of hostility and defiance toward parents and other authorities. However, overt defiance and temper outbursts were infrequent and there was superficial compliance to adults' wishes. Although underachievement and other school difficulties were common, their behavior was not disruptive. Finally, Group IV, withdrawn-socially isolated, was characterized by marked uncommunicativeness and isolation; these patients had few, if any, friends. There was excessive dependence on one or both parents, with notable fears and marked anxiety. These adolescents spent much of their unstructured time in solitary pursuits.

Borderline symptomatology in the latency-age child and the young adolescent tends to be psychoticlike in clinical appearance. Toward the latter part of adolescence, the clinical picture often shifts and begins to resemble that of the borderline adult (Grinker et al. 1968, Grinker and Werble 1977).

TREATMENT

The literature on the treatment of children with borderline and narcissistic disorders remains quite scanty. Among the exceptions are the contributions of Ekstein (1966) and Masterson (1972b, 1973, 1974, 1975, see also Rinsley 1974a), and the brief review chapter by Fuchs and van der Schraaf (1979). Among the reasons for this state of affairs are the unsettled issues of diagnostic nosology and the tendency to label borderline pathology in children as a hyperkinetic syndrome or minimal brain damage. The latter diagnoses generally lead to drug treatment as the sole thereapeutic measure. Treatment difficulties also stem from recent anti-institutional legislation and judicial decrees that considerably complicate the inpatient placement and treatment of seriously disturbed children and youths.

The treatment of borderline and narcissistic children ideally involves the following goals:

1. Establishing and maintaining a stable and predictable environment within which the patient's psychopathology can be resolved, and providing appropriate opportunities for healthy growth and development.

2. Controlling the patient's untoward symptomatic behavior.

3. Working with the patient's family with a view toward unraveling the complex strands of mutually depersonifying communications and interactions from which the identified patient's psychopathology has emerged.

4. Promoting the patient's working through of the unfinished processes of separation-individuation and identity-formation.

The Residential or Inpatient Setting

Residential or inpatient treatment, whether part- or full-time, is reserved for those children and adolescents whose symptomatology precludes effective outpatient therapy. It seeks to provide the stable milieu that these patients lack. The criteria for home removal and admission into therapeutic residence were first stated in 1934 by Potter (1934a,b) and more recently by Easson (1969), Rinsley (1971b, 1974a, 1980b), and Wardle (1974). In brief, these criteria are as follows:

1. The patient's symptomatology, behavior, or conduct is seriously disruptive or bizarre.

2. The patient's ability to utilize home, school, church and other growth-supportive institutions is severely or profoundly compromised.

3. Progressive psychosocial deterioration is occurring despite all efforts to arrest or remit it.

4. The severity of parental-familial psycho-pathology clearly indicates a dysfunctional, pathogenic family nexus.

Residential treatment of a child or adolescent must be highly selective and based on a thorough knowledge of the child, his or her family, and the wider social environment (Szurek et al. 1971). Because such patients tend to express their inner suffering through bizarre, antisocial, destructive, and self-destructive acting out, the inpatient setting must early on control such behavior and assist patients to translate underlying problems into mutually understandable and consensually validated communications.

Outpatient Treatment

The criteria for outpatient treatment of borderline and narcissistic personality disorders are as follows:

1. The patient's symptomatology is devoid of any bizarreness, disruptiveness, or destructiveness severe enough to cause social ostracism or endanger life.

2. The patient shows a reasonable degree of age-appropriate academic achievement.

3. The family setting, despite its pathogenic features, is able to provide elements of ongoing support for the patient's change and growth. The parents recognize the child's need for treatment and cooperate fully with therapeutic requirements (e.g., attending all necessary sessions and paying the requisite fees).

Specific Therapeutic Modalities

INDIVIDUAL PSYCHOTHERAPY. In both inpatient and outpatient settings, dynamically oriented individual psychotherapy is essential to the treatment of borderline and narcissistic children and adolescents. There are usually three stages of treatment (Masterson 1972b; Rinsley 1974a): (1) a resistance or testing stage; (2) an introjective or working-through stage; and (3) a resolution or separation stage. The standards for this difficult work were set forth by Ekstein and his colleagues (1966, 1971), and by Masterson (1972b, 1974). The role of psychotherapy in a residential setting has been reviewed by Greenwood (1955), Hersov (1974), and Robinson et al. (1957).

During the first stage of treatment (resistance or testing), there is as a rule a rapidly developing psychotic transference with a wide range of maneuvers geared toward concealing the patient's autistic pseudocommunity, which often involves pervasive delusional fantasies. For the therapist, the basic task is the development of mutual trust with the patient in order to render the substantive content and the defensive nature of the pseudocommunity available for understanding and interpretation. Critical here is the patient's growing awareness that his or her intimate revelations will not provoke the therapist's rejection or abandonment, or any other fantasized disasters. In time, the contents of the patient's bizarre inner world are revealed and can be used to deal with the family's dysfunctional pattern of depersonifying communications and interpretations.

For example, after more than a year of therapy, a late-latency-age boy with a borderline disorder was able to reveal his fantasy that his mother had placed a terrifying dragon in his penis during his delivery, thus rendering that organ an awful engine of destruction. The fantasy was in part understood as the boy's defense against the mother who viewed him as an essentially phallic extension of herself and whose intense phallic envy found expression in her own hostile fantasies toward male genitalia. The dragon fantasy also served as a defensive warning to the mother not to attempt to appropriate the penis under penalty of her own destruction.

Another example is the 6-year-old borderline girl who, after six months of full-time residential treatment, was able to share with her therapist her fantasy that she had been magically impregnated with millions of unborn babies ("fee-fees") whom she had to keep inside her body so that they would not perish in the cruel world outside. Her fantasy in part expressed her continued reliance on a massive splitting defense ("millions of 'fee-fees'") through introjective identification, with a marked anal-retentive overlay (". . . got to keep them in me"). The defense was designed to ward off danger of her own birth into a hostile, persecutory, ungiving world (failure of separation-individuation). The mutual clinging between the patient and her depressed, borderline mother was viewed as a manifestation of the little girl's fear that growing up would lead to her own death and her mother's death.

The task of the working-through (or introjective) stage of therapy involves insightful interpretation of the patient's manic defenses, persistent infantile megalomania, and desperate need to cling, remain dependent, and not grow up. Basic here is the splitting defense utilized against the underlying abandonment depression and the associated wish for symbiotic reunion (chapter 2, and Masterson 1975). As these defenses are revealed and interpreted within the therapeutic transference, the patient tackles the unfinished work of separation-individuation, which includes completing the rapprochement subphase and beginning to attain object constancy with its attendant sense of separateness and wholeness (chapters 3 and 5). This work is largely completed during the final, or separation, stage of treatment The successful termination process symbolizes the patient's own growing autonomy.

FAMILY THERAPY. In the vast majority of instances, individual treatment of borderline and narcissistic children and adolescents requires concomitant family therapy to be successful. Family therapy exposes the family's pathogenic nexus of depersonifying communications and relationships so that they may be understood, interpreted, and resolved (Zentner and Aponte 1970, Mandelbaum 1977). The family therapist must consider four basic questions in dealing with borderline and narcissistic syndromes: (1) Is the family's pathology such that the surrogate parental figures will support the identified patient's treatment and participate in it as part of a group process? (2) If so, what is the specific nature of the family's depersonifying nexus of communications and interactions? (3) How do these communications and interactions provide insight into the family patterns of confused, distorted, and obfuscated intergenerational, gender, administrative, and nurturant roles and practices? (4) Once these family patterns are identified, how capable are the patient and other family members of changing them?

The family therapist is called upon to deal with critical ethical and psychodynamic issues. The former issues involve both the contemporary pattern of family life discussed earlier and the specific dysfunctional modus vivendi of each family, which reflects the family's alienation and anomie. In order to prove helpful, the family therapist must be a healthy, encultured individual who is able to serve as a trustworthy object for identification. The therapist must be capable of re-parenting the parents so that they can begin to resolve the pathology that arose from their own dysfunctional parenting. Eventually they will be able to provide healthy care for their own children. The psychopathology of at least three successive familial generations is generally involved in such work.

PSYCHOPHARMACOLOGY. The more recent advances in understanding the etiology and dynamics of borderline and narcissistic disorders have not as yet been fully integrated into child psychiatry and pediatric psychoparmacology texts. Major current volumes (Gittelman-Klein 1975, Werry 1978, White 1977) refer to the many unsettled issues of child psychiatric diagnosis and nosology. Borderline cases tend to be included under the rubrics of childhood psychosis or behavior disorder. The narcissistic conditions, which may be considered higher-level borderline syndromes (Ornstein 1974), are even more poorly understood. As Gittelman-Klein et al. (1978) stated it: "A close relationship between drug and diagnosis is . . . uncommon in pediatric psychopharmacology" (p. 139).

The same difficulties appear in the second and third editions of the Diagnostic and Statistical Manual of Mental Disorders (DSM-II 1968, DSM-III 1980). Borderline and narcissistic disorders of children and adolescents are diagnosed as deficit disorders, pervasive developmental disorders, conduct disorders, eating disorders, anxiety disorders, and the like. Treatment with psychoactive agents is by and large empirical. The following generalizations of DSM-III regarding various types of borderline and narcissistic disorders are worthy of note:

1. Children with minimal brain dysfunction or hyperkinetic reaction tend to respond best to stimulants such as amphetamines and methylphenidate. A minority benefit from the use of phenothiazines.

2. Those patients with separation anxiety disorder respond best to imipramine.

3. Patients with chronic motor-tic disorder (Giles de la Tourette's Syndrome) benefit most from haloperidol.

4. The remainder of borderline and narcissistic children and adolescents fall into a polysymptomatic group. They respond differentially to the range of available antipsychotic and antidepressant medications, including the phenothiazines and haloperidol, the tricyclic antidepressants, and the monoamine oxidase inhibitors. The severely borderline adolescent who manifests episodes of grossly psychotic behavior (alloplastic symptomatology) responds best to the antipsychotic agents thioridazine and chlorpromazine. Patients who show autoplastic symptomatology, such as marked motor inhibition, lethargy, and withdrawal, accompanied by psychotic thinking will respond well to antipsychotic medications.

In selected instances, especially when a primary affective (psychotic depressive, manic-depressive) disorder appears during adolescence, tricyclic antidepressants may prove beneficial. The role of lithium salts in the treatment of borderline and narcissistic children and adolescents is still under investigation.

SUMMARY

Over the last twenty years, the traditional values and family patterns in this country have given way to a contemporary laissez-faire system of child rearing. Confusing, highly subjective values, mutual parent-child alienation, and role blurring have led to increasing numbers of children and adolescents with borderline and narcissistic syndromes. This chapter addresses the poorly understood differential diagnosis of this population and offers a range of treatment modalities corresponding to severity of pathology. Emphasized is the importance of the full cooperation of the patient's family with all therapeutic requirements, which frequently include family therapy. Finally, recent psychopharmacological findings are briefly reviewed.

CHAPTER 12

OBJECT-RELATIONS THEORY
AND PSYCHOTHERAPY

This chapter concentrates on the psychoanalytically based treatment applications of object-relations theory to self-disordered patients. Freud's pivotal role as "the first object-relations theorist" and later modifications of his drive-reduction theory are discussed. Object-relations theory is particularly indebted to Freud's (1905, 1915a) differentiation of instinctual aim and instinctual object. Based on his own seminal "Project" (1895), Freud originally conceptualized instinct theory in terms of what latter-day psychologists would term drive-reduction; instinctual aim was accordingly viewed as minimizing the "quantity" of nervous excitation (Freud's somewhat enigmatic "Q"), of "working toward a yield of pleasure" and minimizing unpleasure in accordance with the demands of the pleasure principle (Freud 1911a). But pristine psychoanalytic drive-reduction theory could not account for such diverse phenomena as the perseverative nature of children's play, the so-called traumatic neuroses of war, the characteristics of those individuals "wrecked by success" (Freud 1916), the phenomenon of masochism and, of course, the basis and nature of therapeutic transference; these phenomena led Freud (1920) "beyond the pleasure principle," as he postulated the operation of an even more fundamental characteristic of the psychic apparatus—the repetition-compulsion.

In formulating the concept of the *object* as the instrumentality by and through which the *aim* of an instinct (drive) is achieved, Freud became, in effect, the first object-relations theorist. That his particular biological, Helmholtzian bent caused him to emphasize instinctual aim over instinctual object is certainly not surprising. Nor is it surprising that, in reversing that emphasis and asserting the primacy of object over aim, object-relations theorists should attempt to eschew Freud's biological underpinnings, thereby creating a personology devoid of neurology (chapter 4, and Guntrip 1961, 1968, 1971).

The classical psychoanalytic emphasis on aim over object relates in part to the particular nature of the close-knit Victorian family (Woodward and Mark 1978), whose disturbed members were the first analysands, and in part to the fact that psycho-analytic theory and technique originally evolved from the retro-spective analysis of adult cases. In contrast to today's so-called liberated family structure and child-rearing practices, the fin de siècle European ménage, with its relatively clear-cut age, gender, and generational distinctions, functioned on the basis of the inhibition, renunciation, and displacement of instinctual needs; strict control was considered a prerequisite for the grow-ing child's progressive socialization (Freud 1930). The early psychoanalytic emphasis on the Oedipus complex and its asso-ciated triadic-sexual issues as etiologic for the infantile neurosis and later neuroses evolved from observing the familial hothouse atmosphere, which was governed by guilt over unexpressed instinctual urges. Emergent from such repressive circumstances, the adults whom Freud and his colleagues psychoanalyzed dis-played psychopathology that was originally viewed in terms of unrequited and "repressed" libidinal (sexual) needs and regres-sive, desexualized efforts at mastery (anal defenses) of these needs. As a result, the depth and pervasiveness of many of these early patients' illnesses were underestimated, as the famous cases of Anna O., Dora, the Wolf Man, and the Rat Man amply illustrate.

As Freud's "Project" established psychoanalysis essentially as a drive-reduction theory, it likewise established it as a self-as-process theory, as contrasted with a self-as-object theory (chapter 4, and Rinsley 1962). Basic to the self-as-process view is the notion of endopsychic structures, notably the ego, as impersonal *systems* or *mechanisms* remote from or devoid of direct, intimate, subjective apprehension and experience. Perhaps the most comprehensive statement concerning human personality as a congeries of mechanisms or systems found expression in the so-called American school of ego psychology, epitomized in the writings of Heinz Hartmann (1964) and his associates, who viewed their approach as capable of forging scientific links with nonanalytic "academic" psychology."* American ego psychologists spoke of a *conflict-free ego sphere*, of *ego apparatus*, of *primary* and *secondary autonomy*, and of *neutralized* and *unneutralized drive energies* in an essentially impersonal fashion. Its classical adherents were wont to emphasize the importance of strictly observed, noninterventive analytic technique (Arlow and Brenner 1964, Boyer and Giovacchini 1967).

The origins and development of much of contemporary object-relations theory may be traced to the writings of a small number of highly original investigators beginning with Melanie Klein who, despite admitted theoretical shortcomings (Glover 1945), drew exceedingly close to the inner worlds of her young patients. Federn (1952), who studied perception and attempted to analyze schizophrenics, viewed the ego as no mere abstraction, but rather, as directly accessible to experience. Sullivan (1953, 1962) wrote of "fantastic personifications." And Edith Jacobson's contributions to the metapsychology of (endopsychic) representations (1954a,b,c, 1957, 1964, 1971) further opened the door to a view of personality that was at considerable variance with the

---

*A comprehensive statement of the psychoanalytic systems concept of the human personality is represented in the 1963 work, *The Vital Balance*, by Menninger, Mayman, and Pruyser.

impersonal systems, or self-as-process, view. Interestingly, the academic psychologists called this approach "self-as-object!" In its latter-day form, it comprises an amalgam of the "pure gold" of psychoanalysis and what Eissler (1953, 1958) has termed "parameters," that is, disciplined departures from the strict application of the basic rule (including the rule of abstinence), which is almost impossible for children, borderline patients, and psychotics to observe. Indeed, as the results of the Menninger Foundation Psychotherapy Research Project indicate (Kernberg 1972b) and as Kernberg has affirmed (1975), the borderline patient responds best to therapeutic technique that judiciously combines both support and exploration (uncovering). Support parameters thus help strengthen the patient's ego for the work of analysis. In Simmel's (1929) original concept of the psycho-analytic sanitarium, he expresses the concept of support param-eters for the psychoanalytic treatment of patients who are unable to withstand the rigors of outpatient treatment (Rinsley 1963).* Federn had articulated it by introducing a female (= maternal) colleague into his analyses of schizophrenics; Winnicott's (1950–55, 1960) concept of the "good enough" mother and environment, and Modell's (1968, 1975) concept of the "holding" environment (Kahn 1963) are basic to it.

Freud's formulation of the concept of the repetition-compulsion to account for clinical phenomena that were inexplicable in terms of drive-reduction represented a profound insight. His under-standing of it was ultimately based on the death instinct, which was itself explicable in terms of innate human aggression. Of course, the concept of the repetition-compulsion, of the over-determined tendency to recapitulate, and hence to re-experience, past events, especially those of a traumatic nature, represents an effort to understand the present in terms of the past while retaining the notion of the primacy of instinctual aim over

---

*It should be noted that Kernberg's view of the use of support parameters (1980d) is closely akin to Simmel's in that he relies on the wider social, including hospital, environment for their application and eschews supportive maneuvers within therapeutic hours.

instinctual object. Whether expressed in autoplastic or alloplastic symptoms or behavior, the repetition-compulsion represents an effort to master trauma, to bind its associated dysphoria, and to work it through; it represents an attempt to heal a narcissistic wound or, in other words, to *mourn*. And what is thus mourned? The answer, so eloquently stated in "Mourning and Melancholia" (Freud 1917b), is *object loss*.

When Melanie Klein or Ronald Fairbairn tells us that object assumes primacy over aim, they tell us that it is object relationship that counts, rather than the mere reduction of instinctual tension or the "yield of pleasure" for which the ego works (Freud, 1911a). In object-relations terms, the repetition-compulsion recapitulates *relationship*; thus the phenomena that originally puzzled Freud become understandable in terms of the need to recapture or re-experience relationship rather than merely to feel good.*

When Giovacchini (1979) writes that he doubts that he has ever seen a neurotic individual in analysis or treatment, he reminds us that our psychotherapeutic practices appear to be preponderantly, if not exclusively, devoted to patients whose developmental fixations are of a pre-Oedipal nature. If the phrases *narcissistic wound (trauma)* and *object loss* thus refer to pre-Oedipal events and experiences, then we must ask what those events and experiences are. Again, if Oedipal-triadic determinants of later psychopathology are indeed pathogenic epiphenomena engrafted, as it were, on prior traumas, then what constitutes the latter and how do they come to be expressed in later symptomatology? And finally, how can object-relations theory help us understand them?

Our psychotic, borderline, and narcissistic patients seem to be telling us that something happened, or did not happen, in their early infancy that induced what Balint (1968) has termed a

---

*Thus the masochist, who seeks the experience of pain, counterphobically courts discomfort because it in effect guarantees that some form of relationship is possible, that one has not been abandoned and will indeed survive, albeit uncomfortably.

basic fault; this basic fault has rendered them confused, feeling both impotent and grandiose, and prone to regressive perceptual, cognitive, and affective decomposition or fragmentation. They are fearful that their aggressive and libidinal-affiliative instinctual urges will destroy them or others, or at least will preclude relationships, leaving them bereft, rejected, and abandoned. For them, Oedipal-incestuous rivalries constitute symptomatic luxuries when self-survival is the fundamental issue. They are, indeed, enigmas to themselves and others. The higher-level narcissists (narcissistic personalities) emerge either as inveterate misery- and injustice-collecting masochists or else as detached, loveless tyrants whose families and associates exist for their greater glory as they go on to ever-greater achievements at the frightful expense of those who attempt to care for them (Bursten 1978). Recent clinical investigation indicates that these patients have a common endopsychic structure that places them in the diagnostic-developmental continuum or spectrum known as *disorders of the self* (Kohut 1971, 1977, Ornstein 1974, Rinsley 1980a and chapter 9).

To understand this endopsychic structure, it is necessary to consider the nature of the primal trauma that underlies it. When this is done, then two early infantile phenomena come immediately to mind, viz., the young infant's primitive "all good"-"all bad" perceptual and responsive organization and his enormous vulnerability to those pervasively disruptive, mass-reflexive "affecto-motor storms" that ultimately can only be put to rest through the ministration of a "good enough" mothering figure (Winnicott 1960).

In accordance with the pleasure principle, the infant will "take in" (accept) a "good" food item, such as a dilute sugar solution placed on his tongue, and will "spit out" (reject) a "bad" food item, such as a dilute acetic acid solution placed on his tongue. Acceptance of a good food item signifies its incorporation and ensuing physico-chemical assimilation accompanied by the laying-down of a good (positively valent) memory trace. Likewise, rejection of a bad food item is accompanied by the laying-down of a bad (negatively valent) memory trace.* A preponderance of bad food items is thus seen to result in the build-up of an ever-expanding repository of negatively valent memory traces. These, in turn, fail to damp down the infant's indigenous visceral-autonomic lability, which is episodically expressed in the affecto-motor discharges, resulting in (1) an ongoing or unremitting condition of heightened irritability and tension, and (2) a repository of negative memory traces that progressively consolidate into what will later become a negative identity. These are, of course, the pathological effects of the "bad breast" or, more accurately, the bad breast part-object. As Fairbairn (1954, 1963) has pointed out, this bad breast part-object (what he calls the *rejected object*) undergoes powerful introjection and subsequent splitting (what he calls the *split internalized bad object*); the results of this splitting are Fairbairn's *exciting object* (E.O.) and *rejecting object* (R.O.) (see chapters 4 and 14), which Masterson and I (chapter 2) have termed, respectively, the *rewarding* part-object-representation or part-object image and the *rejecting (withdrawing) part-object-representation* or *part-object image*. From the side of the infant, as it were, are generated two corresponding part-self representations or part-self images, respectively termed by Fairbairn the *libidinal ego* (L.E.) and the *Anti-libidinal ego* (Anti-L.E.), corresponding to Masterson's and my (1975) respective *rewarding* and *rejecting (withdrawing) part-self representations* or *part-self images*; these come into respective association or affiliation with the two corresponding part-object representations, thereby generating two "alliances," as it were, namely the E.O.-L.E. and the R.O.-Anti-L.E.

The *anlage* of the *good breast part-object* (good object), without which the infant's survival would be impossible, likewise undergoes internalization; Fairbairn terms this the *ideal object* (I.O.) which comes to form an "alliance" with what he terms the

---

*It should be remembered that "good" milk may be rendered "bad" if the mother proffers it to the infant with ambivalent, disruptive, or rejecting attitudes and feelings, which may be expressed through muscular tension, inappropriate holding of the infant, and other somatic concomitants of disturbed nurturing.

central ego (C.E.) from the side of the infant. There thus comes into existence a complex endopsychic structure comprised of three "alliances," as it were: the "good" or "accepted" I.O.-C.E. and the "bad" or "rejected" dyadic E.O.-L.E. and R.O.-Anti-L.E. The latter two are maintained apart through the overdetermined operation of the splitting defense and both are, in turn, split from the I.O.-C.E. What thus began as an expression of the reflexive swallowing or spitting out of proffered food becomes imbued with symbolic-representational significance and passes over into a true defense (chapter 4).* Unless otherwise influenced by the intervention of restitutive mothering or, lacking that, by appropriate treatment provided at a later time, there evolves in the growing child an ensuing "all good" vs. "all bad" world view, a symptomatic hallmark of the self-disordered (psychotic, borderline, narcissistic) individual (Ornstein 1974, Rinsley 1980a, 1980b, 1981).

For object-relations theory to have clinical significance and application, however, it needs to be understood in a developmental context. That context is, of course, provided by classical psychosexual stage theory (Abraham 1924, Fenichel 1945), carried to its highest point of development in those contributions of Margaret Mahler and her colleagues (Mahler et al. 1975) devoted to symbiosis and individuation. The interdigitation of object-relations and Mahlerian developmental phase concepts allows for a coherent, developmentally based diagnostic nosology of much greater validity than the one provided by pristine psychosexual stage theory. In addition, it provides the necessary ingredients for a rational approach to psychoanalytic treatment, particularly treatment of the major psychoses and personality (characterologic) disorders, or disorders of the self (Kohut 1971). Indeed, it was Mahler herself (1971) who speculated that borderline phenomena were expressions of failure of separation-individuation, an insight that was to provide the impetus for

---

*For a further, evaluative discussion of these "alliances," see Kernberg (1980b).

Masterson's and my later publications on that subject (chapters 2, 4, 5, and 11, as well as Masterson 1974, 1975, 1976, Rinsley 1980a,b).

The 1975 Masterson-Rinsley paper (see chapter 2) may be said to have rediscovered Fairbairn's split internalized bad object and recognized it as basic to the developmental arrest and ensuing symptomatology of borderline adolescents and adults. In that paper, as well as in its more detailed successors, we could confirm Mahler's (1971) speculations as we antedated the developmental arrest or fixation that underlies borderline personality disorder to the *rapprochement subphase of separation-individuation* (occurring at 16 to 26 months of age). Our inferences were based upon Masterson's and my analytic treatment of both inpatient and outpatient borderline ("symbiotic") adolescents and their families, my own supervisory work in the treatment of similar preadolescents and their families, and my observational study of psychotic and borderline mothers and their preschool children, carried out in the Child Development Center of the Children's Section of Topeka State Hospital between 1970 and 1975.

The endopsychic structure, analogous to Fairbairn's E.O.-L.E. and R.O.-Anti-L.E. alliances, which Masterson and I originally described (chapter 2), is known as the *split object-relations unit* (SORU) of the borderline; it comprises two representational-affect complexes, as described earlier by Kernberg (1966). It originates in the push-pull mother-infant relationship, prominent during the rapprochement subphase of separation-individuation, in which the mother rewards the infant for dependency (hence, for inadequacy) and withdraws from or rejects him in the wake of his efforts toward growth, thereby fixating him at the phase of partial self-object differentiation. The infant's recurrent and resurgent symbiotic needs for refusion or reunion, coexisting with his chronic feelings of frustration, rage, and impotency, constitute what Masterson and I have termed *abandonment depression*. The structure of the SORU comprises the introjective representational precipitates of this twin theme and is basic to the internal object relations and symptomatology of the borderline personality; the SORU is described in detail in chapters 2 and 3.

It is evident that the repetitive self-injurious, self-defeating, essentially masochistic behavior of these self-disordered individuals can only be adequately understood in terms of the primacy of the pathogenic maternal object tie and not in terms of any postulated instinctual aim. When we carefully examine both the higher-level narcissistic personality and the regressed, fragmented psychotic, we discover the presence of a basically similar endopsychic structure. As Ornstein (1974) has clearly pointed out and I have elsewhere affirmed (Rinsley 1980a and chapters 3 and 9), the diagnostic groups of the major psychoses, the borderline disorders, and the narcissistic personalities may be aligned along a continuum based on degree of regressive "fragmentability" of archaic internal self-objects. The persistence of self-objects, of course, bespeaks failure of self-object differentiation and desymbiotization, and the persistence of impaired object constancy (Fraiberg 1969), part-object relations, and the inability to mourn (chapter 5).

APPLICATIONS TO PSYCHOTHERAPY

Fundamental to the practice and goals of psychotherapy is the generation of the therapeutic alliance. The more expeditiously this is accomplished, the more effective the treatment will be. This means, among other things, facilitating the positive transference in order to optimize the self-disordered patient's limited capacity to trust the therapist, and hence, to generate what Goldstein (1959) termed "communion" with him. As Kernberg (1975) has aptly noted, with borderline patients the therapist must employ skillful confrontation, clarification, and, when feasible, interpretation of the negative transference. Masterson and I (chapters 2 and 5, as well as Masterson 1976) describe this approach in terms of relatively early confrontation and clarification of the deleterious nature of the patient's symptomatic behavior, which paves the way for developing insight into the patient's SORU. One also begins psychotherapy with all self-disordered patients with the awareness that they suffer from a relative deficiency of "good internal objects," and hence, of the libidinal energy normally associated with these objects (Federn 1952, Rinsley 1968). Finally, therapeutic approach and technique should be flexibly based on the patient's variable—and often profound—need for support parameters (v. inf.).

EMOTIONAL LABILITY AND UNPREDICTABILITY. With the possible exception of the higher-level narcissistic personality, self-disordered patients often puzzle and confuse their therapists with an array of polar-opposite and rapidly alternating and fluctuating emotions; their often kaleidoscopic "psychotic" transferences readily convey their redoubtable reliance on projective-introjective defenses, epitomized in the "two D's"—Deification and Devaluation. Their complaints of feeling "up-tight," "mixed-up," "a mess," "in total confusion," and the like reflect an ongoing condition of heightened inner tension (anxiety); this condition is readily traced to the persistent affecto-motor storms of the young infant that were never adequately put to rest by a "good enough" mother, which produced a chronic state of visceral-autonomic hyperirritability in the infant. This engendered a chronic state of overalert watchfulness reflected in a persistent "scanning" function, and expressed as a seemingly uncanny ability to intuit the unconscious or unexpressed motives of others, including those of the therapist (chapter 6, and Krohn 1974).

One patient, a 31-year-old borderline man, often prefaced his replies to his therapist's questions with, "Ummm . . . I guess you want me to say . . ." This was most evident when he was pathologically idealizing the therapist while simultaneously viewing himself as the therapist's puppet. Repeated confrontation finally evoked the interpretable fact that, as a child, the patient had concluded that he could only repeat the words and ideas expressed by his sadistic adoptive father and that he had "no right" to those of his own.

Persistent proneness to affecto-motor turmoil finds frequent expression in these patients' problems with sphincter zone specificity, conveyed in polymorphous-perverse sexuality (Kut Rosenfeld and Sprince 1963). Their sexual behavior, including their genital sexuality, is often in the service of primitive pre-Oedipal needs for nurturant warmth and closeness. They will "purchase" the latter at the expense of mature genital relations, sometimes by means of homosexual perversity and other primitively overdetermined sexual actions.

Another patient, a 39-year-old unmarried professional woman, could readily admit that her heterosexual promiscuity served the purpose of temporarily alleviating her chronic, intense feelings of loneliness. Not surprisingly, she was anorgastic and in fact found sexual intercourse to be disgusting, occasionally leading to nausea. With arresting pseudoinsight she commented, "It's like vomiting up my mother!"

The patient often experiences significant relief, accompanied by reinforcement of the positive transference, when the therapist conveys his awareness of the patient's affecto-motor turmoil—that is, the patient's simultaneous mistrust and highly overdetermined, often frightening need for closeness. Following one such communication by the therapist, a middle-aged narcissistic patient replied, "Well . . . I guess it's any port in a storm" (sic).

OBJECT INCONSTANCY AND OBJECT IMPERMANENCY. Adler (1979, 1981) has recently re-emphasized these exceptionally important characteristics of self-disordered patients. Among psychotics and severe borderline cases, failure of evocative memory or recall finds expression in the patient's inability to generate and maintain a stable inner image of the therapist between therapeutic hours (object impermanency); viewed as a defense, it conveys the patient's need to scotomatize or negatively hallucinate the therapist. In higher-level self-disordered patients, including the more purely narcissistic personalities, evocative recall of the therapist's image remains intact, but neither the image nor the actual therapist is consistently invested ("cathected"), which is reflected in the undercurrent of mistrust and suspicion found in these patients (object inconstancy) (chapter 8).

The disruptive significance of object impermanency and object inconstancy in the psychotherapeutic process cannot be overestimated, as it creates numerous peculiar and disturbing varieties of "acting in" and "acting out."

One example is a 27-year-old borderline man who told his therapist, "When you're gone I feel I hate you!" This was followed by a spate of obscene invectives directed at the therapist. When the therapist then confronted the patient's inability to imagine or visualize the therapist in the latter's absence, the patient replied, "Yeah, that's right, and I have to do a lot of things to get in trouble so you'll see me . . ." This statement conveys the disarming pseudoinsight that such self-disordered individuals often display; it likewise conveys failure of self-object (in this case, patient-therapist) differentiation, as expressed by the patient's use of the word "see," which is representative of his projection of scoptophilic partial aims into the therapist.

With such patients, I attempt judiciously to introduce a parameter to facilitate the stabilization of my self-image. First, I direct the patient to close his eyes and picture me "inside," and then to open them and actually see me; next I direct the patient to "make me go away" by closing his eyes again and, when that has been accomplished, to reopen his eyes and look at me again. It is indeed impressive how many of these patients can achieve this with a little practice; further, they experience amazement and relief when they realize that the therapist recognizes and understands their problem. An additional advantage of this particular parameter is its clearly regressive and playful character. As one patient stated, ". . . we used to do this when we were kids . . . you know, open and close your eyes to see if the other kid's really there . . . it was lots of fun only it made me scared when I couldn't get the picture."

FANTASY DEFICIENCY. The self-disordered patient's deficiency both in the amount of fantasy he is able to generate and in his adaptive and creative use of that fantasy has a significant impact on his therapy. Often, if not invariably, the patient's self-depreciative use of such terms as "empty," "hopeless," "meaningless," "confused," "fake," "façade," and the like conveys a self-experience of impoverished inner content that reflects the fantasy-deficient condition. The relationship between waking fantasy ("daydreams") and nocturnal dreaming is underscored by the fact that many of these patients report deficiencies in both; thus, they are unable to utilize fantasy to plan and set realistic goals; nor can they utilize the nocturnal dream to work through unconscious conflict and integrate it with the here-and-now represented in the day residues (chapter 8).

The fantasy deficiency of self-disordered patients is, of course, related to their impaired object permanency and object constancy. As noted, the self-depreciative terms they employ to convey this endopsychic state reflect their inability to summon up "good" mental images or representations. The fantasy deficiency is also related to developmental arrest involving pathological persistence of the transitional object and mode of experience (Modell 1968, Winnicott 1951), reflecting fixation at the level of infantile grandiosity and, of course, of part-object relations.

The self-disordered patient's well-known feeling of "entitlement" reflects the pathological persistence of infantile-grandiosity (infantile-megalomania) seemingly paradoxically coexisting with pervasive feelings of impotency, worthlessness, and hopelessness. Magical expectations of cure reflect profound passive-anaclitic (symbiotic) needs that, in turn, evoke the patient's anxiety, leading to devaluing projective identifications with the therapist and to related angry demands on the therapist.

The therapist's ability to recognize and deal sensitively with the patient's fantasy deficiency and, ultimately, with the patient's fantasies as they are elaborated in the therapeutic transference, constitutes one of the essentials of treatment. The apprehensions of self-disordered patients regarding their evolving fantasies, or their lack of fantasy, are found to center on the following: *any* fantasy is per se dangerous to one's self and to others, most notably to the therapist; having fantasies implies that one is "crazy"; fantasies are secrets which the therapist will steal or otherwise take away (the so-called primal exchange: Modell 1971); fantasies must be acted on and out; and masturbatory and other sexual fantasies, again in relation to the therapist, are particularly fearsome and dangerous. Experience amply demonstrates that as the patient's image of the therapist becomes evocably stabilized and reliable, that is, as the therapeutic alliance becomes strengthened, the patient's "fantasy work" proceeds apace. The major caveat, of course, has to do with the therapist's own developed capacity for such work within the countertransference, such that both he and the patient come to develop a genuine interest and belief in the understandability and interpretability of the patient's evolving and increasingly freely communicated fantasy in the therapeutic hours.

A highly intelligent 15-year-old borderline adolescent girl in full-time residential treatment (*P*) put it succinctly to her male therapist (*T*):

T: I know it's hard to tell me what you think about, or daydream or even fantasize. . . .
P: Yup . . . I'm afraid to.
T: Why is that?
P: Well, because if I tell you about those things you'll have them and I won't have them any more.
T: Uh, uh . . . if you tell me, then you'll have them and I'll have them . . . we'll both have them.
P: Yipe! I never thought of that!

BASIC FAULT. This phrase, as used by Balint (1968), refers to the self-disordered individual's impairment of primary and secondary narcissism and of (internal) object relations based upon defective early mother-infant bonding. In Federn's terms (1952), it refers to defective medial ego feeling, or "prere-flective narcissism," which lies close to the core of the self. It is experienced and conveyed in the patient's abiding feeling that in some indefinable way he is flawed, defective, imperfect, or damaged, that there has long been "something wrong" or "something missing." The phrases "not all there" and "not playing with a full deck" convey this chronic, disquieting self-perception. Metaphorically, basic fault means "I am (feel) bad." In Fairbairn's terms, it reflects ongoing sadistic assaults by the R.O.–Anti-L.E. alliance (Fairbairn's primitive superego) against the L.E.; in Masterson's and my terms it reflects the untrammeled operation of the rejecting (withdrawing) SORU part-unit (i.e., the "alliance" between the rejecting [withdrawing] part-object-image or part-object-representation and the rejecting [withdraw-ing] part-self-image or part-self-representation, with their as-sociated *abandonment depression*).

The self-disordered patient attempts to "make good" this perceived self-defect, in part by means of the welter of approach-avoidance symptomatology he displays, particularly in the thera-peutic transference. The higher-level narcissistic patient usually denies the perceived self-defect; he may project it onto others, viewing them as incompetent and himself as "the greatest"; or, as Bursten (1978) has noted, he may deny it by means of masochistic, injustice-collecting self-aggrandizement.

A 25-year-old divorced male graduate student said, "I never felt right about myself . . . there was always something vaguely wrong . . . missing, and I could never figure out what it was."

The as-if features that the basic fault imparts to the sympto-matology and object relationships of the self-disordered patient are succinctly encompassed in Adler's (1981) comment, "Kohut describes the sense of inner incompleteness that temporarily disappears within a therapeutic relationship when the therapist performs needed functions that the patient does not possess at that moment." When this occurs, the patient temporarily "feels good" and when, at significant therapeutic junctures, it does not, he "feels bad," with ensuing reactivation of affecto-motor turmoil, and hence, of feelings of abandonment, at which times the patient will lash out at the therapist or indulge in self-defeating and self-injurious behavior in a magical attempt to "punish" the therapist and to force him to banish the "bad" feelings.

The case vignette of the 27-year-old borderline woman reported by Masterson and myself (chapter 2, pp. 46–49) illustrates how the patient's perception of abandonment by the therapist provoked symptomatic behavior, especially as therapeutic progress reactivated her fear of loss of the therapist.

Again, judicious confrontation, clarification, and, when possible, interpretation of the components of the SORU as they come to be expressed in the patient's symptomatic communications and behavior during therapeutic hours, as well as in his symptomatic behavior outside them, will expose the pathogenesis of the basic fault.

A 33-year-old borderline man with a history of alcoholism and illicit drug usage told the therapist, "whenever I'd get feisty my mother would always shove food in my mouth . . . lots of times I didn't want it and I'd almost puke but I was afraid she'd hate me or hit me if I didn't eat when she wanted me to . . . she fed me to shut me up. . . . "After over 100 hours of therapy, the patient could say, "I can see that being 'bad' got me food so eating kept me from 'being bad' . . . that's why I used to drink or get stoned . . . to not feel bad . . ." After the therapist asked, "And what else?" the patient replied, "to keep her from leaving me."

LIMITS AND CONTROLS. No discussion of the psychotherapy of the self-disordered patient would be complete without reference to the patient's need for externally imposed limits or controls. A partial exception is the higher-level narcissistic personality, for whom such a need may be rather less important during the course of therapy.

My own experience with these patients, including adolescents and adults, amply underscores their need to have limits set for them relatively early. Among other things, this means that the psychotherapist should never acquiesce in, much less promote, the patient's self-injurious acting-in and acting-out; nor should the therapist assume a permissive or laissez-faire attitude toward symptomatic behavior that the patient invariably, if not admittedly, perceives is harmful to himself. In some cases, this limit setting assumes the form of a direct command, such as to cease all alcohol intake, drug use, or perverse sexual activities; in other cases, it is expressed as disapproval of the deleterious symptomatic act or behavior communicated in the context of acceptance both of the patient as a whole, and of the *need* that underlies the particular act or behavior.

The rule of abstinence plays a significant role in the psychoanalytic treatment of self-disordered patients, much as it does in the case of less seriously disturbed individuals, by promoting the exposure, understanding, and interpretation of the "underlying material" that the symptomatology symbolically conveys and maintains apart from the patient's conscious awareness.* For these patients, since absence of disagreement means agreement, therapeutic failure or needless prolongation of treatment may result when reliance is placed on "strict" analytic technique.

It is amazing how latter-day psychoanalysts and other analytically trained and sophisticated therapists "permit" their patients all varieties of "acting out," including marriages, divorces, and changes in occupation and domicile location, without dealing

---

*As Eissler (1958) has reminded us, the "rule of abstinence" originally referred to the requirement that the analyst refrain from gratifying the patient's wishes and needs within analytic hours. As used here in its more extended sense, it applies to symptomatic behavior that subserves secondary gain *both within and outside therapeutic hours.*

with the enormous resistances they convey. In this connection, one is reminded of the aphorism attributed to Freud, to wit, that "psychoanalysis cannot compete with sex."

SOME FURTHER CONSIDERATIONS OF THERAPEUTIC TECHNIQUE

Basing his conclusions on his own experience as a psychoanalytic clinician, as well as on the findings of the Menninger Foundation Psychotherapy Research Project, Kernberg (1972b, 1975) has affirmed that optimal psychotherapeutic technique with borderline patients combines both exploration (uncovering, transference interpretation) and support.* His diagnostic "structural interview" focuses on the use of confrontation and clarification to generate "tension" and to provoke responses that provide insight into the patient's defenses, identity conflicts, and degree of reality-testing.

In a number of respects, the therapeutic technique that Masterson and I have recommended is similar. Its major focus, moreover, is on the confrontation, clarification, and interpretation of the SORU, with the aim of facilitating the patient's insight into it, as well as on promoting the development of the therapeutic alliance ("healthy object-relations unit") in the therapeutic transference. When successful, this approach uncovers the original mother-infant push-pull relationship that is etiologic for the self-disordered patient's pathological internal object relations and associated symptomatology.

Kohut's (1971, 1977) treatment of higher-level narcissistic patients, whom he differentiates from borderline patients, focuses on his now well-known *grandiose self* and *idealized parental*

---

*To be sure, Kernberg (1980d) avoids the direct use of support parameters within the therapeutic hours; instead, he relies on them being provided "from the outside," including, for example, the hospital environment and associated activities.

image as these come to be expressed within the so-called mirroring transference. His concept of the *self-object* as characteristic of psychotic, borderline, and narcissistic personalities reflects their impaired self-object differentiation (Ornstein 1974, Rinsley 1980a and chapter 9), with the added understanding that the self-objects of the narcissistic personality are relatively stable, that is, resistant to regressive fragmentation, and hence, to repersonification or reanimation (''demetabolization'': Kernberg 1966). My own clinical experience with narcissistic patients confirms both the relative stability of their self-objects and the etiologic importance of the SORU for their symptomatology. The relatively greater stability of the self-objects in such patients accounts for their therapeutic responsiveness to a ''stricter'' analytic technique than borderline and more seriously disorganized patients can tolerate.

SUMMARY

Object-relations concepts are finding increasing application in psychoanalytic and dynamic psychotherapeutic practice in the wake of the increased numbers of pre-Oedipally fixated, self-disordered patients who find their way into the consulting room, psychiatric hospital, or residential treatment facility. In extending and deepening classical psychoanalytic metapsychology, object-relations theory widens the range of clinical therapeutic technique while remaining solidly within the framework of psychoanalysis, which is ultimately the most thoroughgoing theory of personality and of psychopathology that has yet been developed.

CHAPTER 13

THE
MASTERSON-RINSLEY CONCEPT
AND BEYOND

This chapter reconsiders the evolution and further implications of the 1975 Masterson-Rinsley paper (and its revised
[1980] version—see chapter 2) devoted to the development and
endopsychic structure of borderline psychopathology. This
paper, which has emerged as a not insubstantial contribution to
the burgeoning literature on borderline and related "spectrum"
disorders (chapter 9, Stone 1980), represented the conver-
gence of the work of two clinician-investigators who had reached
remarkably similar conclusions independently and in different
clinical settings. From both a personal and a scientific point of
view, Masterson and I felt encouraged by our respective vali-
dation and confirmation of each other's work. It is the aim of
this chapter to place that work in historical perspective and to
consider both its relationship to the ever-expanding literature on
borderline psychopathology and its relevance for the psychoses
and other personality-characterologic pathology among preadults
and adults.

I shall begin by looking back to the 1950s, that "quiet"
decade when psychoanalysis reached the apex of its influence on
American psychiatry. As is well known, psychoanalytic clinicians
had come to view the adolescent years as a period of storm and

stress, of proneness to what Erikson (1963) was to call *identity diffusion*, such that the adolescent, buffeted by protean emotional fluctuations and ever-susceptible to symptomatic and genetic-dynamic regression, was deemed a poor candidate for psychoanalytic treatment. Thus the adolescent's purportedly "weak" ego was cited as the basis for his unanalyzability, while his unanalyzability was cited as evidence of his ego weakness (Rinsley 1965). This rather pejorative view of the adolescent experience, termed the *turmoil school* or *view*, has long since been discredited in the wake of numerous studies pointing to the conclusion that the "normal," modal, or psychologically healthy adolescent is not turmoil-ridden and, conversely, that the turmoil-ridden adolescent is neither "normal," modal, nor psychologically healthy (Rinsley 1972).

One of these studies was the important Symptomatic Adolescent Research Project conducted by Masterson and his colleagues at the Cornell University Medical College-New York Hospital (Masterson 1967a,b, 1968, Masterson et al. 1963, 1966, Masterson and Washburne 1966). It had become abundantly evident to Masterson that the so-called symptomatic adolescents he saw and studied were not merely passing through some sort of time-limited, phasic "adjustment reaction"; rather, they were suffering from serious psychopathology and "they didn't grow out of it."

When I came upon Masterson's writings in the 1960s, I had already reached essentially the same conclusion regarding the psychopathology of adolescents disturbed enough to require inpatient treatment (Rinsley 1963, 1965, 1967a,b). It was also evident that Masterson's expert clinical application of the inpatient or residential milieu closely resembled both Hendrickson's inpatient treatment of seriously disturbed adolescents in Ann Arbor (Hendrickson 1957, Hendrickson and Holmes 1959, Hendrickson et al. 1959) and my own inpatient treatment in Topeka. All three of us emphasized the importance of controlling symptomatic behavior by employing firm limit setting as soon as the adolescent was admitted into residence. By the same token, we all emphasized the totality of the milieu per se as the prime instrumentality of treatment, utilizing the gamut of individual, group, family, occupational, recreational, and educational modalities in accordance with the individualized treatment plan. The general assumption underlying such an approach was that the seriously disturbed adolescent emerged from a pathogenic, dysfunctional family nexus, so that the intensive, interpretive, and comprehensive treatment of the "identified" patient necessarily involved efforts to restructure the wider familial context in the direction of healthy communications, interactions, and relationships. It was essential that the patient be removed from the dysfunctional family environment by means of inpatient or residential admission; then he had to be provided with both "ego support" and "ego interpretation" (Noshpitz 1962). Only in this way could the analysis of the patient's individual psychopathology and the family's dysfunctionality be undertaken. The attempt to provide a comprehensive diagnostic and therapeutic milieu was, of course, not novel; the specific features of Masterson's and my approaches bore a percipient relationship to the pioneering work of such clinicians as Noshpitz (1962), Bettelheim (Bettelheim and Sylvester 1952), and Redl (Redl 1959, Redl and Wineman 1951, 1952). Common to all of them is the concept of the "good enough" or "holding" environment (Modell 1968, Winnicott 1950–55) as applicable within the inpatient or residential setting; that is, for such seriously ill adolescents, appropriate re-parenting *must* accompany analytic treatment—neither element will be optimally effective without the other (Rinsley 1974a, 1980b).

THE RESIDENTIAL PROCESS

However dysfunctional the adolescent's family nexus has been, his removal from it and admission into full-time residence is invariably a traumatic affair. A major component of the patient's and the family's response to the separation is the appearance of a variety of resistances to the new milieu; these resistances comprise an often strenuous and/or protracted attempt to deny the fact and impact of the separation, and thereby to deny and undo the trauma associated with it. Both the patient's and the parents' patterns of resistance assume particular forms or manifestations, as detailed in two early papers I co-authored with Donald Hall and George Inge, respectively (Rinsley and Hall 1962, Rinsley and Inge 1961), and as further developed in several later publications (Rinsley 1968, 1974a,b 1980b).

Our studies of the resistance to staff members as well as to physical features of the treatment, and of the particular, collusive parent-child interactions that prolonged such resistance, led to an understanding of resistance behaviors as manifestations of pre-Oedipal transference. Using the work of Stanton and Schwartz (1954) and, in modified fashion, William Menninger (1936a,b, 1937, 1939), as a springboard, we applied the psychoanalytic concepts of transference and resistance to and within the wider residential context. The clinical problem was to minimize or eliminate the transference-derived resistances in order to motivate the patient and the family to "engage with" the staff and the milieu, to "get them into treatment" as expeditiously and effectively as possible. Only when this had occurred in significant measure could the "identified" patient and the family begin to make lasting, healthy (inner) personality, group-communicative, and group-relationship changes. The pre-Oedipal nature of such families' transference-resistance paradigms was consistent with the increasing evidence that adolescents who needed full-time residential treatment harbored major psychopathology. Careful diagnostic study of the latter invariably ruled out less pervasive "neurotic" illness as well as euphemistic and vague classifications such as "adjustment reaction," "nonspecific ego weakness," and the like.

But primitive, pre-Oedipal transference and related resistance constituted only one of several phenomena that pointed toward our patients' long-standing and pervasive psychopathology. A second, associated phenomenon was their desperate clinging to, and profound immersion in, dysfunctional parent-child relationships that displayed the features of prolonged and unresolved symbioses, and hence, of failure of separation-individuation (Mahler 1968, Rinsley 1964, 1965, 1967a,b, 1972, 1974a,b, 1980b). A third and pervasive phenomenon comprised the triad of deep-seated aggression, depression, and identity diffusion. In short, we found ourselves face to face with psychologically unseparated adolescents whose adaptive-coping mechanisms were either episodically or chronically psychotic. Of course, it was evident that these were not "garden variety" adolescents making their way toward adulthood via some sort of adolescent *Sturm und Drang*; rather, they were seriously developmentally deviant adolescents who had lost their way years before they came into treatment. As already noted, Masterson had long since reached this same conclusion.

In accordance with the nosology of the time, and following Mahler (1952, 1958, 1965a,b), my staff and I diagnosed our inpatient adolescents as suffering from symbiotic psychosis or symbiotic (childhood) schizophrenia (Rinsley 1972). A minority of these patients had never even developed a need-gratifying mother-infant symbiosis, and hence, were even more profoundly and pervasively disturbed as well as difficult to treat; we diagnosed the latter as suffering from autistic-presymbiotic psychosis or (childhood) schizophrenia (Fliess 1961, Mahler 1952, 1958, 1965a).* As our awareness of the significance of the early transference-resistance manifestations developed, it became increasingly obvious that the major therapeutic task was the identification, exposure, and beginning resolution of the patient-parent symbiotic "tie that binds" (Masterson 1967a, 1972b). The period following admission we accordingly termed the *resistance phase*; Masterson (1972b) termed it the *testing phase*.

---

*Because the great majority of the adolescent inpatients under consideration here were suffering from symbiosis-related psychopathology, this discussion will be devoted to them and not to the more developmentally primitive autistic-presymbiotic group, discussion of whom is presented elsewhere (Rinsley 1974a,b, 1980b).

Since both our Adolescent Unit at Topeka State Hospital and Masterson's Adolescent Service at Cornell's Payne Whitney Clinic were long-term and intensive, it was possible to study the ensuing course and natural history of the full-time inpatient or residential process both extensively and intensively, to observe and record the unfolding of any lasting therapeutic intrapersonal and interpersonal-intrafamilial change. Masterson and I, along with a third independent clinician, Jerry Lewis of Timberlawn Hospital in Dallas, agreed about the phasic nature of the inpatient-residential treatment process (Lewis 1970). Following the successfully traversed resistance (testing) phase, there emerged an often prolonged second phase, during which the immensely complex process of desymbiotization was begun and carried through; I called this phase the *definitive* or *introjective phase* (Rinsley 1965, 1974a, 1980b) while Masterson (1972b) termed it the *engagement phase*. In successfully treated cases, this middle phase was followed by a third and final *resolution phase* (Rinsley 1965, 1974a, 1980b) or *separation phase* (Masterson, 1972b).

The initial presentation of this triphasic concept of the residential treatment process was set forth in my 1965 paper devoted to intensive hospital treatment; it was subtitled "an object-relations view." In that publication, considerable attention was accorded the vicissitudes of the second phase of treatment, with its emphasis on the externalization of the adolescent's pervasive underlying depression pari passu the "switching" or exchange of "good" and "bad" objects. It seemed evident, at the time, that the clinical phenomena particular to this phase of treatment bore a discernible relationship to the triphasic natural history that Bowlby (1960a,b, 1961, 1962) had described in the case of prematurely separated infants. Our adolescents thus appeared to be recapitulating Bowlby's *stage of protest* during the resistance phase, his *stage of despair* during the definitive or introjective phase, and, in unsuccessfully treated cases, his *stage of detachment*, as they bordered on but appeared never to enter the third or resolution phase of treatment. Thus, the process of admission into residence, of physical-geographical severing of the parent-child tie, appeared to have set in motion the latter-day manifestations of a healthy separation-individuation process that had gone egregiously awry. The seminal writings of Margaret Mahler and her colleagues would further clarify the early problem of our inpatient adolescents: they had remained essentially symbiotic, never completing the process of healthy separation-individuation (Mahler 1952, 1958, 1965a,b, 1967, 1968, 1971, Mahler and Gosliner 1955, Mahler et al. 1949, 1959, 1975).

Later it was discovered that the depressive manifestations and introjective-projective "switching" or exchanging that consistently characterized the definitive or middle phase of treatment had been described earlier by Fairbairn (1941) as characteristic of his postulated transitional stage of quasi-independence. We seemed indeed to be witnessing in our inpatient adolescents the beginnings of Fairbairn's "dichotomy and exteriorization," including the latter's attendant differentiation of self and object, which endowed the external(ized) object with the quality of reality. In other words, we seemed to be witnessing the reinception of the complex process of separation-individuation within the residential or inpatient setting. In terms of Melanie Klein's (1940, 1946, 1955) view, we were seeing the patient's and the parent's beginning working-through of the infantile depressive position, with its attendant cessation of splitting, generation of whole-object relations, and onset of normal repression. Thus, the significance of the inpatient adolescent's rich variety of resistance metaphors and behavior could be understood in terms of the untrammeled operation of the primitive splitting defense that typified continued developmental arrest at the paranoid-schizoid position.

Object-relations theory had ineluctably entered our thinking in an effort to understand the course and natural history of the intensive, reconstructive residential treatment process; the role of that process as a vehicle for the attainment of lasting, healthy inner personality change could be understood in terms of its use to promote separation-individuation. Psychoanalysis, especially its object-relations offshoot, had provided a comprehensive understanding of the developmental pathogenesis of our patients' individual and familial psychopathology; that understanding would later be extended well beyond our earlier application of it.*

As noted, Masterson had been coming to a similar conclusion regarding the phasic nature of intensive inpatient treatment, and, in particular, had seen the analogy to Bowlby's stages as fundamental to an understanding of the transitional stage phenomena (Fairbairn's quasi-independence) that his patients had been manifesting. Masterson had likewise been deeply impressed with the emergence of depression once the resistance (testing) phase had been traversed and the patient had entered the second or middle (definitive, engagement) phase of treatment. He too had been assimilating Mahler's developmental phase theory. In his landmark book, *Treatment of the Borderline Adolescent: A Developmental Approach* (1972b), Masterson synthesized all of his earlier research and went beyond it, ascribing the emergent definitive- or engagement-phase depression, which he aptly termed *abandonment depression*, to early developmental arrest associated with failure of separation-individuation. As the following will indicate, his diagnostic thinking at that time was more advanced than was my own. When I had managed to catch up with him, the stage was set for a remarkably felicitous collaborative work that led directly to the 1975 Masterson-Rinsley paper.

DIAGNOSTIC CONSIDERATIONS

In accordance with the nosologic ethos associated with the ascendancy of dynamic psychiatry in this country following World War II, diagnostic labeling fell into more than a slight

---

*In 1968 I was recipient of the Edward A. Strecker Memorial Award of the Institute of the Pennsylvania Hospital for this work.

measure of disrepute; indeed some prominent clinicians, Karl Menninger (Menninger et al. 1963) among them, considered it an exercise in futility, perhaps even harmful to patients. During this period, the DSM-I (1952) had evolved into the DSM-II (1968), with its differentiation of the major functional psychoses—the schizophrenias and the major affective disorders (affective psychoses), respectively—in terms of *thought disorder* and *mood disorder*, as well as its array of nonpsychotic personality disorders. The DSM-II also provided an inclusive category, *transient situational disturbances*; the latter had a subcategory called *adjustment reaction of adolescence*, characterized by "irritability and depression associated with school failure and manifested by temper outbursts, brooding, and discouragement," a euphemistic underdiagnosis that many of our inpatient adolescents had received prior to their admission. On the contrary, careful diagnostic study of the adolescents in need of admission into my own service revealed a pattern of long-standing psychopathology, with both thought and mood disorders. As the latter was usually expressed symptomatically in the "impure" form considered typical for adolescents (Rinsley 1965, 1967a,b, 1972), these adolescents were viewed as psychotic and, in conformity with the DSM-II (1968), were diagnosed as suffering from (childhood) schizophrenia (the two terms were used roughly interchangeably at the time).

To represent more than mere labeling, however, diagnosis had to serve as more than a catalogue of symptoms; that is, it had to reflect the natural historical context in which the individual's psychosocial development had gone awry, had deviated, or had become fixated or arrested. The original developmental context was, of course, provided by pristine or classical psychoanalytic (psychosexual) stage theory (see chapter 9); its full potential, however, was only to be realized in the epochal separation-individuation studies of Margaret Mahler and her colleagues (Mahler et al. 1975). Beginning in the 1940s with studies devoted to infantile and child psychosis and schizophrenia, Mahler and her colleagues' ever-expanding contributions

(Mahler 1952, 1958, 1965a,b, 1967, 1968, Mahler and Gosliner 1955, Mahler et al. 1949, 1959) evolved into a comprehensive view of normal and deviant development in the late 1960s; this view of the "psychological birth" of the human infant was based on the now famous phases of autism, separation-individuation, and on-the-way-to-object-constancy, and the separation-individuation subphases of differentiation, practicing, and rapprochement (Mahler et al. 1975). Mahlerian phase theory added new and profound dimensions to classical stage theory (Rinsley 1980a); it also incorporated various components of psychoanalytic object-relations theory and the psychology of mental representations (Jacobson 1964).

It was Mahlerian phase theory that was to provide workers such as Masterson and myself with the requisite understanding of the developmental etiology of our adolescent inpatients' psychopathology, not to mention the basis for their differential diagnosis. In an important series of writings beginning in 1971, Masterson (1971a,b, 1972a,b, 1973, 1974, 1975) fruitfully applied phase-theoretical insights to a diagnostic and in-depth developmental understanding of the symptomatic adolescent, from which emerged his evolving concept of the borderline adolescent. As my 1972 nosology paper will indicate, I moved in this direction rather more slowly. Thus, although the term *borderline* had appeared in my own writings on adolescents as early as the 1965 object-relations paper, I continued to apply the Mahler-derived diagnostic category, *symbiotic psychosis*, to the majority of our inpatient adolescents, regarding it as essentially equivalent to *borderline*.

When I became convinced, however, that Masterson's formulation of the abandonment depression and my patients' ineluctably emergent middle- or definitive-phase depression represented one and the same phenomenon, it became evident that he and I had been witnessing and writing about the major symptomatology accruing from subphase-related developmental arrest in our respective patients. It likewise became evident that, in our successfully treated cases, the triphasic process was reflecting the adolescent's progress from the paranoid-schizoid position to the successfully worked-through depressive position. Our experiences with the highly structured, intensive residential milieu had indeed provided us with a window into our patients' early developmental arrest or deviation. Following Mahler's (1971) own suggestion, we related that developmental arrest to separation-individuation failure that usually began during the practicing subphase (10–16 months) and reached its peak during the rapprochement subphase (16–26 months). The concept *borderline* had indeed come of age, especially as it could be employed to represent a particular form of internal object relations governed by the persistence of the primitive splitting defense (Masterson 1975) which had been described earlier by Fairbairn (1941). Masterson had been working on a manuscript; in 1974, he graciously permitted me to collaborate with him in bringing it to completion. The result was the 1975 paper, a distillate of much that I have just described.

THE DEVELOPMENTAL–DIAGNOSTIC SPECTRUM

It hardly needs to be restated here that American psychiatry, including its child and adolescent subspecialties, has undergone major and permanent change during the last 25 years. The earlier pivotal position of psychodynamic-psychoanalytic ascendancy has given way to an enormous efflorescence of putatively more "basic" and "scientific" biological, biochemical, and physiologic research representative of a recrudescent mind-is-brain view in the best tradition of Wilhelm Griesinger; much of this conveys a behavioristic, nomothetic approach that ignores or denigrates anything that smacks of "psychologizing" and introspection, including the vast body of psychoanalytic teachings. The complex determinants of this trend are embedded in the broader matrix of pervasive social change that has typified American and Western European culture throughout this same period, an enumeration of which, even if thoroughly known and understood, would be well beyond the scope of this discussion (chapters 10–11, and Lasch 1977, 1978). There are, however, significant benefits accruing from this trend, including the effort to understand the physico-chemical substrates of human behavior and psychopathology, and the effort to achieve more accurate diagnosis and prognosis of the range of human mental disorders, as reflected in the DSM-III (1980).

This important diagnostic-prognostic effort, emanating in largest measure from biologically-oriented psychiatrists who are also interested in the hereditary transmission of mental disorders, has produced the important concept of the diagnostic continuum or spectrum (chapter 9, Stone 1980). There is thus the "schizophrenic spectrum" (the various "schizophrenias" and their closely related syndromes), the "schizo-affective spectrum" (combining primary cognitive and affective determinants and clinical features), the "spectrum" of the primary or major affective (manic-depressive, unipolar, bipolar) disorders, and the "spectrum" of the personality or characterologic disorders (chapter 9); each "spectrum" contains a range of symptomatically, and possibly genetically, related syndromes.*

My own departure from child and adolescent psychiatry in 1975 coincided with the publication of the Masterson-Rinsley paper. Since then, I have studied with deepening interest the application of psychoanalytic object-relations and Mahlerian phase theories to an understanding of borderline disorder and, in turn, the latter's relationship to the spectrum of other personality disorders and to the wider continuum of psychopathology. The result of this interest was a series of papers that further explored and developed the concepts basic to the 1975 Masterson-Rinsley paper and extended beyond them to include the major psychoses (chapters 3–7, 9, and 11, as well as Rinsley, 1980a).

---

*This work is admirably discussed and summarized in Stone's recent, comprehensive book, *The Borderline Syndromes: Constitution, Personality, and Adaptation* (1980).

It had indeed seemed possible to attempt an integration of a number of apparently disparate but nonetheless related lines of research that pointed toward the spectrum concept of psychopathology. Emergent from such an attempt was the recognition, developed from both psychodynamic-developmental and biological-genetic sources, of the proximity of the borderline to the major affective disorders, on the one "side" of the developmental continuum, and to the more purely narcissistic personality disorders on the other (Kohut 1971, 1977, Ornstein 1974).

It also seemed possible to place the work that had led to the 1975 Masterson-Rinsley paper in a more rational diagnostic perspective. So far as the nosology set forth in the 1972 paper was concerned, *symbiotic psychosis of adolescence*, as I had then labeled it, could be seen to comprise no less than three diagnostically differentiable syndromes: (1) a regressive symbiotic process reflective of childhood schizophrenic disorder and akin to Mahler's original symbiotic psychosis (schizophrenia) of childhood, manifesting *predominant thought disorder*; (2) a group of "dysthymic," schizo-affective psychotic cases, including some now recognized as adolescent-onset, unipolar and bipolar affective disorder (Carlson and Strober 1979), manifesting *predominant mood disorder*; and (3) a group of cases reflecting disordered internal object relations and considered *borderline* by the criteria of the 1975 Masterson-Rinsley paper. It now appeared that the earlier effort toward diagnosis had not been off the mark and that the attempt to ground it firmly on a knowledge of development, specifically the separation-individuation process, had been both necessary and fruitful.

SUMMARY

The clinical cross-validation provided by Masterson's and my own intensive work with seriously disturbed adolescents places our work in the wider context of evolving research into the pathogenesis and treatment of the range of preadult and adult psychopathology. In that context, both psychodynamic-developmental and biological-genetic data and inferences are required for a comprehensive view of the etiology, diagnosis, and treatment of mental illness. It is exciting to consider how much more is known now concerning the diagnosis and treatment of mental disorder than was known 25 years ago, and to consider how contemporary multidisciplinary research will continue to add comprehensively to that knowledge.

CHAPTER 14

FAIRBAIRN'S OBJECT RELATIONS AND CLASSICAL CONCEPTS OF DYNAMICS AND STRUCTURE

In his review chapter, "Freud's Concepts of Splitting," Grotstein (1981) succinctly summarizes the progress of clinical experiences that led Freud (1914a) to de-emphasize the concept of (dissociative) splitting in favor of "a process of repelling which . . . I called 'defence,' and later, 'repression.'" Freud's decision to supplant the concept of dissociation with the concept of defensive repression was indeed fateful for the evolution of his ideas on psychopathogenesis; it foreshadowed the later topographic, dynamic and economic concepts and laid the foundation for psychoanalytic metapsychology, the antecedents of which Freud had already set down in the "Project" (1895).

The concept of dissociative splitting to account for hysterical symptomatology had originated with Janet (1907), who had postulated that an "exaggerated" psychological state or idea had become separated ("dissociated") from consciousness, causing an uncontrollable "automatic" symptom to appear; Janet further suggested that such fragmentation of the personality resulted from an otherwise obscure deficiency of unifying energy, a condition he termed *psychasthenia* (weakness of the mind). The notion of fragmentation or decomposition of the personality or of mental functioning was, of course, not new with Janet. With respect to the major psychoses, and in particular schizophrenia, such terms as *dementia sejunctiva, dementia dissecans* (Pruyser 1975), *intrapsychic ataxia* (Stransky 1909) and *folie discordante* (Chaslin 1912) had since come into use. Of particular significance was the conclusion of the psychoanalyst, Federn (1952) who, differing reluctantly with Freud, later came to the view that schizophrenia resulted, not from a regressive reinvestment of the ego with narcissistic libido, but rather from a deficiency of ego libido per se.

That the concept of dissociative splitting by no means disappeared from Freud's later, ongoing work is amply attested to in a number of his ensuing publications. Associated with both serious and less serious forms of impairment of reality, splitting reappeared in such diverse writings as: "On Narcissism: An Introduction" (1914b), "Mourning and Melancholia" (1917b), *The Ego and the Id* (1923), "Neurosis and Psychosis" (1924b), "Moses and Monotheism" (1939), *An Outline of Psycho-Analysis* (1940a) and in the two papers most often cited in this connection, "Fetishism" (1927) and "Splitting of the Ego in the Process of Defence" (1940b). From these may be gleaned the view that splitting characterizes the ego, not only in psychosis, but as well in neurosis and in connection with everyday events and experiences during which the temporary or short-lived abrogation of reality serves useful adaptive purposes.

For Melanie Klein (1935, 1940, 1946, 1948), splitting served as a defense against anxiety originating in the death instinct and reinforced by the trauma of birth and the frustration of bodily needs. Its effect, according to her view, is to divide objects into all-good (idealized) and all-bad (persecutory) entities characteristic of the paranoid-schizoid position. Although Melanie Klein (1952, 1958) came close to equating splitting and repression, she developed the view that only when the depressive position is successfully traversed does splitting give way to repression, associated momentously with which are the inception of whole-object relations and the capacity to mourn.

Fairbairn's view of, respectively, splitting and repression are succinctly set forth in claims 9–13 of his 1963 *Synopsis* (chapter 4):

9. TWO ASPECTS OF THE INTERNALIZED OBJECT, VIZ., ITS EXCITING AND ITS FRUSTRATING ASPECTS, ARE SPLIT OFF FROM THE MAIN CORE OF THE OBJECT AND REPRESSED BY THE EGO.

10. THUS THERE COME TO BE CONSTITUTED TWO REPRESSED INTERNAL OBJECTS, VIZ., THE EXCITING (OR LIBIDINAL) OBJECT AND THE REJECTING (OR ANTILIBIDINAL) OBJECT.

11. THE MAIN CORE OF THE INTERNALIZED OBJECT, WHICH IS NOT REPRESSED, IS DESCRIBED AS THE IDEAL OBJECT OR EGO IDEAL.

12. OWING TO THE FACT THAT THE EXCITING (LIBIDINAL) AND REJECTING (ANTILIBIDINAL) OBJECTS ARE BOTH CATHECTED BY THE ORIGINAL EGO, THESE OBJECTS CARRY INTO REPRESSION WITH THEM PARTS OF THE EGO BY WHICH THEY ARE CATHECTED, LEAVING THE CENTRAL CORE OF THE EGO (CENTRAL EGO) UNREPRESSED, BUT ACTING AS THE AGENT OF REPRESSION.

13. THE RESULTING INTERNAL SITUATION IS ONE IN WHICH THE ORIGINAL EGO IS SPLIT INTO THREE EGOS—A CENTRAL (CONSCIOUS) EGO ATTACHED TO THE IDEAL OBJECT (EGO-IDEAL), A REPRESSED LIBIDINAL EGO ATTACHED TO THE EXCITING (OR LIBIDINAL) OBJECT, AND A REPRESSED ANTILIBIDINAL EGO ATTACHED TO THE REJECTING (OR ANTILIBIDINAL) OBJECT.

The heuristic difficulties associated with the foregoing claims have been discussed at some length in chapter 4; some of them, however, deserve restatement for the purposes of the present discussion.

First of all, there is a multiplicity of egos, the nature of some of which is obscure, of others not so obscure. As I attempted to point out in chapter 4, the libidinal ego (L.E.) and the antilibidinal ego (Anti-L.E.) respectively correspond to the rewarding and rejecting (withdrawing) part-self representations associated with the *split object-relations unit* (SORU) originally described in borderline patients (chapter 2), which are directly observable within the therapeutic transferences which these patients quickly and labilely develop. Again, the central ego (C.E.), unrepressed according to Fairbairn, was considered to comprise a whole-self representation that corresponds to Freud's reality ego. But nowhere does Fairbairn further or adequately explicate the original ego (claim 12) by which the exciting object (E.O.) and the rejecting object (R.O.) are presumably cathected. Fairbairn's formulations regarding these egos leaves no doubt, however, that what he terms the original ego (which shall here be designated as the O.E.) exists ab initio, later to be sundered (split) into the L.E., Anti-L.E. and C.E. which are, in turn, affiliated with their corresponding E.O., R.O. and I.O (claim 13). Is, therefore, the postulated O.E. *whole* (that is, unsplit) from the beginning? If so, then it is difficult to imagine how a self-representation can start out as a whole-self representation prior to the time whole-self and whole-object representations have evolved by way of working-through of the later depressive position.

Second, there is the recursive matter of understanding the respective processes of splitting and repression and here, once again, the problem of their relationship, that runs like a thread throughout Freud's writings, resurfaces. On the one hand, Fairbairn seems to equate them (chapter 4), yet he writes at times as if he recognizes them to be different, as in claim 9 (". . . split off and repressed . . ."). In this connection, it is apropos to quote from Grotstein's (1981) review of Freud's thoughts on the subject:

> Freud held . . . for a splitting of consciousness accompanied by the formation of separate psychical groups, as if to suggest that these were two different things. Freud had greater regard

for Breuer's propositions which gave splitting of consciousness a secondary place. The patient intended to split the content of consciousness, not consciousness itself, but, according to Freud, the act backfired [p. 22].

In accordance with this view, the patient (Fräulein Elisabeth von R.) had begun with the splitting of conscious content, which proceeded by extension to encompass the splitting of consciousness per se. Following Freud's (Breuer and Freud 1893–1895) reasoning, we are left with the conclusion that the splitting of the mental content of consciousness, a "willed" or "intended" psychical act serving as a resistance against the association of components of that content, had led to a more encompassing splitting of consciousness itself. The latter process is noted to occur when consciousness remains "attached to" certain mental contents, while it becomes "detached from" other mental contents, rendering the latter, by definition, unconscious. Thus, despite Freud's de-emphasis of splitting (Breuer's "hypnoid states": Breuer and Freud 1893) in favor of repression as a defense, the duality persisted throughout many of his ensuing writings, as noted before, as evidence that Freud had never adequately resolved the issue in his own mind.

That the same duality continues to resurface in Melanie Klein's and Fairbairn's writings therefore comes as no surprise. The greater prominence which they and other British object-relations writers accorded splitting over repression, however, parallels two other, related changes of emphasis, namely, the greater significance attached to pre-Oedipal factors, experiences and determinants and, within the context of instinct theory, the primacy of object as over against aim. Again, from an historical standpoint, the emphasis on objects, object-seeking and object-relatedness had led these psychoanalysts toward the development of a body of observations and inferences that was to constitute the anlagen of a theory of mental representations, later to be elaborated with thoroughness and elegance by Edith

Jacobson (1964). Accordingly, the earliest splitting carried out by the infant could be viewed as a natural consequence of the operation of the pleasure principle (chapter 4), as a defense (Klein 1935, 1940, 1946, 1948) and, certainly, as representative of otherwise healthy ego growth (Rosenfeld 1965).

The theory of mental representations that developed from these prior object-relations considerations (Jacobson 1964, Kernberg 1966) was to serve as one of two major anchor points for the later contributions of Masterson (1976) and Rinsley (chapters 3 and 5) to the elucidation of the pathogenesis of borderline personality disorder and, as well, of other disorders of the self (chapter 9); the other anchor point was provided by the seminal developmental studies of Mahler and her colleagues (Mahler et al. 1975).

A third difficulty has to do with what Fairbairn means by such terms as the main core of the object (claim 9) and the central core of the ego (claim 12). From reading these claims it becomes apparent that there exists some sort of primal object, the internalization of which yields an unrepressed "main core" from which the E.O. and the R.O. are split off *and* repressed. Our previous question concerning how an "original ego" (O.E.) could possibly start out as a whole-self representation is equally applicable to how such a primal object could possibly start out as a whole-object representation. In the case of the latter, however, the matter is not quite as obscure if the postulated primal object is considered even to antedate Spitz's (1965) infantile pre-object, serving as a dimly and inconsistently perceived proto-object which object-relations theory postulates that the neonate proceeds to "seek" from the beginning. Of course, the existence of such a primal object entails the existence of a corresponding primal self; the latter may be considered to constitute a primitive, global (undifferentiated), coenesthetic self-representation that typifies the phase of absolute autism (birth to one month postnatally) and much if not most of the symbiotic phase prior to the earliest beginning differentiation of part-self and part-object representations (Mahler et al. 1975).

A PRELIMINARY SYNOPSIS OF EGOS AND OBJECTS

Let us now summarize what we have thus far set forth in respect to Fairbairn's various egos and objects. As gleaned from his cited claims, there exists from the beginning an entity called the *original ego* (O.E.); there likewise exists from the beginning a corresponding (primal) object, to which we attach the name, *original object* (O.O.) with which the O.E. very early comes into relationship. As a consequence of the infant's very early object-seeking and owing to its alternatively gratifying (i.e., tension-reducing) and frustrating (i.e., nontension-reducing; tension-enhancing) characteristics as dimly perceived by the infant, the O.O. undergoes internalization (introjection) and subsequent splitting into an *exciting object* (E.O.), a *rejecting object* (R.O.) and what Fairbairn termed the main core of the internalized object, the *ideal object* (I.O.) or ego ideal. From the side of the infant there proceed to come into association with these, respectively, the *libidinal ego* (L.E.), the *antilibidinal ego* (Anti-L.E.) and what Fairbairn termed the central core of the ego, the *central ego* (C.E.). The result of all this is no less than three "alliances," namely, the E.O.-L.E., the R.O.-Anti-L.E. and the I.O.-C.E. Note that Fairbairn held that the first two of these are repressed, whereas the I.O.-C.E. alliance is unrepressed; Fairbairn also held that the C.E. acts as the "agent of repression," but inasmuch as the C.E. is affiliated with the I.O., then the agent of repression must be the I.O.-C.E. More will be said concerning Fairbairn's use of the term, repression, in this connection later on in this discussion.

My previous conclusion (chapter 4) about Fairbairn's claims was that his various egos and objects are certainly nothing less than *representations*; thus the L.E., Anti-L.E. and C.E. are self-representations while the E.O., R.O. and I.O. are nothing less than object-representations; and further that these various representations are built up in the infant as a consequence of the vicissitudes of his very early relationship with the mother. Of significance is the fact that the E.O. and the R.O. are split-off components of the "bad" or "rejected" aspects of the O.O., whereas the I.O., the "good" or "accepted" component of the O.O., is not split-off. Similarly, the L.E. and the Anti-L.E. are split-off, whereas the C.E. is not. It follows, therefore, that split-off (bad) representations are repressed, whereas unsplit-off (good) representations are not.

In contrast to the view of Melanie Klein, Fairbairn (1944) originally held that only the bad object was initially introjected and split, the purpose of which was to "remove" and gain mastery over an external persecutor; he later (1951a) revised this view by postulating the initial introjection of a preambivalent object, neither "all good" nor "all bad." We may take this to mean, therefore, that what we have termed the O.O. undergoes introjection in toto and thereby comes into affiliation with what we have termed the O.E.; and further, that from this O.O.-O.E. "alliance" are in turn derived the respective "bad" alliances, the E.O.-L.E. and the R.O.-Anti-L.E., and the "good" alliance, the I.O.-C.E.

RELATIONS TO CLASSICAL STRUCTURES

Fairbairn's effort to relate his various egos and objects to classical metapsychological structures is evidenced in his 1944 paper:

> Actually, the "super-ego" corresponds not so much to the . . . "antilibidinal ego"* as it does to a compound of this structure and its associated object. . . . At the same time the "antilibidinal ego"* is unlike the "super-ego" in that it is . . . devoid of all moral significance . . . it seems to me impossible to offer any satisfactory psychological explanation of guilt in the absence of the super-ego; but the super-ego must be regarded as originating at a higher level of mental organization than that at which the antilibidinal ego* operates. Exactly how the activities

---

*I have taken the liberty of replacing Fairbairn's original term "internal saboteur," as used in this passage, with his later, more acceptable term, "antilibidinal ego."

of these two structures are related must in the meantime remain an open question (pp. 106–107).

We now come to Fairbairn's claims 15 and 16:

15. THE ANTILIBIDINAL EGO, BY VIRTUE OF ITS ATTACHMENT TO THE REJECTING (ANTILIBIDINAL) OBJECT, ADOPTS AN UNCOMPRO-MISINGLY HOSTILE ATTITUDE TO THE LIBIDINAL EGO, AND THUS HAS THE EFFECT OF POWERFULLY REINFORCING THE REPRESSION OF THE LIBIDINAL EGO BY THE CENTRAL EGO.

16. WHAT FREUD DESCRIBED AS THE "SUPEREGO" IS REALLY A COMPLEX STRUCTURE COMPRISING (A) THE IDEAL OBJECT OR EGO IDEAL, (B) THE ANTILIBIDINAL EGO, AND (C) THE REJECTING (OR ANTI-LIBIDINAL) OBJECT.

Thus, in 1963 Fairbairn attempts to provide at least a provisional answer to his "open question" of 1944. From claim 16 may be derived the further assumption that the harsh, sadistic com-ponent of the (classical) superego is comprised of the R.O.-Anti-L.E. as well as the assumption that the C.E. (actually, the I.O.-C.E. in conformity with our revised formulation, *supra*) comprises the superego's ethical-moral component.

Derived as they are from Fairbairn's analytic work, and in particular from his analyses of dreams, these formulations are no mere exercises in purely abstract theory construction. That *these various egos and objects are in fact representations (percepts; images) linked to predominant affects* (chapter 2, and Jacobson, 1964, Kernberg, 1966) will become the more evident when claims 15 and 16 are considered in greater detail.

My initial inference (chapter 4) was to the effect that Fair-bairn's L.E. is analogous to Freud's (1911a, 1923) purified pleasure ego, the aim of which is the willy-nilly discharge of impulse (tension), hence to obtain a "yield of pleasure" (Freud 1911a). The "uncompromisingly hostile attitude" adopted by the superego's harsh, sadistic component, the R.O.- Anti-L.E. toward the L.E. actually represents the affect component of unneutralized aggression, with the R.O.-Anti-L.E. serving as a split-off internal persecutor derived from the primal introjection and subsequent splitting of the preambivalent object, the O.O.

In my initial inference (chapter 4), I also noted that, in contrast to the nature of the E.O.-L.E. and the R.O.-Anti-L.E., which are *part-representations*, the I.O.-C.E. is a *whole-representation*. My original puzzlement over Fairbairn's conclusion that the C.E. (really, the I.O.-C.E.) should be regarded as unrepressed now gives way to the realization that his conclusion amounted to an assertion that the I.O.-C.E. bears a particular relation to reality. And the reality-related nature of the I.O.-C.E. is in turn supported by the conclusion (chapter 4) that the I.O. and the C.E. are to be regarded as whole-representations. In following this line of reasoning, we are left with the conclusion that the C.E., comprising a whole-self-representation, is indeed analogous to Freud's (1911a) reality ego which, together with its affiliated I.O. and with the neutralized ("sublimated") instinctual drive (affect) component associated with it, both mediates and modulates the individual's capacity to bring narcissistic needs into relationship with the requirements and demands of the external world. And, of course, a major aspect of the success of that adaptive relationship has to do with the individual's capacity to respond to ethical-moral imperatives, internally rather than externally imposed.

FURTHER COMMENTS ON SPLITTING, REPRESSION, AND THE STRUCTURE OF THE SUPEREGO

The concept of the I.O.-C.E. as comprising the ethical-moral component of the superego now requires further examination. At various times, Freud wrote of an *ideal ego*, an *ego ideal* (1914b) and a *superego* (1923). The ideal ego referred to the ego of the infant and child that experiences itself as "at one with the id," a state of exceptionally regressive fusion, echoes of which are discernible in regressed manic and catatonic states. In virtue of their similarity, the ideal ego and Freud's (purified) pleasure ego may be considered akin to each other and subsumable under Fairbairn's L.E.. Throughout his writings, Freud often blurred the distinction between what he termed the ego ideal and the superego (1917b, 1921). In the *New Introductory Lectures* (1933), however, he differentiated them: the ego "measures itself" against the ego ideal, of which the superego serves as "vehicle." Overall, the ego ideal survives as the introjective precipitate of the loved parents (the "good object"), hence is libidinal in affective valence and emerges as providing approval or approbation. Its "vehicle," the superego, survives as the introjective precipitate of the hated, punitive parents or of the original "bad object," hence is aggressive in affective valence and emerges as cruel, sadistic and terrifying. Freud's conclusion (1923) that the superego is derived from the child's earliest object relationships is affirmed in Melanie Klein's (1933, 1958) evolving and seemingly ultimately contradictory concept of its origin. The classical view of the superego as "heir" of the Oedipus complex may therefore further be understood in terms of the Kleinian view that oral frustration engenders a premature Oedipal development, of which an earlier, terrifyingly sadistic, precursory "superego" is "heir." Irrespective of whether such a precursory superego is comprised of "unassimilated" or "undemetabolized" forerunners (Jacobson 1964, Kernberg 1966) or is comprised of the triadic components ordinarily associated with the classical superego, the fact remains that those forerunners or components are self-. and object-representations linked to aggressive and libidinal drive derivatives (affects).

We are now prepared to examine further the superego's ethical-moral component. To begin with, there is much to suggest that the processes of internalization that contribute so importantly to the evolution of that component are closely linked to the achievement of object constancy (chapter 8). We thus bring to Fairbairn's object-relations concepts not only a representational point of view, but also a developmental point of view. The latter naturally evolves from the contributions of Margaret Mahler and her associates (1975).

As the child passes from the separation-individuation phase (ages 6 to 30 months) and into the on-the-way-to-object-constancy phase (c. 30 months and beyond), the progressive differentiation of self- and object-representations characteristic of the rapprochement subphase (16 to 30 months) leads to the consolidation of the child's awareness of his separateness, that self and object are, as it were, distinct and, further, that they are stable. The fundamental stability of self- and object-representations is in turn reflected in the child's transition from reliance on recognitory memory to reliance on evocative memory (Fraiberg 1969) and further that the images thus evoked are preponderantly benevolent, hence reliably drive-reducing or need-satisfying. Irrespective of when one's theoretical a prioris dictate that the depressive position sets in, the child's successful transit of the rapprochement subphase signifies its largely having been worked through. And along with the achievement of object constancy as an essential ingredient of that working-through, there occurs the generation of whole-object relations, the mourning for the "lost" symbiotic "dual unity" and entrance into the Oedipal stage of psychosexual development. Finally at this time, there is considered to occur a shift from reliance on the splitting defense to reliance on the defense of repression. And, of course, concomitant with these processes of change goes a profound augmentation of the child's capacity to sense and test reality.

Inasmuch as Fairbairn's object-relations theory lacks a developmental chronology to account for the emergence and consolidation of his various egos and objects, it is necessary to supply one, however preliminary it must be. As already noted (chapter 4), the C.E. bears a powerful relation to reality; and as I have analogized the C.E. to Freud's reality ego, it follows that a major aspect of that relation comprises the I.O., which which the C.E. comes into affiliation as the I.O.-C.E. In conformity with our previous formulation (chapters 2, 3, and 4), the I.O.-C.E. is linked to a mix of neutralized ("sublimated") aggressive and libidinal affects, therewith generating a "whole" object-relations unit that comes into existence when the child has largely successfully transited the rapprochement subphase. It is thus possible to infer, from claim 12, that when Fairbairn holds the C.E. (actually, the I.O.-C.E.) to be unrepressed, he means unsplit, and hence, whole in the sense of whole-self- and whole-object-representations. Acting as the "agent of repression," the C.E. (actually, the I.O.-C.E.) serves as the "agent" of the ongoing splitting of the E.O.-L.E. and the R.O.-Anti-L.E.

As noted earlier (chapters 2, 3, and 5, as well as Masterson 1976), the so-called healthy object-relations unit that develops during the course of the successful treatment of borderline patients, thus forming the therapeutic alliance, is comprised of whole-self- and whole-object-representations. Its progressive consolidation progressively augments the patient's insight into his unrequited wish for symbiotic reunion (refusion) and into the symptomatic behavior that has both articulated and concealed that wish.

Whether Fairbairn surmised something of the whole-representational nature of the I.O.-C.E. one cannot say. But his selection of the alternate term, ego ideal, for the I.O. cannot have been fortuitous. For, indeed, the progressively consolidating I.O.-C.E. (the "healthy object-relations unit") that is so evident clinically serves as the agency by which the patient ultimately comes to control, then to eliminate his repertoire of self-defeating, symptomatic behavior as he "measures himself," as it were, against others and proceeds to bring his behavior into compliance with the demands of the "external" objects from which his treatment has at last assisted him in differentiating himself. *It may therefore be concluded that Fairbairn's C.E. (better, his I.O.-C.E.) comprises the ethical-moral component of the classical superego.*

Our discussion now turns to Fairbairn's claims 15 and 16. In the light of the foregoing, claim 16 may be revised as follows: *what Freud described as the "superego" is really a complex structure comprising (a) the I.O.-C.E., and (b) the R.O.-Anti-L.E.* Having concluded that the I.O.-C.E. comprises the ethical-moral component of the superego, what remains, the R.O.-Anti-L.E., is considered to comprise its harsh, sadistic component. Claim 15 may be revised in accordance with this view: *acting together with the I.O.-C.E., the R.O.-Anti-L.E. brings about and maintains the splitting of the E.O.-L.E. from itself.* The aggression which the R.O.-Anti-L.E. directs toward the E.O.-L.E. is derived from the former's aggressively valent affect component, in turn an amalgam of the perceived aggression of the introjected "bad" object and the infant's indigenous aggression directed at that object in the wake of the latter's frustrating aspects.

It should be remembered, moreover, that the economic moiety that binds the E.O.-L.E. and the R.O.-Anti-L.E. respectively together is libidinal, not aggressive in affective valence. In the case of the R.O.-Anti-L.E., it is this libidinal moiety that, together with the aggression associated with the R.O.-Anti-L.E., provides for its sadism in addition to its aggression-related harshness.

We are now prepared to offer a reconsideration of the fundamental issue surrounding the relationship of splitting to repression. Such a reconsideration begins with the fact that the components of the R.O.-Anti-L.E. and the E.O.-L.E. are part-representations, whereas the components of the I.O.-C.E. are whole-representations. It also begins with the recognition of the E.O.-L.E. as a hedonic self-object (a revision of the definition of the L.E. as the pleasure ego) that unremittingly strives for discharge, that is, for a "yield of pleasure." Finally, it begins with the prior assumption that the I.O.-C.E. comes into full function only upon the child's successful transit of the rapprochement subphase.

In accordance with our formulations, it comes as no surprise that the later-evolving I.O.-C.E. represses the R.O.-Anti-L.E. and the E.O.-L.E. For if, as we believe, repression ("horizontal splitting") evolves as a higher-order defense than ("vertical") splitting, and begins to function at the time whole-object relations have their inception (i.e., the I.O.-C.E.), then repression has to do with the splitting of the mental content of consciousness. That Fairbairn must have perceived this becomes evident upon even casual inspection of his well-recognized diagram (1954, p. 105) which clearly depicts the horizontal layering underneath the superimposed C.E. It may therefore be concluded that the effect of the I.O.-C.E.'s repression of the R.O.-Anti-L.E. and the E.O.-L.E. is to "detach" these latter from consciousness (hence, to render them "unconscious").

By comparison, then, the aggression directed against the E.O.-L.E. by the R.O.-Anti-L.E. represents what must be regarded as the mechanism of (vertical) splitting. In contrast to the horizontal or repressive splitting of the content of consciousness brought about by the I.O.-C.E., that which is brought about by the action of the R.O.-Anti-L.E. upon the E.O.-L.E. leads to the splitting of consciousness itself; the resulting products remain and continue as dynamically active endopsychic structures that coexist and co-function "alongside" and apart from each other. As Fairbairn pointed out in claim 14 (chapter 4, pp. 88–89), the resulting "internal situation represents a basic schizoid position which is more fundamental than the depressive position described by Melanie Klein." In describing the "more fundamental internal situation" to which Fairbairn refers, we may with good reason add the terms, earlier and more primitive, the former in view of the fact that the paranoid-schizoid position antedates the depressive position; and the latter in view of the fact that the persistent, unresolved splitting of consciousness yields the more serious forms of psychotic and personality disorder that exemplify significant degrees of failure of separation-individuation (chapter 9).

THE GENERATION OF WHOLE OBJECTS

As we have noted, the aggression directed against the E.O.-L.E. by the R.O.-Anti-L.E. maintains the process of vertical splitting by means of which the latter self-object structure proceeds to deny a "yield of pleasure" to the former self-object structure. Put another way, the harsh, sadistic component of the superego attempts thereby to inhibit or preclude the pleasure ego's self-indulgence, as it were, to block the pleasure ego's access to motility.

A variety of symptoms may be seen to result from this process. Thus, the E.O.-L.E. may attempt to "escape" from the R.O.-Anti-L.E.'s assault by means of hysterical dissociation, therewith widening the split between the two, as expressed in seizures, somnambulisms, fugues, "automatisms" and the like. Or the E.O.-L.E. may retreat into paralysis, with ensuing catalepsy or severe depression. Again, the E.O.-L.E. may counterphobically attempt a reunion with its antagonist, resulting in mania, with its unbridled psychomotor overactivity so evidently tinged with the R.O.-Anti-L.E.'s sadism. Finally, the E.O.-L.E. may adopt a state of overalert watchfulness toward the R.O.-Anti-L.E., resulting in paranoia.

It is recognized that these phenomena typify the period of infancy and early childhood characterized by the persistence of the self-object, hence by persistent failure of self-object differentiation. Inasmuch as the full functioning of the I.O.-C.E. has not yet developed during this period, its function of horizontal splitting, i.e., repression, has likewise not yet fully developed. The persistence of these endopsychic phenomena into adulthood underlies the well-recognized "failure of repression" that typifies the psychotic and borderline conditions associated with them.

With the full flowering of horizontal splitting (repression) accompanying the working-through of the depressive position following the close of the rapprochement subphase, the phenomena associated with vertical splitting become separated from consciousness, albeit they remain active in what Freud was to term the Ucs. In neurotic states, repression serves as the major defense mechanism, associated with which are a significant degree of self-object differentiation and the capacity for whole-object relations. It is in these cases and, of course, in the essentially healthy personality where the repressive, reality-related I.O.-C.E. functionally predominates. Likewise in these cases, the E.O.-L.E. and the R.O.-Anti-L.E. have become significantly differentiated. When this has occurred, the L.E. and the Anti-L.E. have proceeded to consolidate, thereby generating the "bad" self with its alloplastic, hedonistic aspect (the L.E.) and its hostile, sadistic aspect (the Anti-L.E.). Similarly, the E.O. and the R.O. have proceeded to consolidate, thereby generating the "bad" object, with its seductive, alluring aspect (the E.O.) and its hostile, persecutory aspect (the R.O.).

It will be evident that the consolidation of the E.O.-R.O. and the L.E.-Anti-L.E. will have now sundered the antecedent E.O.-L.E. and R.O.-Anti-L.E. self-objects; the result is to greatly attenuate the aggression of the R.O.-Anti-L.E. (the harsh, sadistic component of the classical superego) directed toward the E.O.-L.E., hence to greatly attenuate the mechanism of vertical splitting.

The final turn of events in the development of endopsychic structure now takes place upon the child's transit of the Oedipal period. The consolidated "bad" self ("bad" self-representation), the L.E.-Anti-L.E., comes into relationship with the "good" self ("good" self-representation), the C.E., and together these generate the whole-self-representation. Concomitantly, the consolidated "bad" object ("bad" object-representation), the E.O.-R.O., comes into relationship with the "good" object ("good" object-representation), the I.O., and together these generate the whole-object representation. Thus,

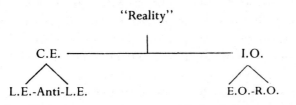

"Reality"

C.E. ———————— I.O.

L.E.-Anti-L.E.   E.O.-R.O.

Whole-self-representation   Whole-object representation

The topographic nature of the foregoing diagram portrays the (horizontal) repression of the E.O.-R.O. and the L.E.-Anti-L.E. by the I.O.-C.E. Our initial formulation to the effect that the I.O. and the C.E. are whole-representations now emerges more clearly when it is understood that, in beginning to function toward the end of the Oedipal period, the I.O.-C.E. comes into association with, and proceeds to hold in repression, its respective part-self and part-object representations. Self-representations and object-representations are thus brought together, thereby putting an end to the "good-bad" perceptual-cognitive dichotomy in terms of which the pre-Oedipal, object-inconstant child views himself and his surroundings. It should be emphasized, moreover, that this is the process that characterizes the successful psychoanalytic treatment of borderline personalities (chapters 2,3, and 5).

FALSE SELF

I proposed in Chapter 4 that Winnicott's false self is comprised of the L.E. and the Anti-L.E., a formulation that now requires further examination in the light of the foregoing discussion. As also noted elsewhere (chapter 11, and Rinsley 1980a) the false self is considered to arise as a consequence of the dysfunctional mother's (and, of course, family's) perception and expectations of, and interaction with, the developing child as if he were something or somebody other than what he in fact is (Rinsley, 1971a). The child's pseudocomplementary response repertoire to this depersonifying or appersonative interactive process is to evolve and become developmentally arrested in terms of a self-object that is reflective of that perception and those expectations, to the detriment of his indigenous self-representation.

The various forms of such depersonification, leading in the end to psychotic, borderline and narcissistic disorders, have been described in detail elsewhere (chapter 11, and Rinsley 1971a). In such cases, the net result is to powerfully fixate the "bad" self-objects, namely, the E.O.-L.E. and the R.O.-Anti-L.E. In the case of the borderline children and adults we have studied and treated, Masterson and I (chapter 2) termed these "bad" self-objects *the split object-relations unit* (SORU). Irrespective of terminology, the part-self representations associated with the "bad" self-object, namely the L.E. and the Anti-L.E. continue their dynamic activity, hence continue to contribute to the observable symptomatology that typifies these patients, in whom both the internal and external ego boundaries remain permeable to the "material" associated with them (chapter 1). This "permeability" in turn reflects both the mechanisms of projection and introjection across the external boundary, and the readiness with which Ucs material traverses the internal boundary and enters consciousness (failure of repression).

In classical terms, therefore, false self implies the persistence of (vertical) splitting, abetted by the endlessly repetitive endopsychic conflict between the pleasure ego (L.E.) and the harsh, sadistic superego (R.O.-Anti-L.E.).

OEDIPAL ISSUES

The decades-long dispute among psychoanalysts over Melanie Klein's back-dating of the Oedipus complex to the first postnatal year of life shows no signs of waning. Irrespective of such fulsome arguments as Glover's (1945) pejorative view of what he termed the "Klein system of child psychology," it was Melanie Klein's (1940, 1945) observation that ". . . the Oedipus complex begins to emerge with, and is part and parcel of, the depressive position." (Segal 1979, p. 129). The apparent, relative neglect of Oedipal issues in many latter-day writings devoted to borderline and narcissistic psychopathology has received a needed correction in terms of the concept of subphase adequacy; particularly relevant is the related view of the Oedipus complex as the "fourth organizer of the psyche" in addition to Spitz's (1959, 1965) first three "organizers," namely the three-month smiling response, the eight-month (stranger) anxiety and the acquisition of speech (Mahler and Kaplan 1977). Although a detailed consideration of the fourth Oedipal organizer is beyond the scope of the present discussion, its pivotal significance for the development of the ego's synthetic function, including the emergence of higher-order operational thought, should be borne in mind (Kaplan 1980).

Melanie Klein's insight into the relationship between the emergence of the Oedipus complex and the events of the depressive position is of particular relevance to our inference concerning the emergence and significance of the I.O.-C.E. Allowing for the consideration that her chronology of that relationship was based upon her clinical observations of Oedipal and depressive-position *precursors* or *forerunners* derived from her analyses of pre-Oedipal children, the full flowering of the triadic Oedipal constellation and its accompanying depressive working through are noted to occur on or about the close of the rapprochement subphase, roughly coincident with the child's entrance into the phallic-Oedipal stage. And, as we have noted, it is at this time when the ethical-moral component of the superego, the I.O.-C.E., attains a degree of development that sets in motion its function of (horizontal) repression. Again, as Melanie Klein pointed out (1945), the Oedipal-stage child perceives the mother and the father as whole-objects, in terms of whose conjugal relationship the child's triadic jealousy normally proceeds to supercede his more primitive dyadic envy.

SUMMARY

This chapter has sought to relate the self- and object-representational components underlying Fairbairn's endopsychic structures to the classical psychoanalytic structures, with particular emphasis on the components of the superego. Particular attention has been accorded the nature of the relationship between splitting and repression from both classical and object-relations points of view, the latter as developed and expressed within the body of Fairbairn's writings. Finally, this chapter attempted to extend and expand the author's prior effort (chapter 4) to apply representational and developmental concepts to Fairbairn's concepts of dynamics and structure.

REFERENCES

Abenheimer, K. M. (1955), Critical observations on Fairbairn's theory of object relations. *Br. J. Med. Psychol.*, 28: 29–41.

Abraham, K. (1912), Notes on the psycho-analytical investigation and treatment of manic-depressive insanity and allied conditions. In: *Selected Papers on Psycho-Analysis*, trans. D. Bryan & A. Strachey. London: Hogarth Press, pp. 137–156.

————— (1916), The first pregenital stage of the libido. In: *Selected Papers of Karl Abraham*. London: Hogarth Press, 1927, pp. 248–279.

————— (1921), Contributions to the theory of the anal character. In: *Selected Papers of Karl Abraham*. London: Hogarth Press, 1927, pp. 370–392.

————— (1924), A short study of the development of the libido, viewed in the light of mental disorders. In: *Selected Papers of Karl Abraham*. London: Hogarth Press, 1927, pp. 418–501.

Abrams, R., Taylor, M. A., & Gaztanaga, P. (1974), Manic-depressive illness and paranoid schizophrenia. *Arch. Gen. Psychiatry*, 31: 640–642.

Ackerman, N. W. (1958), *The Psychodynamics of Family Life*. New York: Basic Books.

————— (1962), Adolescent problems: A symposium of family disorder. *Family Process*, 1: 202–213.

————— (1967), The future of family psychotherapy. In: *Expanding Theory and Practice in Family Therapy*, ed. N. W. Ackerman et al. New York: Family Service Assn. of America, pp. 3–16.

Adler, G. (1979), The myth of the alliance with borderline patients. *Amer. J. Psychiatry*, 136: 642–645.

———— (1981), The borderline-narcissistic personality disorder continuum. *Amer. J. Psychiatry*, 138: 46–50.

Aichhorn, A. (1925), *Wayward Youth*. New York: Viking, 1935.

Akiskal, H. S. & Puzantian, V. R. (1979), Psychotic forms of depression and mania. In: *Affective Disorders: Special Clinical Forms*, ed. H. S. Akiskal. *The Psychiatric Clinics of North America*, 2: 419–439.

Alexander, F. (1930), The neurotic character. In: *The Scope of Psychoanalysis, 1921–1961: Selected Papers of Franz Alexander*. New York: Basic Books, 1961, pp. 56–73.

———— & Healy, W. (1935), *Roots of Crime: Psychoanalytic Studies*. New York: Knopf.

Anthony, E. J. (1968), The developmental precursors of adult schizophrenia. In: *The Transmission of Schizophrenia*, ed. D. Rosenthal & S. Kety. Oxford: Pergamon Press, pp. 293–316.

Arlow, J. & Brenner, C. (1964), *Psychoanalytic Concepts and the Structural Theory*. New York: International Universities Press.

Balint, M. (1968), *The Basic Fault: Therapeutic Aspects of Regression*. London: Tavistock.

Barker, P. (ed.) (1974), *The Residential Psychiatric Treatment of Children*. New York: Wiley.

Bateson, G. (1972), *Steps to an Ecology of Mind*. New York: Ballantine.

———— et al. (1968), Toward a theory of schizophrenia. In: *Communication, Family, and Marriage* (Human Communication, Vol. 1), ed. D. D. Jackson. Palo Alto, Ca.: Science & Behavior Books, pp. 31–54.

Beck, R. & Weiss, H. B. (eds.) (1974), *The Rights of Children* (Harvard Educational Review Reprint Series No. 9). Cambridge, Ma.: Harvard Educational Review.

Bender, L. (1959), The concept of pseudopsychopathic schizophrenia in adolescents. *Amer. J. Orthopsychiatry*, 29: 491–512.

Benson, H. (1975), *The Relaxation Response*. New York: Morrow.

————, Beary, J. F., & Carol, M. P. (1974), The relaxation response. *Psychiatry*, 37: 37–46.

————, Kotch, J. B., Crassweller, K. D., & Greenwood, M. M. (1977), Historical and clinical considerations of the relaxation response. *Amer. Scientist*, 65: 441–445.

Beres, D. (1968), The humanness of human beings: Psychoanalytic considerations. *Psychoanal. Q.*, 37: 487–522.

Bergman, P. & Escalona, S. (1949), Unusual sensitivities in very young children. *The Psychoanal. Study of the Child*, 3/4: 333–352.

Berne, E. L. (1961), *Transactional Analysis in Psychotherapy*. New York: Grove Press.

Bettelheim, B. & Sylvester, E. (1952), A therapeutic milieu. *Amer. J. Orthopsychiatry*, 22: 314–334.

Bleuler, E. (1911), *Dementia Praecox or the Group of Schizophrenias*. Trans. J. Zinkin. New York: International Universities Press, 1950.

Bloch-Hoell, N. (1964), *The Pentecostal Movement*. London: Allen & Unwin.

Blofeld, J. (1977), *Mantras: Sacred Words of Power*. New York: Dutton.

Bowen, M. (1960), A family concept of schizophrenia. In: *The Etiology of Schizophrenia*, ed. D. D. Jackson. New York: Basic Books, pp. 346–372.

———— (1968), Family psychotherapy. In: *Theory and Practice of Family Psychiatry*, ed. J. G. Howells. Edinburgh: Oliver & Boyd, pp. 843–862.

Bowlby, J. (1953), Some pathological processes set in train by early mother-child separation. *J. Ment. Sci.*, 99: 265–272.

———— (1960a), Grief and mourning in infancy and early childhood. *The Psychoanal. Study of the Child*, 15: 9–52.

———— (1960b), Separation anxiety. *Internat. J. Psycho-Anal.*, 41: 89–113.

———— (1961), Processes of mourning. *Internat. J. Psycho-Anal.*, 42: 317–340.

————— (1962), Childhood bereavement and psychiatric illness. In: *Aspects of Psychiatric Research*, ed. D. Richter et al. London: Oxford University Press, pp. 262–293.

Boyer, L. B. & Giovacchini, P. L. (1967), *Psychoanalytic Treatment of Characterological and Schizophrenic Disorders*. New York: Science House.

Brazelton, T. B. (1969), *Infants and Mothers*. New York: Dell.

Brende, J. O. (1974), Speaking in tongues: A psychological study. In: *Psychiatric Assessment by Speech and Hearing Behavior*, ed. C. L. Rousey. Springfield, Ill.: Charles Thomas.

————— & Rinsley, D. B. (1979), Borderline disorder, altered states of consciousness, and glossolalia. *J. Amer. Acad. Psychoanal.*, 7: 165–188.

Brentano, F. (1874), *Psychologie vom empirischen Standpunkte*. Leipzig: Meiner.

Breuer, J. & Freud, S. (1893), On the psychical mechanism of hysterical phenomena. In: Studies on hysteria, *Standard Edition*, 2: 3–17. London: Hogarth Press, 1957 (1955).

————— & ————— (1893–1895), Studies on hysteria. *Standard Edition*, 2: 135–181. London: Hogarth Press, 1957 (1955).

Brown, B. B. (1970), Recognition of aspects of consciousness through association with EEG alpha activity represented by a light signal. *Psychophysiology*, 6: 442–452.

————— (1974) *New Mind, New Body: Bio-feedback: New Directions for the Mind*. New York: Harper & Row.

Brown, N. O. (1959), *Life Against Death*. Middletown, Cn.: Wesleyan University Press.

Buber, M. (1958), *I and Thou*. New York: Scribner's.

Bursten, B. (1978), A diagnostic framework. *Internat. Rev. Psycho-Anal.*, 5: 15–31.

Cannon, W. B. (1929), *Bodily Changes in Pain, Hunger, Fear, and Rage*, 2nd ed., Boston: Branford, 1953.

Carlson, G. & Strober, M. (1979), Affective disorders in adolescence. *The Psychiatric Clinics of North America*, 2: 511–526.

Carrington, P. & Ephron, H. S. (1975), Meditation as an adjunct to psychotherapy. In: *New Dimensions in Psychiatry: A World View*, ed. S. Arieti & G. Chrzanowski. New York: Wiley.

Chaney, R. B. & Webster, J. C. (1966), Information on certain multidimensional sounds. *J. Acoustic Soc. Amer.*, 40: 447–455.

Chaslin, P. (1912), *Elements de Semiologie et Cliniques Mentales.* Paris: Asselin and Houzeau.

Chiland, C. & Lebovici, S. (1977), Borderline or prepsychotic conditions in childhood—A French point of view. In: *Borderline Personality Disorders: The Concept, the Syndrome, the Patient*, ed. P. Hartocollis. New York: International Universities Press, pp. 143–154.

Chodoff, P. (1972), The depressive personality: A critical review. *Arch. Gen. Psychiatry*, 27: 666–673.

Claparède, E. (1911), Recognition and "me-ness." In: *Organization and Pathology of Thought*, ed. D. Rapaport. New York: Columbia University Press, 1951.

Creak, E. M. (1963), Childhood psychosis: A review of 100 cases. *Br. J. Psychiatry*, 109: 84–89.

Deikman, A. J. (1966), Implications of experimentally induced contemplative meditation. *J. Nerv. Mental Dis.*, 142: 101–117.

Deutsch, H. (1942), Some forms of emotional disturbance and their relationship to schizophrenia. In: *Neuroses and Character Types*. New York: International Universities Press, 1965, pp. 262–281.

Dickes, R. (1978), Parents, transitional objects, and childhood fetishes. In: *Between Reality and Fantasy: Transitional Objects and Phenomena*, ed. S. A. Grolnick et al. New York: Aronson, pp. 307–319.

DSM-I (1952), *Diagnostic and Statistical Manual of Mental Disorders.* 1st ed. Washington, D.C.: American Psychiatric Association.

DSM-II (1968), *Diagnostic and Statistical Manual of Mental Disorders.* 2nd ed. Washington, D.C.: American Psychiatric Association.

DSM-III (1980), *Diagnostic and Statistical Manual of Mental Disorders.* 3rd ed. Washington, D.C.: American Psychiatric Association.

Durup, G. & Fessard, A. (1936), L'electren-cephalogramme de l'homme. Observations psychophysiologiques relatives de l'action des stimuli visuels et auditifs. *Ann. Psychol.*, 36: 1–32.

Easson, W. M. (1969), *The Severely Disturbed Adolescent: Inpatient, Residential, and Hospital Treatment.* New York: International Universities Press.

Eisenberg, L. (1968), The interaction of biological and experiential factors in schizophrenia. In: *The Transmission of Schizophrenia*, ed. S. Kety & D. Rosenthal. Oxford: Pergamon Press, pp. 403–409.

Eissler, K. R. 1953), The effect of the structure of the ego on psychoanalytic technique. *J. Amer. Psychoanal. Assn.*, 1: 104–143.

——— (1958), Remarks on some variations in psychoanalytic technique. *Internat. J. Psycho-Anal.*, 39: 222–229.

Ekstein, R. (1966), *Children of Time and Space, of Action and Impulse.* New York: Appleton-Century-Crofts.

——— (1971), *The Challenge: Despair and Hope in the Conquest of Inner Space.* New York: Brunner/Mazel.

Engel, M. (1963), Psychological testing of borderline psychotic children. *Arch. Gen. Psychiatry*, 8: 426–434.

——— (1972), *Psychopathology in Childhood: Social, Diagnostic, and Therapeutic Aspects.* New York: Harcourt Brace Jovanovich.

Erikson, E. H. (1956), The problem of ego identity. *J. Amer. Psychoanal. Assn.*, 4: 56–121.

——— (1963), *Childhood and Society.* Rev. ed. New York: Norton.

Esman, A. H. (1980), Adolescent psychopathology and the rapprochement process. In: *Rapprochement: The Critical Subphase of Separation-Individuation*, ed. R. F. Lax, S. Bach, & J. A. Burland. New York: Aronson, pp. 285–297.

Fairbairn, W. R. D. (1940), Schizoid factors in the personality. In: *An Object-Relations Theory of the Personality*. New York: Basic Books, 1954, pp. 3–27.

—— (1941), A revised psychopathology of the psychoses and the psychoneuroses. In: *An Object-Relations Theory of the Personality*. New York: Basic Books, 1954, pp. 28–58.

—— (1943), The repression and the return of bad objects (with special reference to the "war neuroses"). In: *An Object-Relations Theory of the Personality*. New York: Basic Books, 1954, pp. 59–81.

—— (1944), Endopsychic structure considered in terms of object-relationships. In: *An Object-Relations Theory of the Personality*. New York: Basic Books, 1954, pp. 82–136.

—— (1946), Object-relations and dynamic structure. In: *An Object-Relations Theory of the Personality*. New York: Basic Books, 1954, pp. 137–151.

—— (1949), Steps in the development of an object-relations theory of the personality. In: *An Object-Relations Theory of the Personality*. New York: Basic Books, 1954, pp. 152–161.

—— (1951a), Addendum to 1944 work op. cit., pp. 133–136.

—— (1951b), A synopsis of the development of the author's views regarding the structure of the personality. In: *An Object-Relations View of the Personality*. New York: Basic Books. 1954, pp. 162–179.

—— (1954), *An Object-Relations Theory of the Personality*. New York: Basic Books.

—— (1963), Synopsis of an object-relations theory of the personality. *Internat. J. Psycho-Anal.*, 44: 224–225.

Fast, I. (1975), Aspects of work style and work difficulty in borderline personalities. *Internat. J. Psycho-Anal.*, 56: 397–403.

Federn, E. (1962), The therapeutic personality, as illustrated by Paul Federn and August Aichhorn. *Psychiat. Q.*, 36: 29–43.

Federn, P. (1952), 1. Ego psychological aspect of schizophrenia; 2. The ego in schizophrenia. In: *Ego Psychology and the Psychoses*, ed. E. Weiss. New York: Basic Books, pp. 212–240.

Fenichel, O. (1945), *The Psychoanalytic Theory of Neurosis*. New York: Norton.

Fischer, R. (1971), A cartography of ecstatic and meditative states. *Science*, 174: 897–904.

Fliess, R. (1961), *Ego and Body Ego: Contributions to their Psychoanalytic Psychology*. New York: Schulte.

Fraiberg, S. (1969), Libidinal object constancy and mental representation. *The Psychoanal. Study of the Child*, 24: 9–47.

Frankel, S. A. (1977), The treatment of a narcissistic disturbance in childhood. *Internat. J. Psychoanal. Psychother.*, 6: 165–186.

Freud, A. (1960), Discussion of Dr. John Bowlby's paper. *The Psychoanal. Study of the Child*, 15: 53–62.

———— (1968), Panel discussion held at the 25th Congress of the International Psycho-Analytical Association, Copenhagen, July, 1967. *Internat. J. Psycho-Anal.*, 49: 506–512.

———— & Dann, S. (1951), An experiment in group upbringing. *The Psychoanal. Study of the Child*, 27: 621–625.

Freud, S. (1895), Project for a scientific psychology. *Standard Edition*, 1: 283–397. London: Hogarth Press, 1966.

———— (1905), Three essays on the theory of sexuality. *Standard Edition*, 7: 135–245. London: Hogarth Press, 1953.

———— (1911a), Formulations on the two principles of mental functioning. *Standard Edition*, 12: 218–226. London: Hogarth Press, 1958.

———— (1911b), Psycho-analytic notes on an autobiographical account of a case of paranoia (dementia paranoides). *Standard Edition*, 12: 9–82. London: Hogarth Press, 1958.

———— (1914a), On the history of the psychoanalytic movement. *Standard Edition*, 14: 7–66. London: Hogarth Press, 1957.

———— (1914b), On narcissism: An introduction. *Standard Edition*, 14: 73–102. London: Hogarth Press, 1957.

———— (1915a), Instincts and their vicissitudes. *Standard Edition*, 14: 117–140. London: Hogarth Press, 1957.

———— (1915b), Repression. *Standard Edition*, 14: 146–158. London: Hogarth Press, 1957.

——— (1916), Some character types met with in psycho-analytic work. *Standard Edition*, 14: 311–333. London: Hogarth Press, 1957.

——— (1917a), Introductory lectures on psycho-analysis, Part III. *Standard Edition*, 16: 243–448. London: Hogarth Press, 1957.

——— (1917b), Mourning and melancholia. *Standard Edition*, 14: 243–258. London: Hogarth Press, 1957.

——— (1920), Beyond the pleasure principle. *Standard Edition*, 18: 7–64. London: Hogarth Press, 1955.

——— (1921), Group psychology and analysis of the ego. *Standard Edition*, 18:69–143. London: Hogarth Press, 1957 (1955).

——— (1923), The ego and the id. *Standard Edition*, 19: 12–66. London: Hogarth Press, 1961.

——— (1924a), The loss of reality in neurosis and psychosis. *Standard Edition*, 19: 183–187. London: Hogarth Press, 1961.

——— (1924b), Neurosis and psychosis. *Standard Edition*, 19: 149–153. London: Hogarth Press, 1961.

——— (1926), Inhibitions, symptoms, and anxiety. *Standard Edition*, 20: 87–172. London: Hogarth Press, 1959.

——— (1927), Fetishism. *Standard Edition*, 21: 152–157. London: Hogarth Press, 1968.

——— (1930), Civilization and its discontents. *Standard Edition*, 21: 64–145. London: Hogarth Press, 1968.

——— (1933), New introductory lectures on psycho-analysis. *Standard Edition*, 22: 5–193. London: Hogarth Press, 1964.

——— (1939), Moses and monotheism. *Standard Edition*, 23: 7–137. London: Hogarth Press, 1964.

——— (1940a), An outline of psycho-analysis. *Standard Edition*, 23: 144–207. London: Hogarth Press, 1964.

——— (1940b), Splitting of the ego in the process of defence. *Standard Edition*, 23: 275–278. London: Hogarth Press, 1964.

Frosch, J. (1960), Psychotic character. *J. Amer. Psychoanal. Assn.*, 8: 544–551.

——— (1964), The psychotic character. *Psychiat. Q.*, 38: 81–96.

————— (1970), Psychoanalytic considerations of the psychotic character. *J. Amer. Psychoanal. Assn.*, 18: 24–50.

Fuchs, R. R. & van der Schraaf, A. H. (1979), Borderline conditions. In: *Clinician's Handbook of Childhood Psychopathology*, ed. M. M. Josephson & R. T. Porter. New York: Aronson, pp. 69–82.

Galin, D. & Ornstein, R. E. (1972), Lateral specialization of cognitive mode: An EEG study. *Psychophysiology*, 9: 412–418.

Gellhorn, E. (1967), *Principles of Autonomic-Somatic Integrations: Physiological Basis and Psychological and Clinical Implications.* Minneapolis: University of Minnesota Press.

————— & Kiely, W. F. (1972), Mystical states of consciousness: Neurophysiological and clinical aspects. *J. Nerv. Mental Dis.*, 154: 399–405.

Giovacchini, P. L. (1979), *Treatment of Primitive Mental States.* New York: Aronson.

Gittelman-Klein, R. (ed.) (1975), *Recent Advances in Child Psychopharmacology* (Child Psychiatry and Psychology Series). New York: Human Sciences Press.

————— et al. (1978), Diagnostic classifications and psychopharmacological indications. In: *Pediatric Psychopharmacology: The Use of Behavior-Modifying Drugs in Children*, ed. J. S. Werry. New York: Brunner/Mazel, pp. 136–167.

Glover, E. (1945), Examination of the Klein system of child psychology. *The Psychoanal. Study of the Child*, 1: 75–118.

————— (1949), The position of psycho-analysis in Great Britain. In: *Selected Papers on Psycho-Analysis, Vol I: On the Early Development of the Mind.* New York: International Universities Press, 1956, pp. 352–363.

————— (1968), *The Birth of the Ego: A Nuclear Hypothesis.* New York: International Universities Press.

Glueck, B. C. & Stroebel, C. F. (1975), Biofeedback and meditation in the treatment of psychiatric illness. *Comprehensive Psychiatry*, 16: 303–321.

Goldfarb, W. (1945), Psychological privation in infancy and subsequent adjustment. *Amer. J. Orthopsychiatry*, 15: 247–255.

———— (1961), *Childhood Schizophrenia*. Cambridge, Mass.: Harvard University Press.

Goldstein, K. (1959a), Functional disturbances in brain damage. In: *American Handbook of Psychiatry*, Vol. 1, ed. S. Arieti. New York: Basic Books, pp. 770–794.

———— (1959b), The organismic approach. In: *American Handbook of Psychiatry*, Vol. II, ed. S. Arieti. New York: Basic Books, pp. 1333–1347.

Goldstein, M. J. & Jones, J. E. (1977), Adolescent and familial precursors of borderline and schizophrenic conditions. In: *Borderline Personality Disorders: The Concept, the Syndrome, the Patient*, ed. P. Hartocollis. New York: International Universities Press, pp. 213–229.

Goodman, F. D. (1972), *Speaking in Tongues*. Chicago: University of Chicago Press.

Gottesman, I. I. (1968), Severity/concordance and diagnostic refinement in the Maudsley-Bethlehem schizophrenic twin study. In: *The Transmission of Schizophrenia*, ed. D. Rosenthal & S. Kety. Oxford: Pergamon Press, pp. 37–48.

———— & Shields, J. (1972), *Schizophrenia and Genetics: A Twin Study Vantage Point*. New York: Academic Press.

Greenhill, M. H. (1976), The self-destruction of psychiatry. *Res. Commun. Psychol. Psychiat. Behav.*, 1: 347–354.

Greenwood, E. D. (1955), The role of psychotherapy in residential treatment. *Amer. J. Orthopsychiatry*, 25: 692–698.

Grinker, R. R. & Werble, B. (1977), *The Borderline Patient*. New York: Aronson.

————, ————, & Drye, R. (eds.) (1968), *The Borderline Syndrome: A Behavioral Study of Ego Functions*. New York: Basic Books.

Group for the Advancement of Psychiatry (1976), *Mysticism: Spiritual Quest or Psychic Disorder?*, Vol. 9, no. 97.

Grotstein, J. S. (1981), *Splitting and Projective Identification*. New York: Aronson.

Guntrip, H. J. S. (1961), *Personality Structure and Human Interaction: The Developing Synthesis of Psychodynamic Theory.* New York: International Universities Press, 1964.

———— (1968), *Schizoid Phenomena, Object Relations, and the Self.* New York: International Universities Press.

———— (1971), *Psychoanalytic Theory, Therapy, and the Self.* New York: Basic Books.

Haley, J. (1963), *Strategies of Psychotherapy.* New York: Grune & Stratton.

Harper, M. (1965), *As at the Beginning: The Twentieth Century Pentecostal Revival.* Plainfield, N.J.: Logos International.

Hartmann, H. (1950), Comments on the psychoanalytic theory of the ego. In: *Essays on Ego Psychology.* New York: International Universities Press, 1964, pp. 113–141.

———— (1952), The mutual influences in the development of ego and id. In: *Essays on Ego Psychology.* New York: International Universities Press, 1964, pp. 155–182.

———— (1955), Notes on the theory of sublimation. In: *Essays on Ego Psychology.* New York: International Universities Press, 1964, pp. 215–240.

———— (1956a), The development of the ego concept in Freud's work. In: *Essays on Ego Psychology.* New York: International Universities Press, 1964, pp. 268–296.

———— (1956b), Notes on the reality principle. In: *Essays on Ego Psychology.* New York: International Universities Press, 1964, pp. 241–267.

———— (1964), *Essays on Ego Psychology: Selected Problems in Psychoanalytic Theory.* New York: International Universities Press.

Healy, W. & Bronner, A. F. (1936), *New Light on Delinquency and Its Treatment.* New Haven, Ct.: Yale University Press.

Hendrickson, W. J. (1957), Adolescent Service, Neuropsychiatric Institute, University of Michigan. *Bulletin of the Michigan Society for Mental Health*, 13: 1–9.

———— & Holmes, D. J. (1959), Control of behavior as a crucial factor in intensive psychiatric treatment in an all-adolescent ward. *Amer. J. Psychiatry*, 115: 969–973.

——, ——, & Waggoner, R. W. (1959), Psychotherapy of the hospitalized adolescent. *Amer. J. Psychiatry*, 116: 527–532.

Hersov, L. A. (1974), Neurotic disorders with special reference to school refusal. In: *The Residential Psychiatric Treatment of Children*, ed. P. A. Barker. New York: Wiley, pp. 105–141.

Hess, W. R. (1957), *Functional Organization of the Diencephalon*. New York: Grune & Stratton.

Hewitt, L. E. & Jenkins, R. L. (1964), *Fundamental Patterns of Maladjustment: The Dynamics of Their Origin*. Springfield, Il.: State of Illinois Publications.

Hinsie, L. E. & Campbell, R. J. (1970), *Psychiatric Dictionary*, 4th ed. New York: Oxford University Press.

Hoch, P. H. & Polatin, P. (1949), Pseudoneurotic forms of schizophrenia. *Psychiatric Q.*, 23: 248–276.

Horton, W. H. (1966), *The Glossolalia Phenomenon*. Cleveland, Tn.: Pathway Press.

Irwin, O. C. (1948), Infant speech: Development of vowel sounds. *J. Speech Hear. Disorders*, 13: 31–34.

Jackson, D. D. & Weakland, J. H. (1961), Conjoint family therapy: Some considerations on theory, technique, and results. *Psychiatry*, 24 (supplement to no. 2): 30–45.

Jacobson, E. (1954a), Contribution to the metapsychology of psychotic identifications. *J. Amer. Psychoanal. Assn.*, 2: 239–262.

—— (1954b), On psychotic identifications. *Internat. J. Psycho-Anal.*, 35: 102–108.

—— (1954c), The self and the object world: Vicissitudes of their infantile cathexes and their influence on ideational and affective development. *The Psychoanal. Study of the Child*, 9: 75–127.

———— (1957), Denial and repression. *J. Amer. Psychoanal. Assn.*, 5: 61–92.

———— (1964), *The Self and the Object World*. New York: International Universities Press.

———— (1971), *Depression*. New York: International Universities Press.

Janet, P. (1907), *The Major Symptoms of Hysteria*. New York: Macmillan.

Johnson, A. B. (1977), A temple of last resorts. In: *The Narcissistic Condition*, ed. M. C. Nelson. New York: Human Sciences Press, pp. 27–65.

Johnson, A. M. (1949), Sanctions for superego lacunae of adolescents. In: *Searchlights on Delinquency*, ed. K. R. Eissler. New York: International Universities Press, pp. 225–245.

———— (1959), Juvenile delinquency. In: *American Handbook of Psychiatry*, Vol. I, ed. S. Arieti. New York: Basic Books, pp. 840–856.

———— & Szurek, S. A. (1952), The genesis of antisocial acting out in children and adults. *Psychoanal. Q.*, 21: 323–343.

Jones, E. (1913), The significance of the grandfather for the fate of the individual. In: *Papers on Psycho-Analysis*, 4th ed. London: Bailliere, Tindall & Cox, 1938, pp. 519–524.

Kaplan, L. J. (1980), Rapprochement and oedipal organization: Effects on borderline phenomena. In: *Rapprochement: The Critical Subphase of Separation-Individuation*, ed. R. F. Lax et al. New York: Aronson, pp. 39–63.

Kelsey, M. T. (1964), *Tongue Speaking*. Garden City, N.Y.: Doubleday.

Kernberg, O. F. (1966), Structural derivatives of object relationships. *Internat. J. Psycho-Anal.*, 47: 236–253.

———— (1967), Borderline personality organization. *J. Amer. Psychoanal. Assn.*, 15: 641–685.

———— (1968), The treatment of patients with borderline personality organization. *Internat. J. Psycho-Anal.*, 49: 600–619.

———— (1970a), Factors in the psychoanalytic treatment of narcissistic personalities. *J. Amer. Psychoanal. Assn.*, 18: 51–85.

———— (1970b), A psychoanalytic classification of character pathology. *J. Amer. Psychoanal. Assn.*, 18: 800–822.

———— (1971a), New developments in psychoanalytic object-relations theory. (Paper read to the American Psychoanalytic Association, Washington, D.C.)

———— (1971b), Prognostic considerations regarding borderline personality organization. *J. Amer. Psychoanal. Assn.*, 19: 595–635.

———— (1972a), Early ego integration and object relations. *Annals N.Y. Acad. Sci.*, 193: 233–247.

———— (1972b), Summary and conclusions. Psychotherapy and psychoanalysis: Final report of The Menninger Foundation's Psychotherapy Research Project. *Bull. Menninger Clin.*, 36: 181–195.

———— (1975), *Borderline Conditions and Pathological Narcissism*. New York: Aronson.

———— (1977), The structural diagnosis of borderline personality organization. In: *Borderline Personality Disorders: The Concept, the Syndrome, the Patient*, ed. P. Hartocollis. New York: International Universities Press, pp. 87–121.

———— (1979a), Contributions of Edith Jacobson: An overview. *J. Amer. Psychoanal. Assn.*, 27: 793–819.

———— (1979b), Some implications of object-relations theory for psychoanalytic technique. *J. Amer. Psychoanal. Assn.*, 27 (supplement): 207–239.

———— (1980a), Developmental theory, structural organization, and psychoanalytic technique. In: *Rapprochement: The Critical Subphase of Separation-Individuation*, ed. R. F. Lax et al. New York: Aronson, pp. 23–38.

———— (1980b), Fairbairn's theory and challenge. In: *Internal World and External Reality: Object-Relations Theory Applied*. New York: Aronson, pp. 57–84.

———— (1980c), Regression in leaders. In: *Internal World and External Reality: Object-Relations Theory Applied*. New York: Aronson, pp. 253–273.

———— (1980d), A theory of psychoanalytic psychotherapy. In: *Internal World and External Reality: Object-Relations Theory Applied.* New York: Aronson, pp. 181–208.

Kety, S. et al. (1968), Mental illness in the biological and adoptive families of adopted schizophrenics. In: *The Transmission of Schizophrenia,* ed. D. Rosenthal & S. Kety. Oxford: Pergamon Press, pp. 345–362.

Khan, M. M. R. (1963), The concept of cumulative trauma. *The Psychoanal. Study of the Child,* 18: 286–306.

Kildahl, J. P. (1972), *The Psychology of Speaking in Tongues.* New York: Harper & Row.

Kimura, D. (1973), The asymmetry of the human brain. *Scientific Amer.,* 228: 70–78.

Klein, D. F. (1975), Psychopharmacology and the borderline patient. In: *Borderline States in Psychiatry,* ed. J. E. Mack. New York: Grune & Stratton, pp. 75–92.

———— (1977), Psychopharmacological treatment and delineation of borderline disorders. In: *Borderline Personality Disorders: The Concept, the Syndrome, the Patient,* ed. P. Hartocollis. New York: International Universities Press, pp. 365–383.

———— & Davis, J. (1969), *Drug Treatment and Psychodiagnosis.* Baltimore: Williams & Wilkins.

Klein, M. (1932), *The Psycho-Analysis of Children.* London: Hogarth Press.

———— (1933), The early development of conscience in the child. In: *Melanie Klein: Love, Guilt and Reparation & Other Works, 1921–1945.* New York: Delacorte Press/Seymour Lawrence, 1975, pp. 248–257.

———— (1935), A contribution to the psychogenesis of manic-depressive states. In: *Melanie Klein: Love, Guilt and Reparation & Other Works, 1921–1945.* New York: Delacorte Press/Seymour Lawrence, 1975, pp. 262–289.

———— (1940), Mourning and its relation to manic-depressive states. In: *Melanie Klein: Love, Guilt and Reparation & Other Works, 1921–1945.* New York: Delacorte Press, 1975, pp. 344–369.

———— (1945), The Oedipus complex in the light of early

anxieties. In: *Melanie Klein: Love, Guilt and Reparation & Other Works, 1921–1945*. New York: Delacorte Press, 1975, pp. 370–419.

———— (1946), Notes on some schizoid mechanisms. In: *Melanie Klein: Envy and Gratitude & Other Works, 1946–1963*. London: Hogarth Press/New York: Delacorte Press/Seymour Lawrence, 1975, pp. 1–24.

———— (1948), On the theory of anxiety and guilt. In: *Melanie Klein: Envy and Gratitude & Other Works, 1946–1963*. New York: Delacorte Press/Seymour Lawrence, 1975, pp. 25–42.

———— (1952), Some theoretical conclusions regarding the emotional life of the infant. In: *Melanie Klein: Envy and Gratitude & Other Works, 1946–1963*. New York: Delacorte Press/Seymour Lawrence, 1975, pp. 61–93.

———— (1955), On identification. In: *Melanie Klein: Envy and Gratitude & Other Works, 1946–1963*. New York: Delacorte Press/Seymour Lawrence, 1975, pp. 141–175.

———— (1958), On the development of mental functioning. In: *Melanie Klein: Envy and Gratitude & Other Works, 1946–1963*. New York: Delacorte Press/Seymour Lawrence, 1975, pp. 236–246.

Knight, R. P. (1953), Borderline states. *Bull. Menninger Clin.*, 17: 1–12.

———— (1954), Management and psychotherapy of the borderline schizophrenic patient. In: *Psychoanalytic Psychiatry and Psychology*, ed. R. P. Knight & C. R. Friedman. New York: International Universities Press, pp. 110–122.

Kohut, H. (1971), *The Analysis of the Self*. New York: International Universities Press.

———— (1977), *The Restoration of the Self*. New York: International Universities Press.

Kolb, L. C. (1973), *Modern Clinical Psychiatry*, 8th ed. Philadelphia: Saunders.

Kris, A. O. (1976), On wanting too much: The "exceptions" revisited. *Internat. J. Psycho-Anal.*, 57: 85–95.

Kris, E. (1952), *Psychoanalytic Explorations in Art*. New York: International Universities Press.

———— (1955), Neutralization and sublimation: Observations on young children. *The Psychoanal. Study of the Child*, 10: 30–46.

Krohn, A. (1974), Borderline "empathy" and differentiations of object representations. *Internat. J. Psychoanal. Psychother.*, 3: 142–165.

Kumin, I. M. (1978), Emptiness and its relation to schizoid ego structure. *Internat. Rev. Psychoanal.*, 5: 207–216.

Kut Rosenfeld, S. K. & Sprince, M. P. (1963), An attempt to formulate the meaning of the concept "borderline." *The Psychoanal. Study of the Child*, 18: 603–635.

L'Abate, L. (1976), *Understanding and Helping the Individual in the Family*. New York: Grune & Stratton.

Laing, R. D. (1967), *The Politics of Experience*, New York: Pantheon Books.

Lasch, C. (1977), *Haven in a Heartless World: The Family Besieged*. New York: Basic Books.

———— (1978), *The Culture of Narcissism: American Life in an Age of Diminishing Expectations*. New York: Norton.

Lax, R., Bach, S., & Burland, J. A. (eds.) (1980), *Rapprochement: The Critical Subphase of Separation-Individuation*. New York: Aronson.

Lesh, T. V. (1970), Zen meditation and the development of empathy in counselors. *J. Human. Psychol.*, 10: 39–74.

Lewis, D. O. & Balla, D. A. (1976), *Delinquency and Psychopathology*. New York: Grune & Stratton.

Lewis, J. M. (1970), The development of an adolescent inpatient service. *Adolescence*, 5: 303–312.

Lidz, T., Fleck, S., & Cornelison, A. R. (1965), *Schizophrenia and the Family*. New York: International Universities Press.

————, ————, & ———— (1968), Schism and skew in the families of schizophrenics. In: *A Modern Introduction to the Family*, rev. ed., ed. N. W. Bell & E. F. Vogel. New York: Free Press, pp. 650–662.

Liebowitz, M. R. & Klein, D. F. (1979), Hysteroid dysphoria. In:

Affective Disorders: Special Clinical Forms, ed. H. S. Akiskal. *The Psychiatric Clinics of North America*, 2: 555–575.

Loewald, H. W. (1974), Current status of the concept of infantile neurosis: Discussion. *The Psychoanal. Study of the Child*, 29: 183–188.

Lovekin, A. & Malony, H. N. (1977), Religious glossolalia: A longitudinal study of personality changes. *J. Sci. Study Religion*, 16: 383–393.

Mahler, M. S. (1952), On child psychosis and schizophrenia: Autistic and symbiotic infantile psychoses. *The Psychoanal. Study of the Child*, 7: 286–305. Reprinted in *The Selected Papers of Margaret S. Mahler*, Vol. 1. New York: Aronson, 1979, pp. 132–153.

——— (1958), Autism and symbiosis: two extreme disturbances in identity. *Internat. J. Psycho-Anal.*, 39: 77–83. Reprinted in *The Selected Papers of Margaret S. Mahler*, Vol. 1. New York: Aronson, 1979, pp. 169–181.

——— (1963), Thoughts about development and individuation. *The Psychoanal. Study of the Child*, 18: 307–324. Reprinted in *The Selected Papers of Margaret S. Mahler*, Vol. 2. New York: Aronson, 1979, pp. 3–19.

——— (1965a), On early infantile psychosis: The symbiotic and autistic syndromes. *J. Amer. Acad. Child Psychiatry*, 4: 554–568. Reprinted in *The Selected Papers of Margaret S. Mahler*, Vol. 1. New York: Aronson, 1979, pp. 155–168.

——— (1965b), On the significance of the normal separation-individuation phase with reference to research in symbiotic child psychosis. In: *Drives, Affects, Behavior*, Vol. 2, ed. M. Schur. New York: International Universities Press, pp. 161–169. Reprinted in *The Selected Papers of Margaret S. Mahler*, Vol. 2. New York: Aronson, 1979, pp. 49–57.

——— (1967), On human symbiosis and the vicissitudes of individuation. *J. Amer. Psychoanal. Assn.*, 25: 740–763. Reprinted in *The Selected Papers of Margaret S. Mahler*, Vol 2. New York: Aronson, 1979, pp. 77–97.

———— (1968), *On Human Symbiosis and the Vicissitudes of Individuation, Vol. 1: Infantile Psychosis*. In collaboration with M. Furer. New York: International Universities Press.

———— (1971), A study of the separation-individuation process and its possible application to borderline phenomena in the psychoanalytic situation. *The Psychoanal. Study of the Child*, 26: 403–424. Reprinted in *The Selected Papers of Margaret S. Mahler*, Vol. 2. New York: Aronson, 1979, pp. 169–187.

———— (1972a), On the first three subphases of the separation-individuation process. *Internat. J. Psycho-Anal.*, 53: 333–338. Reprinted in *The Selected Papers of Margaret S. Mahler*, Vol. 2. New York: Aronson, 1979, pp. 119–130.

———— (1972b), Rapprochement subphase of the separation-individuation process. *Psychoanal. Q.*, 41: 487–506. Reprinted in *The Selected Papers of Margaret S. Mahler*, Vol. 2. New York: Aronson, 1979, pp. 131–148.

———— (1974), Symbiosis and individuation: The psychological birth of the human infant. *The Psychoanal. Study of the Child*, 29: 89–106.

———— & Furer, M. (1963), Certain aspects of the separation-individuation phase. *Psychoanal. Q.*, 32: 1–14. Reprinted in *The Selected Papers of Margaret S. Mahler*, Vol. 2. New York: Aronson, 1979, pp. 21–34.

————, ————, & Settlage, C. F. (1959), Severe emotional disturbances in childhood: Psychosis. In: *American Handbook of Psychiatry*, Vol. 1, ed. S. Arieti. New York: Basic Books, pp. 816–839.

———— & Gosliner, B. J. (1955), On symbiotic child psychosis: Genetic, dynamic, and restitutive aspects. *The Psychoanal. Study of the Child*, 10: 195–212. Reprinted in *The Selected Papers of Margaret S. Mahler*, Vol. 1. New York: Aronson, 1979, pp. 109–129.

———— & Kaplan, L. (1977), Developmental aspects in the assessment of narcissistic and so-called borderline personalities. In: *Borderline Personality Disorders: The Concept, the Syndrome, the Patient*, ed. P. Hartocollis. New York: International Universities Press, pp. 71–85.

———— & LaPerriere, K. (1965), Mother-child interaction during separation-individuation. *Psychoanal. Q.*, 34: 483–498. Reprinted in *The Selected Papers of Margaret S. Mahler*, Vol. 2. New York: Aronson, 1979, pp. 35–48.

———— & McDevitt, J. B. (1968), Observations on adaptation and defence *in statu nascendi*: Developmental precursors in the first two years of life. *Psychoanal. Q.*, 37: 1–21. Reprinted in *The Selected Papers of Margaret S. Mahler*, Vol. 2. New York: Aronson, 1979, pp. 99–117.

————, Pine, F., & Bergman, A. (1970), The mother's reaction to her toddler's drive for individuation. In: *Parenthood: Its Psychology and Psychopathology*, ed. E. J. Anthony & T. Benedek. Boston: Little, Brown, pp. 257–274.

————, Pine F., & Bergman, A. (1975). *The Psychological Birth of the Human Infant: Symbiosis and Individuation*. New York: Basic Books.

————, Ross, J. R., & DeFries, Z. (1949), Clinical studies in benign and malignant cases of childhood psychosis (schizophrenialike). *Amer. J. Orthopsychiatry*, 19: 295–305.

Mandelbaum, A. (1977), The family treatment of the borderline patient. In: *Borderline Personality Disorders: The Concept, the Syndrome, the Patient*, ed. P. Hartocollis. New York: International Universities Press, pp. 423–438.

Marcuse, H. (1955), *Eros and Civilization*. Boston: Beacon Press, 1965.

Masterson, J. F. (1967a), *The Psychiatric Dilemma of Adolescence*. Boston: Little, Brown.

———— (1967b), The symptomatic adolescent five years later: He didn't grow out of it. *Amer. J. Psychiatry*, 123: 1338–1345.

———— (1968), The psychiatric significance of adolescent turmoil. *Amer. J. Psychiatry*, 124: 1549–1554.

———— (1971a), Diagnosis and treatment of the borderline syndrome in adolescents. *Confrontations Psychiatriques*, 7: 125–155.

——— (1971b), Treatment of the adolescent with borderline syndrome: A problem in separation-individuation. *Bull. Menninger Clin.*, 35: 5–18.

——— (1972a), Intensive psychotherapy of the adolescent with a borderline syndrome. *Cuadernos de la Asociacion Argentina de Psiquiatria y Psicologia de la Infancia y de la Adolescencia*, 3: 15–50.

——— (1972b), *Treatment of the Borderline Adolescent: A Developmental Approach.* New York: Wiley-Interscience.

——— (1973), The borderline adolescent. *Adol. Psychiatry*, 2: 240–268.

——— (1974), Intensive psychotherapy of the adolescent with a borderline syndrome. In: *American Handbook of Psychiatry*, 2nd ed., Vol. 2, ed. S. Arieti. New York: Basic Books, pp. 250–263.

——— (1975), The splitting defense mechanism of the borderline adolescent: Developmental and clinical aspects. In: *Borderline States in Psychiatry*, ed. J. E. Mack. New York: Grune & Stratton, pp. 93–101.

——— (1976), *Psychotherapy of the Borderline Adult: A Developmental Approach.* New York: Brunner/Mazel.

——— (1977), Primary anorexia nervosa in the borderline adolescent: An object-relations view. In: *Borderline Personality Disorders: The Concept, the Syndrome, the Patient*, ed. P. Hartocollis. New York: International Universities Press, pp. 475–494.

——— (1979), Borderline and narcissistic disorders: Developmental considerations. Paper presented at a workshop sponsored by The Menninger Foundation and Smith, Kline & French Laboratories on "Borderline and Narcissistic Disorders." Vail, Colorado, March 3–10, 1979.

——— & Rinsley, D. B. (1975), The borderline syndrome: The role of the mother in the genesis and psychic structure of the borderline personality. *Internat. J. Psycho-Anal.*, 56: 163–177. Reprinted in this book, Chapter 2.

———, Tucker, K., & Berk, G. (1963), Psychopathology in

adolescence. IV. Clinical and dynamic characteristics. *Amer. J. Psychiatry*, 120: 357–366.

———, ———, & ——— (1966), The symptomatic adolescent: Delineation of psychiatric syndromes. *Comprehensive Psychiatry*, 7: 166–174.

——— & Washburne, A. (1966), The symptomatic adolescent: Psychiatric illness or adolescent turmoil? *Amer. J. Psychiatry*, 122: 1240–1248.

Maulsby, R. L. (1971), An illustration of emotionally evoked theta rhythm in infancy: Hedonic hypersynchrony. *Electroencephal. Clin. Neurophysiol.*, 31: 157–165.

McDevitt, J. B. (1980), The role of internalization in the development of object relations during the separation-individuation phase. In: *Rapprochement: The Critical Subphase of Separation-Individuation*, ed. R. F. Lax et al. New York: Aronson, pp. 135–149.

Menninger, K. A., Mayman, M., & Pruyser, P. W. (1963), *The Vital Balance*. New York: Viking.

Menninger, W. C. (1936a), Individuation in the prescription of nursing care of the psychiatric patient. *J. Amer. Med. Assn.*, 106: 756–761.

——— (1936b), Psychiatric hospital treatment designed to meet unconscious needs. *Amer. J. Psychiatry*, 93: 347–360.

——— (1937), Psychoanalytic principles applied to the treatment of hospitalized patients. *Bull. Menninger Clin.*, 1: 35–43.

——— (1939), Psychoanalytic principles in psychiatric hospital therapy. *Southern Med. J.*, 32: 348–354.

Metcalf, D. R. & Spitz, R. A. (1978), The transitional object: Critical developmental period and organizer of the psyche. In: *Between Reality and Fantasy: Transitional Objects and Phenomena*, ed. S. A. Grolnick et al. New York: Aronson, pp. 99–108.

Milner, P. (1962), Laterality effects in audition. In: *Interhemispheric Relations and Cerebral Dominance*, ed. V. B. Mountcastle. Baltimore: Johns Hopkins University Press.

Modell, A. H. (1963), Primitive object relationships and the predisposition to schizophrenia. *Internat. J. Psycho-Anal.*, 44: 282–292.

———— (1968), *Object Love and Reality: An Introduction to a Psychoanalytic Theory of Object Relations.* New York: International Universities Press.

———— (1971), The origin of certain forms of pre-Oedipal guilt and the implications for a psychoanalytic theory of affects. *Internat. J. Psycho-Anal.*, 52: 337–346.

———— (1975), The ego and the id fifty years later. *Internat. J. Psycho-Anal.*, 56: 57–68.

Morse, S. J. (1972), Structure and reconstruction: A critical comparison of Michael Balint and D. W. Winnicott. *Internat. J. Psycho-Anal.*, 53: 487–500.

Nagera, H. (1966), Sleep and its disturbance approached developmentally. *The Psychoanal. Study of the Child*, 21: 393–447.

Nelson, M. C. (ed.) (1977), *The Narcissistic Condition.* New York: Human Sciences Press.

Nemiah, J. & Sifneos, P. (1970), Affect and fantasy in patients with psychosomatic disorders. In: *Modern Trends in Psychosomatic Medicine*, Vol. 2, ed. D. W. Hill. London: Butterworth, pp. 26–35.

Noshpitz, J. D. (1962), Notes on the theory of residential treatment. *J. Amer. Acad. Child Psychiat.*, 1: 284–296.

Nunberg, H. (1955), *Principles of Psychoanalysis.* New York: International Universities Press.

Olds, J. & Milner, P. (1954), Positive reinforcement produced by electrical stimulation of septal area and other regions of the rat brain. *J. Compar. Physiol. Psychol.*, 47: 419–427.

Ornstein, P. H. (1974), On narcissism: Beyond the introduction, highlights of Heinz Kohut's contributions to the psychoanalytic treatment of narcissistic personality disorders. *Ann. Psychoanal.*, 2: 127–149.

Ornstein, R. E. (1972), *The Psychology of Consciousness*. San Francisco: Freeman.

Otis, L. S. (1974), If well-integrated but anxious, try TM. *Psychol. Today*, 7: 45–46.

Ovesey, L. (1969), *Homosexuality and Pseudohomosexuality*. New York: Science House.

Parens, H. & Saul, L. J. (1971), *Dependency in Man: A Psychoanalytic Study*. New York: International Universities Press.

Penfield, W. & Roberts, L. (1959), *Speech and Brain-Mechanisms*. Princeton, N.J.: Princeton University Press.

Peterfreund, E. (1971), Information, systems, and psychoanalysis: An evolutionary biological approach to psychoanalytic theory. *Psychological Issues*, 7(1/2), Monogr. 25/26. New York: International Universities Press.

Piaget, J. (1937), *The Construction of Reality in the Child*. New York: Basic Books, 1954.

Pine, F. (1974a), Libidinal object constancy: A theoretical note. *Psychoanal. and Contemporary Sci.*, 3: 307–313. New York: International Universities Press.

——— (1974b), On the concept "borderline" in children: A clinical essay. *The Psychoanal. Study of the Child*, 29: 341–368.

Potter, H. W. (1934a), A service for children in a psychiatric hospital. *Psychiatric Q.*, 8: 16–31.

——— (1934b), The treatment of problem children in a psychiatric hospital. *Amer. J. Psychiatry*, 91: 869–880.

Pribram, K. H. & Gill, M. M. (1975), *Freud's "Project" Re-assessed: Preface to Contemporary Cognitive Theory and Neuropsychology*. New York: Basic Books.

Pruyser, P. W. (1975), What splits in "splitting"? A scrutiny of the concept of splitting in psychoanalysis and psychiatry. *Bull. Menninger Clin.*, 39: 1–46.

——— (1977), The seamy side of current religious beliefs. *Bull. Menninger Clin.*, 41: 329–348.

Rado, S. (1928), The problem of melancholia. *Internat. J. Psycho-Anal.*, 9: 420–438.

———— (1956), *Psychoanalysis of Behavior: Collected Papers*. New York: Grune & Stratton.

———— (1962), Theory and therapy: The theory of schizotypal organization and its application to the treatment of decompensated schizotypal behavior. In: *Psychoanalysis of Behavior: Collected Papers*, Vol. 2. New York: Grune & Stratton, pp. 127–140.

Redl, F. (1959), Life space interview techniques. *Amer. J. Orthopsychiatry*, 29: 1–18.

———— & Wineman, D. (1951), *Children Who Hate*. Glencoe, Il.: Free Press of Glencoe.

———— & ———— (1952), *Controls from Within*. Glencoe, Il.: Free Press of Glencoe.

Richardson, J. T. (1973), Psychological interpretation of glossolalia: A reexamination of research. *J. Sci. Study Religion*, 12: 199–207.

Rinsley, D. B. (1962), A contribution to the theory of ego and self. *Psychiat. Q.*, 36: 96–120.

———— (1963), Psychiatric hospital treatment with special reference to children. *Archives of General Psychiatry*, 9: 489–496. Reprinted in *Treatment of the Severely Disturbed Adolescent*. New York: Aronson, 1980, pp. 39–52.

———— (1964), Psychiatric hospital treatment with special reference to children. *Current Psychiatric Therapies*, 4: 69–73.

———— (1965), Intensive psychiatric hospital treatment of adolescents: An object-relations view. *Psychiat. Q.*, 39: 405–429.

———— (1967a), The adolescent in residential treatment: Some critical reflections. *Adolescence*, 2: 83–95. Reprinted in *Treatment of the Severely Disturbed Adolescent*. New York: Aronson, 1980, pp. 53–63.

———— (1967b), Intensive residential treatment of the adolescent. *Psychiat. Q.*, 41: 134–143.

———— (1968), Theory and practice of intensive residential treatment of adolescents. *Psychiat. Q.*, 42: 611–638. Revised and reprinted in *Adolescent Psychiatry*, 1: 479–509. Reprinted in *Treatment of the Severely Disturbed Adolescent*. New York: Aronson, 1980, pp. 103–130.

—— (1971a), The adolescent inpatient: Patterns of depersonification. *Psychiat. Q.*, 45: 3–22. Reprinted in *Treatment of the Severely Disturbed Adolescent*. New York: Aronson, 1980, pp. 185–212.

—— (1971b), Theory and practice of intensive residential treatment of adolescents. *Adol. Psychiatry*, 1: 479–509.

—— (1972), A contribution to the nosology and dynamics of adolescent schizophrenia. *Psychiat. Q.*, 46: 159–186. Reprinted in *Treatment of the Severely Disturbed Adolescent*. New York: Aronson, 1980, pp. 213–239.

—— (1974a), Residential treatment of adolescents. In: *American Handbook of Psychiatry*, 2nd Ed., Vol. 2. New York: Basic Books, pp. 353–366. Reprinted in *Treatment of the Severely Disturbed Adolescent*. New York: Aronson, 1980, pp. 161–181.

—— (1974b), Special education for adolescents in residential psychiatric treatment. *Adol. Psychiatry*, 3: 394–418. Reprinted in *Treatment of the Severely Disturbed Adolescent*. New York: Aronson, 1980, pp. 131–160.

—— (1980a), The developmental etiology of borderline and narcissistic disorders. *Bull. Menninger Clin.*, 44: 127–134.

—— (1980b), Principles of therapeutic milieu with children. In: *Emotional Disorders in Children and Adolescents*, ed. G. P. Sholevar, R. M. Benson, & B. J. Blinder. New York: SP Medical and Scientific Books, pp. 191–208.

—— & Hall, D. D. (1962), Psychiatric hospital treatment of adolescents: Parental resistances as expressed in casework metaphor. *Arch. Gen. Psychiatry*, 7: 286–294. Reprinted in *Treatment of the Severely Disturbed Adolescent*. New York: Aronson, 1980, pp. 22–38.

—— & Inge, G. P., III (1961), Psychiatric hospital treatment of adolescents: Verbal and nonverbal resistance to treatment.

Bull. Menninger Clin., 25: 249–263. Reprinted in *Treatment of the Severely Disturbed Adolescent.* New York: Aronson, 1980, pp. 3–21.

Ritvo, S. (1974), Current status of the concept of infantile neurosis: Implications for diagnosis and technique. *The Psychoanal. Study of the Child*, 29: 159–181.

Robinson, J. F. et al. (eds.) (1957), *Psychiatric Inpatient Treatment of Children.* Washington, D.C.: American Psychiatric Association.

Rodnick, E. H. & Goldstein, M. J. (1974), A research strategy for studying risk for schizophrenia during adolescence and early childhood. In: *Children at Psychiatric Risk*, ed. E. J. Anthony & C. Koupernik. New York: Wiley, pp. 507–526.

Rolfe, R. M. & MacClintock, A. U. (1976), The due process rights of minors "voluntarily admitted" to mental institutions. *J. Psychiat. Law*, 4: 333–375.

Rosenfeld, H. (1965), *Psychotic States.* New York: International Universities Press.

Rosse, I. C. (1887), Illustrations of error in the diagnosis of some nervous diseases. *J. Nerv. Ment. Dis.*, 14: 681–701.

Rousey, C. L. (1974), *Psychiatric Assessment by Speech and Hearing Behavior.* Springfield, Il.: Thomas.

———— & Moriarty, A. E. (1965), *Diagnostic Implications of Speech Sounds.* Springfield, Il.: Thomas.

Satir, V. M. (1967), *Conjoint Family Therapy: A Guide to Theory and Technique*, Rev. Ed. Palo Alto, Ca.: Science & Behavior Books.

———— (1972), *Peoplemaking.* Palo Alto, Ca.: Science & Behavior Books.

Schacter, S. & Singer, J. E. (1962), Cognitive, social, and physiological determinants of emotional states. *Psychol. Rev.*, 69: 377–399.

Schafer, R. (1968), *Aspects of Internalization.* New York: International Universities Press.

———— (1976), *A New Language for Psychoanalysis*. New Haven, Ct.: Yale University Press.

Schilder, P. (1935), *The Image and Appearance of the Human Body*. London; Paul, Trench, Trubner.

———— (1953), *Medical Psychology*. New York: International Universities Press.

Schimel, J. L. (1974), Problems of delinquency and their treatment. In: *American Handbook of Psychiatry*, rev. ed., Vol. 2, ed. S. Arieti. New York: Basic Books, pp. 264–274.

Schmideberg, M. (1947), The treatment of psychopaths and borderline patients. *Amer. J. Psychotherapy*, 1: 45–55.

Segal, H. (1979), *Melanie Klein*. New York: Viking Press.

Settlage, C. F. (1980), The psychoanalytic understanding of narcissistic and borderline personality disorders: Advances in developmental theory. In: *Rapprochement: The Critical Subphase of Separation-Individuation*, ed. R. F. Lax et al. New York: Aronson, pp. 77–100.

Shafii, M. (1973), Adaptive and therapeutic aspects of meditation. *Internat. J. Psychoanal. Psychother.*, 2: 364–382.

Shankweiler, D. & Studdert-Kennedy, M. (1967), Identification of consonants and vowels presented to left and right ears. *Q. J. Exp. Psychol.*, 19: 59–63.

Shapiro, E. R. et al. (1975), The influence of family experience on borderline personality development. *Internat. Rev. Psychoanal.*, 2: 399–411.

Shapiro, T. (1974), The development and distortion of empathy. *Psychoanal. Q.*, 43: 4–25.

Shaw, C. R. & McKay, H. D. (1931), Social factors in juvenile delinquency. National Commission on Law Observance and Enforcement, Report No. 13. Washington, D.C.: U.S. Government Printing Office.

Sifneos, P. (1973), The presence of "alexithymic" characteristics psychosomatic patients. *Psychother. & Psychosomatics*, 22: 255–262.

———— (1975), Problems of psychotherapy of patients with

alexithymic characteristics and physical disease. *Psychother. &
Psychosomatics*, 26: 65–70.
Simmel, E. (1929), Psycho-analytic treatment in a sanitarium.
Internat. J. Psycho-Anal., 10: 70–89.
Singer, M. T. & Wynne, L. C. (1965a), Thought disorder and
family relations of schizophrenics, III: Methodology using
projective techniques. *Arch. Gen. Psychiatry*, 12: 186–200.
———— & ———— (1965b), Thought disorder and family relations
of schizophrenics, IV: Results and implications. *Arch. Gen.
Psychiatry*, 12: 201–212.
Sperry, R. W. (1968), Hemisphere deconnection and unity in
conscious awareness. *Amer. Psychol.*, 23: 723–733.
Spitz, R. A. (1945), Hospitalism: An inquiry into the genesis of
psychiatric conditions of early childhood. *The Psychoanal.
Study of the Child*, 1: 53–74.
———— (1946), Hospitalism: A follow-up report. *The Psychoanal.
Study of the Child*, 2: 113–117.
———— (1957), *No and Yes: On the Genesis of Human Communication*.
New York: International Universities Press.
———— (1959), *A Genetic Field Theory of Ego Formation*. New York:
International Universities Press.
———— (1965), *The First Year of Life*. New York: International
Universities Press.
———— & Wolf, K. M. (1946), Anaclitic depression: An inquiry
into the genesis of psychiatric conditions of early child-
hood, II. *The Psychoanal. Study of the Child*, 2: 313–342.
Stagg, F., Hinson, E. G., & Oates, W. E. (1967), *Glossolalia*.
Nashville & New York: Abingdon Press.
Stanton, A. & Schwartz, M. S. (1954), *The Mental Hospital*.
New York: Basic Books.
Stone, M. H. (1980), *The Borderline Syndromes: Constitution, Per-
sonality, and Adaptation*. New York: McGraw-Hill.
Stransky, E. (1909), *Über die Dementia Praecox*. Wiesbaden: J. F.
Bergmann.
Studdert-Kennedy, M. & Shankweiler, D. (1970), Hemispheric

specialization of speech perception. *J. Acoust. Soc. Amer.*, 48: 579–594.

Sullivan, H. S. (1953), *The Interpersonal Theory of Psychiatry*, ed. H. S. Perry & M. L. Gawel. New York: Norton.

———— (1962), Schizophrenia as a Human Process. In: *The Collected Works of Harry Stack Sullivan*, Vol. 2. New York: Norton, pp. 7–363.

Synan, V. (1975), *Aspects of Pentecostal-Charismatic Origins*. Plainfield, N.J.: Logos International.

Szasz, T. S. (1961), *The Myth of Mental Illness*. New York: Hoeber-Harper.

———— (1965), *Psychiatric Justice*. New York: Macmillan.

———— (1974), *The Myth of Mental Illness*, rev. ed. New York: Harper & Row.

Szurek, S. A. et al. (eds.) (1971), *Inpatient Care for the Psychotic Child* (Langley Porter Child Psychiatry Series, 5). Palo Alto, Ca.: Science & Behavior Books.

Tart, C. T. (1969), *Altered States of Consciousness*. New York: Wiley.

Toffler, A. (1970), *Future Shock*. New York: Random House.

Topping, R. (1943), Treatment of the pseudosocial boy. *Amer. J. Orthopsychiatry*, 13: 353–360.

Vivier, L. (1960), Glossolalia. Unpublished thesis, Department of Psychiatry, University of Witwatersrand. Microfilm of the University of Chicago and Union Theological Seminary.

Voth, H. M. (1977), *The Castrated Family*. Kansas City, Ks.: Sheed, Andrews & McMeel.

Waelder, R. (1976), *Psychoanalysis: Observation, Theory, Application*. New York: International Universities Press.

Wallace, R. K. (1970), Physiological effects of transcendental meditation. *Science*, 167: 1751–1754.

Wardle, C. J. (1974), Residential care of children with conduct disorders. In: *The Residential Psychiatric Treatment of Children*, ed. P. A. Barker. New York: Wiley, pp. 48–104.

Weil, A. P. (1970), The basic core. *The Psychoanal. Study of the Child*, 25: 442–469.

Weiss, E. (1950), *Principles of Psychodynamics*. New York: Grune & Stratton.

——— (1960), *The Structure and Dynamics of the Human Mind*. New York: Grune & Stratton.

Werry, J. S. (ed.) (1978), *Pediatric Psychopharmacology: The Use of Behavior Modifying Drugs in Children*. New York: Brunner/Mazel.

White, J. H. (1977), *Pediatric Psychopharmacology: A Practical Guide to Clinical Application*. Baltimore: Williams & Wilkins.

Wierville, V. P. (1967), *Receiving the Holy Spirit Today*. Boston: Branden Press.

Wilkerson, D. (1963), *The Cross and the Switchblade*. Westwood, N.J.: Revell.

Winnicott, D. W. (1949), Mind and its relation to the psyche-soma. In: *Collected Papers: Through Paediatrics to Psycho-Analysis*. London: Tavistock, 1958, pp. 243–254.

——— (1950–1955), Aggression in relation to emotional development. In: *Collected Papers: Through Paediatrics to Psycho-Analysis*. London: Tavistock, 1958, pp. 204–218.

——— (1951), Transitional objects and transitional phenomena. In: *Collected Papers: Through Paediatrics to Psycho-Analysis*. London: Tavistock, 1958, pp. 229–242.

——— (1960), Ego distortion in terms of true and false self. In: *The Maturational Processes and the Facilitating Environment: Studies in the Theory of Emotional Development*. New York: International Universities Press, 1965, pp. 140–152.

Woodward, K. L. & Mark, R. (1978), The new narcissism. *Newsweek*, January 30, pp. 70–72.

Wynne, L. C. (1961), The study of intrafamilial alignments and splits in exploratory family therapy. In: *Exploring the Base for Family Therapy*, ed. N. W. Ackerman et al. New York: Family Service Assn. of America, pp. 95–115.

———— & Singer, M. T. (1963a), Thought disorder and family relations of schizophrenics, I: A research strategy. *Arch. Gen. Psychiatry*, 9: 191–198.

———— & ———— (1963b), Thought disorder and family relations of schizophrenics, II: A classification of forms of thinking. *Arch. Gen. Psychiatry*, 9: 199–206.

Yerevanian, B. I. & Akiskal, H. S. (1979), "Neurotic," characterological, and dysthymic depressions. In: *Affective Disorders: Special Clinical Forms*, ed. H. S. Akiskal. *The Psychiatric Clinics of North America*, 2: 595–617.

Zentner, E. B. & Aponte, H. J. (1970), The amorphous family nexus. *Psychiatric Q.*, 44: 91–113.

ACKNOWLEDGMENTS

CHAPTER 1. Rinsley, D. B. (1968). Economic aspects of object relations. *Internat. J. Psycho-Anal.*, 49:38–48.

CHAPTER 2. Masterson, J. F. & Rinsley, D. B. (1975). The borderline syndrome: The role of the mother in the genesis and psychic structure of the borderline personality. In: *Rapprochement: The Critical Subphase of Separation-Individuation*, ed. R. Lax et al. New York: Aronson, 1980, pp. 299–329.

CHAPTER 3. Rinsley, D. B. (1977). An object-relations view of borderline personality. In: *Borderline Personality Disorders*, ed. P. Hartocollis. New York: International Universities Press, pp. 47–70.

CHAPTER 4. Rinsley, D. B. (1979). Fairbairn's object-relations theory: A reconsideration in terms of newer knowledge. *Bull. Menninger Clin.*, 43:489–514.

CHAPTER 5. Rinsley, D. B. (1978). Borderline psychopathology: A review of aetiology, dynamics, and treatment. *Internat. Rev. Psycho-Anal.*, 5:45–54.

CHAPTER 6. Carter, L. & Rinsley, D. B. (1977). Vicissitudes of "empathy" in a borderline adolescent. *Internat. Rev. Psycho-Anal.*, 4:317–326.

CHAPTER 7. Brende, J. O. & Rinsley, D. B. (1979). Borderline disorder, altered states of consciousness, and glossolalia. *J. Amer. Acad. Psychoanal.*, 7:165–188.

CHAPTER 8. Rinsley, D. B. (in press). Object constancy, object permanency, and personality disorder. In: *Self and Object Constancy*, ed. R. F. Lax et al. New York: Aronson.

CHAPTER 9. Rinsley, D. B. (1981). Dynamic and developmental issues in borderline and related "spectrum" disorders. *The Psychiatric Clinics of North America*, 4:117–132.

CHAPTER 10.   Rinsley, D. B. (1978). Juvenile delinquency: A review of the past and a look at the future. *Bull. Menninger Clin.*, 42:252–260.

CHAPTER 11.   Adapted from Rinsley, D. B. (1980). Diagnosis and treatment of borderline and narcissistic children and adolescents. *Bull. Menninger Clin.*, 44:147–170.

CHAPTER 13.   Adapted from Rinsley, D. B. (1981). Borderline psychopathology: The concepts of Masterson and Rinsley and beyond. *Adolescent Psychiatry*, 9:259–274.

INDEX

Abandonment depression, 40n–41n,
    67, 161, 162, 225, 232
  defense against, 41
  departure of, 71–72
Abenheimer, K. M., 75, 77
Abraham, K., 15, 17, 173, 184, 224
  on depression, 59–60, 82, 184
Abrams, R., 184
Abstinence, rule of, 234n
Ackerman, N. W., 118, 192
Acting in, 229
Acting out, 191, 229
Active ego feelings, 5
Adler, A., 78
Adler, G., 163, 228, 232–233
Adolescence
  adjustment reaction of, 245
  psychopathology of, 238–239
  and residential treatment process,
    239–244
  symbiotic psychosis of, 249
  turmoil school of, 238
Affect
  assimilation to mental representa-
    tions, 11
  linked, 70
  pseudo, 165
Affective communication, 143
Affectomotor storms, 80, 177, 223,
    227
  failure to tone down, 104n, 131n
  and feeding experience, 155
  vulnerability to, 222
Aggression
  failure to neutralize, 28

infantile, 13
and neutralized energy, 20
oral, see oral aggression
projection of, 59
as reaction to frustration or
    deprivation, 80
of superego, 82
Aichhorn, A., 190
  "Wayward Youth," 189
Akiskal, H. S., 184
Alexander, F., 190
Alexander the Great, 164
Alexithymia, 163
  see also fantasy deficiency
All good-all bad perceptual
    organization, 63–64, 73, 99–
    100, 111–113, 115, 154–156,
    175, 179–181, 222
Alliances
  Anti-L.E.-R.O., 43, 85, 87–88, 91,
    253, 257, 258, 260, 262–269
  C.E.-I.O., 85, 87–88, 91, 95, 253,
    257, 258, 260, 262–269
  E.O.-R.O., 267
  Fairbairn's, 85–88
  L.E.-Anti-L.E., 266–267
  L.E.-E.O., 43n, 85, 90, 253, 257,
    258, 260, 262–269
  between rewarding part-unit and
    pleasure ego, 109
Alpha waves, 139–140
Altered states of consciousness
    (ASC), 135–138, 150–152
  brain wave accompaniments to,
    138–141

307

Defenses
  against abandonment depression,
    41
  infantile, 12–15
  internalization of object as, 82–83
  primitive mechanisms of, 8
  projective–introjective, 116
  and the SORU, 37, 100, 119, 177
  splitting, 162
Definitive phase, 242
Defusion of instincts, 16, 22
Deification, 227
Deikman, A. J., 137
Denial, 13–14
Dependence, 61
Depersonalization, 7
  and ego weakness, 8
  and perceptual alienation, 19
Depersonification, 62, 117–119
  and juvenile delinquency, 191–194
  patterns of, 201–203
    less severe, 202–203
    psychotic and severe, 201–202
Depression (melancholia), 184
  see abandonment depression
  early studies of, 59–61
  and object loss, 82
Depressive dysphoria, 176
Depressive position, 17, 22, 60,
    87–89
  arrest at, 101
  working through in inpatient
    setting, 243
Derealization, see estrangement
Desymbiotization, 163, 242
  inhibition of, 100, 156
Deutsch, H., 20, 58
Devaluation, 227
Developmental–diagnostic spectrum,
    247–249
Diagnosis, 205–208
Diagnostic labeling, 244–245
Diathesis-stress model, 173
  applied to schizophrenia, 172
  nature–nurture and, 186–187

Disorders of the self, see self,
    disorders of
Double bind, 191
Double introjection, 60
Dream, ego boundary in, 6–7
Drive, and instinct, 76–77
Drye, R., 58
DSM I (*Diagnostic and Statistical
    Manual of Mental Disorders*),
    245
DSM III, 184–185, 214, 248
DSM II, 214
Durup, G., 139
Dyad, fixation at level of, 158–161
Dysphoria, 162, 176

Early ego functions, 79
Easson, W. M., 207, 209
Economics, and object relations, 1–23
Ego(s)
  antilibidinal, see antilibidinal ego
  bodily, 7
  central, see central ego
  characterized by splitting, 252
  early, 79
  Fairbairn's multiplicity of, 77
  fixation of, 27–29, 72
  fragmentation of, 81
  fundamentally object-seeking, 81
  inherent experientiality of, 5
  intertranslatability with repre-
    sentations, 92
  libidinal, see libidinal ego
  libido as function of, 79–80
  and objects, 257–258
  original, see original ego
  pathological, 40–41
  perceptibility of, 4–5
  pleasure, see pleasure ego
  present from birth, 79
  progressive growth of, 87
  reality, see reality ego
  regression in the service of, 150
  split, see split ego

Mother (*continued*)
  libidinal availability of, 30
    in borderline's development,
      35–36
    Mahler's understanding of,
      32–35, 56
    and the SORU, 36–38, 42–43,
      99, 177, 225
    and the split ego, 38–42
  mirroring function of, 33–34
  psychotic, 98
  role of, 25–26
  whole-image concept of, 27
Mother-infant interaction
  ambivalent, 98–99
  and internalization, 86
  push-pull quality of, 35
Mourning
  failure to develop capacity for, 101
  and repetition-compulsion, 221
"Mourning and Melancholia" (Freud),
  221, 252
Mutual cuing, 33

Nagera, H., 153
Narcissism, 3
  "new," 135, 199
  pathologically persistent, 58
  psychology of, 160
Narcissistic children and adolescents,
  199–215
Narcissistic personality
  and borderline personality,
    165–166
  desymbiotization by, 163
  of leaders, 164–165
  object inconstancy of, 162
Narcissistic wound, 221
Nature–nurture, 29–31, 186–187
  and diathesis-stress, 186–187
Negative introjection, 28–29
Negativism, childhood, 22
Nelson, M. C., 193, 199
Nemiah, J., 163
Neurology, 78

Neurosis, veridicality of, 171–172,
  221
Neutralization, failure of, 28, 73, 119
Neutralized energy
  dearth of, 102
  sources of, 20–23
Nonself, differentiation from self, 12
Normal autism, 63
  borderline mother's enjoyment of,
    97–98
Noshpitz, J. D., 239
Not-me, 12–13
Nunberg, H., 8

Object-cathexis, 8
Object constancy, 66, 153–169
  affective component of, 153
  mnemonic component of, 153
  and object permanency, 153–154
Object impermanency, 161–166,
  228–230
Object inconstancy, 178
  and object impermanency,
    161–166, 228–230
Object loss
  Freud on, 16–17
  and melancholia, 82
  and repetition-compulsion,
    220–221
Object permanency, 153–154
  and internalization, 167
Object-related communication, 143
Object relations, 57–73
  developmental-diagnostic
    spectrum in terms of,
    179–186
  economic aspects of, 1–23
  healthy, 70–71
  impairment of, 8
  of late oral stage, 88
  normal, 25–27
    mother's libidinal availability in
      development of, 32–35
  shift toward, 2
  stages of, 26
  structural derivatives of, 11

Reductionism, 80
Reflective ego feelings, 5
Regression
  and analysis, 107
  controlled, 139
  deepest, 14
  in leaders, 164
  pre-Oedipal, 62–63
  in the service of the ego, 150
Reintrojection, 16–17
  from side of the Ucs, 21
Rejected object, 223
Rejecting object (R.O.), 62, 82,
    84–88, 91–92, 94, 223–225,
    254, 257–260, 263–269
  antilibidinal ego attached to, 85,
    253
Relationship psychology, 76
Relaxation response, 135, 150–151
Repetition-compulsion, 220–221
Representational development, 86
Representations
  intertranslatability with egos, 92
  self and object, 11–12
Repression, 18–21
  and the ego, 84–85
  failure of, 8
  Fairbairn's concept of, 93
  of libinal ego, 90
  onset of, 87
  and part-object-representations,
    86
  and splitting, 251, 254–255,
    261–265
Residential process, 239–244
  phases of, 241–242
Resistance, family's, 239–240
Resistance phase, 241
Resolution phase, 242
Retention, and obsessional mode, 16
Reunion, fantasies of, 41, 120
Rewarding part-unit, 38–39
  alliance with pleasure ego, 48–49,
    55–56
Richardson, J. T., 145–146
Riddance mechanism, 84

Rinsley, D. B., 30, 36, 63, 76, 97, 98,
    103, 109, 116, 118, 172, 174,
    182, 183, 191, 209, 211, 225,
    226, 237, 238, 240, 242, 245,
    268
Ritvo, S., 58
Roberts, L., 140
Robinson, J. F., 211
Rolfe, R. M., 197
Rosenfeld, H., 256
Rosse, I. C., 104
Rousey, C. L., 138, 142, 144

Sadomasochism, 102, 159–160
Sartre, J. P., 5
Satir, V. M., 192
Saul, L. J., 25
Scanning capacity, 104
Scapegoating, 190–191
  and the identified patient,
    203–204
Schacter, S., 136
Schafer, R., 78, 154
Schilder, P., 7, 12n
Schimel, J. L., 190
Schizo-affective syndromes, 174
Schizoid factors, 94
Schizophrenia, 2
  etiology of, 65
  familial basis of, 191–192
  "pseudoneurotic," 57
  symbiotic, 185
Schmideberg, M., 171
van der Schraaf, A. H., 209
Schwartz, A., 240
Segal, H., 269
Self
  of borderline individual, 119–120
  differentiation from nonself, 12
  disorders of, 174
    endopsychic structure of, 222
    increase in, 199
  failure to differentiate, 60
  false, *see* false self
  fusion with object, 100
  grandiose, 160

Treatment (*continued*)
  inpatient, 209–210, 239–244
  outpatient, 210
  stages of, 211
Trieb, Brill's translation of, 76
Trophotropic response, 135–136

Valence, 11, 17
Vivier, L., 145–146
Voth, H. M., 196, 200
Vowels
  in glossolalia, 144–145
  infant's use of, 142

Waelder, R., 75
Wallace, R. K., 136, 137
Wardle, C. J., 209
Wayward Youth (Aichhorn), 189
"Weak" ego, 8–10
Weakland, J. H., 192
Webster, J. C., 143
Weiss, E., 2, 95
  on Federn's conception of ego
    states, 10
Weiss, H. B., 197

Werble, B., 58, 163, 171, 173, 184,
    208
Werry, J. S., 213
White, J. H., 213
Whole-objects
  aims, 16
  cathected as if part-objects, 28n,
    88, 101
  generation of, 265–268
  maternal concept, 27
  and repression, 87
Wierville, V. P., 146
Wilkerson, D., 146
Wineman, D., 239
Winnicott, D. W., 81, 99, 156–157,
    166, 167, 177, 191, 220, 230,
    239, 268
Withdrawing part-unit, 38–39
Wolf, K. M., 26
Women's liberation, 195–196, 200
Woodward, K. L., 199, 218
Wordsworth, W., 9n
Wynne, L. C., 192, 201, 203

Yerevanian, B. I., 184

Zentner, E. B., 213